Scott Thompson – Safe journeys.

1993 R.I.P

Mark Thompson

OUT OF HOURS

AUSTIN MACAULEY PUBLISHERS™

LONDON * CAMBRIDGE * NEW YORK * SHARJAH

A CIP catalogue record for this title is available from the British Library.

ISBN 9781788485661 (Paperback)
ISBN 9781788485678 (Hardback)
ISBN 9781528954549 (ePub e-book)

www.austinmacauley.com

First Published 2022
Austin Macauley Publishers Ltd®
1 Canada Square
Canary Wharf
London
E14 5AA

To those who believe in me

3B12 Ludo Club

To the kindness of strangers

Table of Contents

Prologue

'Hurry up, Bernie, we haven't got all night,' Jacques urged him.

'I can only go as fast as the mag drill, can't I?' Bernie snapped back.

'Put some more cutting oil on the drill bit.'

'I got plenty on it, Mac.'

'How's the coast looking, Jacques?' I asked.

'We got two people passing on the opposite side of the street but they won't be able to hear us up here, trust me.'

'It would have been a big help if Harry had given us the combination to the safe too,' Bernie grumbled.

'He gave us the door keys and the code for the alarm, so let's not quibble,' I reminded him.

Bernie (aka The Bolt) continued drilling the safe with the magnetic (mag) drill, only stopping to lubricate the drill bit with cutting oil, aiding the 32mm diamond-tipped drill bit to cut easily and also to prevent it from blunting. The magnetic drill is a marvellous piece of equipment; it is powered by electricity that has a magnetic base plate that when switched on, magnetises itself to any flat metal surface. As Jacques had pointed out, time was getting on even though it was only 9:30 pm on a quiet Sunday night.

'That's it, we're through,' Bernie announced smiling through his ski mask.

I took the weight of the mag drill whilst Bernie de-magnetized it from the safe. I carefully lowered it to one side away from the safe door. Bernie turned on his pen light and shone it in the hole we had just drilled.

'Bingo! Here, you take a look, Mac,' he said excitedly, handing me the pen light.

I shone it in the hole and said, 'Okay, it looks to be good. We're through the locking plate.'

'Excuse me, gentlemen,' said Jacques clamping a pair of 36-inch Stillson to the safe handle and slowly applying pressure, turned the safe handle anti-clockwise until we heard a click.

'Shall I?' Bernie asked, his pearly white teeth showing through the mouth hole in his ski mask.

'The pleasure is all yours, Bolt,' Jacques told him.

'Fingers crossed, Bernie,' I whispered.

Bernie grasped the handle and pulled the safe door towards him, opening it an inch then he opened the door all the way with joyful whispers of 'YES' from each of us as we all looked inside. There staring us in the face were huge bundles of cash; we filled a small hold-all with all the cash and then quickly placed the mag drill and Stillson in a larger hold-all that Jacques slung over his shoulder. We made our way down from the offices to street level, stopping at the rear door of the premises and removed our overshoes, ski masks and overalls, placing them all in a bag only, keeping our gloves on, removing them once we are outside away from the building.

'Jacques?'

'Yes, Mac.'

'You take all the equipment and clothes. And don't forget to burn them.'

'Check,' he replied.

'Bernie, you take care of the cash.'

'Okay, Mac, but what about you?'

'I'll damage the door first then reset the alarm and kick the door in to set off the alarm in five minutes' time and catch a taxi off the rank back to the house. By the time the police arrive, we'll be long gone.'

'What then?' Jacques asked me anxiously.

'We'll give Harry his cut tomorrow and then its Seychelles, here we come,' I replied laughing.

Chapter 1

Blasts from the Past

You know when something occurs to you? I had known this group of particular people all my life except for a few that I had only met on certain contracts regarding engineering companies who I had worked for, but never had the privilege of working with them out of hours, though we all had something in common – we liked money and plenty of it! On this particular morning, after smoking two cigarettes and drinking two cups of tea whilst watching the news, I showered and got dressed, then headed uptown to pay a few bills.

As the day progressed to just past noon, I went into my local bar called the White Horse and said hello to a few regular customers who I seldom have anything to do with apart from when they make conversation with me, as I like to keep my circle small, and ordered a pint at the bar. I took my pint and pulled out a courtesy newspaper from the news rack on the wall and sat at a corner table where I can see everyone in the bar coming and going. I took a sip of my pint then got my head stuck in the newspaper reading an article on global warming – boring, I know but it takes my interest – when suddenly a voice said in an astonished tone, 'Hello, mate.'

I looked up and to my astonishment, stood there in front of me with a beaming smile upon his face was my old friend Mick Jones, whom I had not seen since I was a 16-year-old lad.

'Well, stone the bloody crows,' I said leaping up from my chair and gave Mick a solid handshake and a man hug. 'Have a seat,' I asked him ecstatically.

Mick instantly sat down and we spent the next hour sipping on our beers quickly reminiscing about our youth and up to the present day. Mick explained that he had to move away with his father and mother to Germany to an army base as his dad was in the forces and that there was no time for goodbyes, as they moved during the summer holidays when most of us were away on holiday with our families. Mick had got a trade as a locksmith whilst living in Germany, not liking the army life much to the dismay of his parents especially his father, and after a few years Mick set up his own locksmith business. One day he got a call to open a safe as the owner, the dozy idiot, kept the combination on his mobile phone but he had got pick-pocketed along with a bunch of keys and now he couldn't open his safe without the combination or the key. Mick arrived and the owner, in his mid-30s, escorts him inside his premises and into a room where he shows Mick the safe.

'Not a problem,' Mick told the man, continuing, 'Just give me thirty minutes and I'll have it open for you.'

'That quick?' the owner replied, quite shocked.

'Give or take five minutes,' Mick told him smiling.

'Splendid. I'll leave you to it then?'

'Yes, that would be appreciated, thank you,' Mick told him.

Thirty minutes and a cup of coffee later, Mick had the safe open but for the first time in his career, Mick wanted to have a good peek inside the safe. When he did, he reckons there must have been fifty grand in cash, stocks, bonds and a little black velvet bag. Curiosity killed the cat, so Mick opened the little black velvet bag and peeked inside, and to his amazement, the bag contained lots of small diamonds all staring back at him.

Mick was now sweating and smiling as he removed ten diamonds out of the black velvet bag, wrapping them up in his handkerchief which he put back in his pocket and then informed the owner that his safe was open, much to the owner's delight. Mick replaced the lock and told the owner how to set a new combination code. The owner thanked Mick, who told the man that he had other pressing affairs to attend to and collected his payment for his work, and fucked off promptly in a mild panic, grinning to himself.

Two days had passed by without incident after he had the diamonds. Mick was peacefully sat at home in the evening when his doorbell rang and upon opening the front door, two burly men with rugged faces dressed in black suits quickly looked Mick up and down from head to toe, before they smashed him in the face with their fists and began kicking the shit out him, demanding all ten diamonds be handed back over to them or he would lose his fingers. Mick, who had never been hit in his life, was not going to play Jack the Lad with these guys and deny all knowledge of the diamonds' whereabouts; instead, he instantly put his hand in his pocket and handed the diamonds back, still wrapped up in his handkerchief, over to the two burly thugs with a weak smile on his face.

Mick took another brash kicking and got pampered for the next two weeks in hospital, and his locksmith business was razed to the ground by these geezers, who now demanded £50,000 cash from him as a gesture of goodwill for the inconvenience he caused to the rightful owner of the diamonds. Mick of course paid up, he changed his name and left Germany to sit in the sun for two months trying to work out where it had all gone wrong and for his injuries to fully heal.

Mick decided to come back to the U.K. and to his old town Barry Island in Wales, in the hope that he wasn't to be found again by the German guys, bless. So here we were, sipping our beers and laughing when Fox Filly made her entrance and walked over to me and asked, 'Alright, love?'

'Now I am,' I replied sitting up straight.

'You and your mate fancy another beer or a glass of champagne?' she asked smiling.

Me and Mick raised an eye brow at each other and I said, 'Don't mind if we do, thanks.'

Fox Filly, or her full title Melody Fox-Wright, turned around and quickly made her way to the bar, said something to the barman and quickly made her way back to us.

'Who the hell is that?' Mick asked earnestly.

'You'll find out in a minute, Mick.'

'She got some form on her mate,' Mick remarked eyeing her up and down.

'That's not the only form she's got, mate,' I said coyly.

'I heard that but I'll take that as a compliment,' Fox said smiling as she sat down at the end of our table.

'Heard what? I asked.

'Your friend's compliment, Mac.'

The barman quickly put three fluted glasses and an ice bucket on the table, and popped the cork of the champagne and placed the bottle in the ice bucket then retired back behind the bar.

'Who's your friend, Mac?' Fox asked inquisitively.

'This, love, is an old friend of mine, Mick Jones, and Mick, this is the beautiful Melody Fox-Wright, otherwise known as Fox.'

'Nice to meet your acquaintance, Fox,' Mick said holding out his hand.

'Likewise,' Fox replied, coldly ignoring Mick's outstretched hand then turned her attention on me.

'So, Mac, how have you been keeping, I thought you had forgotten all about me?' she said whilst pouring the champagne into the flutes.

'I'm better now you're here.'

'A toast,' Fox declared.

'Too whom?' I asked.

'To friends, old,' Fox let out a sigh and looked at Mick adding, 'and new. And to you, Mac, for fucking ruining my life for the last two years!!' And with that said, she threw her champagne in my face, winked at Mick and stormed off calling me a prick over her shoulder.

'What the hell was that all about?' Mick gasped in astonishment.

'It's a long story,' I replied. 'She has just been released from a two-year jail sentence and blames me for her incarceration for robbing the bank she worked for, which was all her own doing, I can assure you. She stole £1.5 million of her customers' money, and because I never sent her letters, only postcards, she's got the hump with me, I suppose?'

Mick replied puzzled, 'OH, I see ... More champagne, Mac?'

'No, you go ahead and polish it off. I'll stick to the beer thanks, Mick.'

'Are you sure?'

'Yes, it's okay. Enjoy it, it's on Fox,' I replied to him whilst wiping the champagne off me with a serviette.

'Tell me, Mick.'

'Yes, Mac.'

'What did you change your name to?'

'Ah well, you see, it's kind of funny really,' he chuckled. 'I changed it to DeBeers, on the account of the diamonds I stole from that guy. I just thought it appropriate at the time.'

'Very appropriate,' I replied in agreement with him.

We both laughed and raised our glasses to each other.

It was at that moment Jacques walked in the bar.

'Okay, Mac. How are you today, mate?'

'I've had drier days.'

'Alright, pal?' he said to Mick.

'Yeah, fine, pal,' Mick replied with a wry look on his face.

'So do you guys want drinks?' Jacques asked.

'I'm fine, thanks,' I replied.

'Me too,' said Mick, raising his flute of champagne.

'Suit yourselves.'

Jacques went to the bar and came back with three double Bacardi and cokes – typical of him. I introduce Mick to Jacques and soon they were talking football and getting on like a house on fire (as they were both Man U fans) and more Bacardi followed by more Bacardi, and Mick told Jacques his diamond story and we all laughed at Fox Filly throwing her champagne over me.

'She's out then,' Jacques said smiling.

'She sure is,' I replied grinning from ear to ear.

Mick got himself a nice little two-bed apartment overlooking Barry Docks on the waterfront and invited me and Jacques back for a few more drinks and more banter, and to watch some porn as Mick's fucked up on porn stars and states that if he had a ten-inch dick, he'd be in the porn business himself, doing more women than Ron the man. Whoever that is?

Jacques was getting on well with Mick and that's rare for him on a first meeting, but hey, Mick didn't know Jacques, and after Mick told Jacques about his locksmiths business, I was wondering if Jacques was just looking after his interests or was he really getting on with Mick? On the other hand, Mick was just an easy-going guy that couldn't see life the way we could as he'd been out of the town too long and had not grown with the changes here. Mick insisted we crash at his place as it was 12.30am and he had a half bottle of vodka left that he wanted us to share with him, but me and Jacques declined his invitation and called a taxi instead, and left him watching his porn in the privacy of his own rhapsodic mastered choke!

I woke up later that Friday afternoon at around 2.15pm with a thumping headache from the day before with my chance meeting with my old friend Mick and my good mate Jacques, and our little drinking session. But the only person on my mind was of course Fox Filly and how I had missed her over the last two years. This woman was in a league of her own when it came to earning money and leading men astray with seduction as she had the assets to do it with. At a tad off six feet, with legs longer than the Nile, long black raven hair as shiny as polished ebony, with a bum so pert, it would be a sin to look at another, along with breasts you swear had implants but were very much all hers. Her face would not look out of place on the front cover of *Vogue* magazine and then there were her eyes, pure jade green with a purplish pupil and the best part: she was as cold as ice when it came down to it.

But as a lady, she was elegant, graceful coupled with an angelic innocence, not to mention charming. Still, a lot of men and women have fallen foul of her charms including me about twelve years ago when we first met. We were both at Barry College where I was studying Engineering and Fox was studying Business Management and Accounts.

We got to know each other pretty well and soon enough we were having a fling that went on for over two years before she shot off to university to further her career and then the phone calls between us dilapidated into nothing. I guess that's the way things go trying to have a long-distance relationship?

Anyways, four years later, Fox-Filly turned up in the Seychelles with a load of her mates on some sort of gap year round the world happening, along with her then boyfriend Ollie. Jacques, me and our long-time friend Bernie had been given some money for a little work we had done with a magnetic drill on a safe, so we decided to go scuba diving and snorkelling, and generally toss it off for three weeks on Mahé in the Seychelles.

'Hey, Mac, is that you?' I heard a woman's voice say.

I turned my head in the direction of the voice and there she was, fitter than ever her, body all toned, with her raven black hair tied back, breasts in your face and a sarong wrapped around her waist but low enough to show off them child bearing hips – only in the Seychelles, I thought, but what a sight.

'Fox, is that you, it can't be?'

'Yes, Mac, it's me alright,' she replied with a huge blushing smile on her face.

'Of all the places to bump into you, love,' I said.

I got up out of my hammock and walked the few steps towards her, and as we met, she leaned into me with a cwtch and kissed me on my neck just below the ear, which sent a tingling sensation all the way down my spine, producing goose bumps all over my body. It felt good–*real* good – as she always had that effect on me.

Fox explained briefly the last four years of her life and I likewise explained mine but leaving out a few major details whilst we sat sipping cocktails at the beach bar, and all I could do was sit there admiring her beauty.

'Hey, Mel, where have you been and who's this? 'a dumpy looking blonde guy asked.

'Hi, honey. This is Mac, we're old friends from college.'

'Oh hi, I'm Ollie. Melody's fiancé. Where is the men's room?' he asked.

'Over there to your left about 20 meters away,' I pointed out to him.

'Fox. What the hell are you doing with that guy?'

'WOW…I haven't been called Fox in four years, and as for Ollie, he's bloody loaded,' she paused but went on, 'I met him in university six months ago, he just spends money on me and he thinks that's love? But it's something, I suppose, and anyhow, he's paid for this gap year so I would be a fool to have turned him down. But just go along with it, Mac, and you may be rewarded for your silence, 'she said winking at me.

'You haven't changed a bit in the last four years, love. Are you playing this guy or what?' I asked her with a shameful look on my face.

Fox snapped back at me instantly, 'Leave it out, Mac. It's my business. Remember why I left that little town and what I went to university for?'

'Keep your lid on, honey,' I told her.

Fox grimaced, took a sip of her cocktail and said, 'It's business, Mac, that's all.'

I sat their looking into her hypnotic eyes in total awe. I couldn't help but feel admiration for her and yet pity for poor Ollie. But she had a point, I suppose?

'How long are you staying in Mahé for? 'I asked her, changing the subject.

'We've got two weeks here, two weeks in the Maldives and then we go onto Goa in India,' she replied, lowering her sunglasses.

It was just then that Jacques and Bernie appeared returning back from snorkelling and were heading towards us when I called out to them both, 'How was the fish down there?'

'Wet and colourful,' Bernie called back grinning.

Fox called out to Jacques, 'Hello, stranger.'

'Christ, Fox! Is that you? 'Jacques cried out in astonishment.

Fox stood up with her arms outstretched to greet him and said, 'Sure is, mate.'

They greeted each other with a hug and a kiss on the cheek just as Ollie came back from the gents and again he asked who Jacques and Bernie were. After more introductions, we all decided to meet up later that night in the Beraya Beau Valere Sea restaurant for dinner and a chance for us all to get acquainted a little more.

The evening went well meeting the rest of her group of friends travelling with her, as did the rest of our stay, and when it came time for Fox and her friends to depart, it was kind of sad to see them go, especially Fox. But when she hugged me good bye and kissed my neck, she whispered, 'Check your top pocket,' then boarded the waiting sea plane. She turned back smiled and winked at me. The door shut and the sea plane skied along the waters and rose into the sky, and she was gone. I put my left hand in my top right pocket of my shirt and pulled out a piece of paper, unfolding it and reading:

Thanks for a wonderful time last night. Four years is a long time to wait for a real good fuck. Thank Jacques for getting Ollie blinding drunk and putting him to bed for us. Tell Bernie he's sweet and to wash my lipstick of his cheek that he's been wearing for the past three days. Here's my phone number, stay in touch and watch out for the sharks when you dive. I've missed you so much, Mac.

All my love,
Fox
x-X-x.

Jacques spoke first, 'You still miss her, don't you, Mac?'
'More now than ever.'
'Well, let's go drown our sorrows,' Bernie suggested.
'Sure sounds good to me,' Jacques answered.
'What sorrows have you got to drown, Bolt? 'I asked him.
'Quite a bit, Mac.'
Inquisitively, I asked him, 'How come?'
'I've been shagging Fox's mate Violet for the last three nights and I'm going to miss her sweet lips tonight, 'he replied glumly.
'So, it was Violet's lipstick on your cheek and not Fox's?'
'Eh?' Bernie replied puzzled.
'I'll explain it at the bar,' I told him smiling to myself.
So on that note, we headed to the beach bar and ordered three cocktails, and the rest is history.
We spent the rest of our holiday lazing around diving and snorkelling as planned, but I still could not get Fox out of my head. As for Jacques and Bernie, they chased any new girls that came to the Seychelles and got laid more there in three weeks than they had done in the last three months back home, though they wouldn't admit it if they were asked to on their own admission. After a long

flight back to Heathrow and the long drive back to Wales, we all agreed to meet up in a few days and then get back to work in more ways than one. We are all time-served tradesman in our jobs and all three have something in common, that is we all come from an engineering background. I myself have a HNC in pipefitting and have worked for some of the biggest engineering companies in the U.K. as well as overseas.

Jacques is a top-class welder who has worked all over the world and is rated as one of the best in his field. And Bernie (The Bolt) is a class 1 mechanic in a league of his own with an HND, and can repair or modify anything that's thrown at him. So, seeming we three have been burning and drilling through steel for x-amount of our lives and know the weakest points in structures, the tools and equipment that we use is predominantly unknown to the majority of criminal minds, therefore we have a greater advantage over other guys in this business.

Plus, we get flown all over the world by our employers present and past so we have the perfect cover to look for out-of-hours work that brings in a lot more rewards than being made up in a big company for a relatively good salary, a company car and a quality health plan.

It may sound secure for some people but for what we want in life. it's not enough by any standards.

Now… all that remains is for us to go and get it, if you catch my drift. But for now, we have to get some rest as it had been a long flight and long drive home.

Chapter 2

The Glasgow Ranger

Other than phone calls, we did not see each other for a few days as to get over our jet lag and generally recoup from our time in the Seychelles. Bernie went back to the south of France to take care of our little project over there whilst I just sat around the apartment watching the same old crap on the *Discovery* channel and drinking lots of juice; I was tired and bored out of my mind to say the least. But the next morning I got a phone call from Jacques at around 10 am.

'Hello, mate, everything okay?' I asked him.

'Mac, we got to meet up later for a chat.'

'Sure, Jacques. Where do you want to meet?'

'Say 2:30 in Sam's bar, and try not to be late. I want you to meet a good friend of mine from Glasgow.'

'Sure, so long as he's okay and not full of himself.'

'That's one thing he is not, 'Jacques replied.

'Okay, 2:30 it is, catch you later, mate,' I said ending the call.

I know what's coming when I get there, but it's a case of what we are going to do abroad as we don't crap on our own door step, and to tell you the truth, Europe is the easiest place to steal almost anything. So what if the police carry guns there, they do here in the U.K. nowadays. It took me a long time to convince Jacques and Bernie to work overseas as the ponds are bigger and the pickings richer, easier too.

I arrived at Sam's bar fifteen minutes late as always, kind of my trademark on meets, unless some serious shit had gone down then I would arrive fifteen minutes early for good measure.

'Same as ever, never on time,' Jacques remarked.

'I know, I know, forgive me.'

'Allow me to introduce you to Robbie Duggan. Robbie, this is Mac,' Jacques announced.

'Good to meet your acquaintance. I take it you and Jacques have worked together before?' I inquired.

'Ooch I, Mac. We worked in Dubai and Angola onshore and the occasional jobs off-shore on the oil rigs in the North Sea and in the Norwegian sector for the last eight years, and I tell you this, he's fucking ace at welding, 'he waffled.

'Okay, enough, what'll you have to drink, Mac?' Jacques asked.

'Pint of lager, mate, thanks.'

'I'll have another, pal,' Robbie piped in.

Jacques made his way over to the bar and left me with the Jock, who was a robust chap of about five foot eight in height, with shoulder length ginger curly hair and Armani glasses that looked out of place on his pale puffy face. Totally pro Rangers, as you can always tell by the blue football shirt they sport, but if he's a friend of Jacques then he must be sound, as Jacques is of sound nature and has remarkable judgment of people. A quality he has possessed since we first met and managed to retain it very well, especially in our game of working here and there for years with companies and not falling foul of drink and bad substances that some idiots do, all too often getting off their faces and regretting it the next day or even for weeks down the line, sometimes ending people's careers.

Jacques returned with our drinks and sat down and as the conversation flowed, Robbie quite inadvertently asked, 'Right, down to business. So, are you lot in or are you out?'

I looked at Jacques in total disbelief and in stunned silence, and then double clocked the Jock as if to say, 'Is this guy for fucking real?' Now for one thing, if I remember rightly, this Jock had not even mentioned why he was there, never mind what for, and for the likes of me, I can't remember how much money was involved or where the fucking hell we were getting it from. Now I've worked with plenty of Scottish people and I know they are renowned for their drinking, and the only time you can tell when they're pissed drunk is when they're brawling and smashing up pubs if Celtic or Rangers lose in football, but this guy just broke my attention by scratching my head. And I thought Jacques had a brilliant gift for weighing people up!

It was then Jacques intervened, 'For fuck's sake, Robbie! Keep it real, will you?'

'How much has he had to drink and at what time this morning did he start, more to the point?' I demanded. But before Jacques could answer, the Jock interrupted.

'Now listen here, pal' The Jock started, 'I'll not be taking kindly for that talk about me, it's just I've been enjoying myself here in Wales and I think Cardiff is a great city, and you Welsh people here are so friendly and welcoming, I apologize to both of yous.'

'Mac—' Jacques started.

I held up my hands and said, 'Why did you want me to meet this guy? I can understand if he had just landed on a job, spent five hours doing an induction and wanted to go and find digs, but this is bollocks, Jacques. No offence, pal,' I added sarcastically.

'Mac, mate, just hear the man out.'

'He's off his tits,' I told him.

The Jock scowled at me and growled, 'Who's off his titties, pal?!'

Jacques shook his head then turned to the Jock and said, 'Now Robbie, enlighten Mac about your recent trip to Norway and leave out the parts of the oil refinery you were working on and just tell Mac the important details.'

'No problem, pal,' he replied and began filling us in on the details.

The Jock told us of his exploits whilst working in Norway anyway, and as the Jock went on, I began to listen more intently and with more interest to what was coming out of his mouth, which by now for some reason he seemed normal again. Whilst on his days off, Robbie liked to go sightseeing like most contractors do and it was on one of these little trips out that Robbie stumbled across our out-of-hours work. As it happened, there was a trip organized to Bergen by his employer and when Robbie arrived in Bergen and was wandering around taking in the sights, he found this lovely little number in the form of a jeweller's shop that specialised in diamonds for the up-market Norwegians. The thing is, in Norway they have almost zero crime, with the majority being very honest people. (You can actually go window shopping at 3 am and view what's on offer through the shop windows, seeming there are no shutters on the windows which is a rare thing in the U.K these days.) Thanks to today's technology, Robbie managed to take a few sly photographs on his mobile phone of what's in the jeweller's window. He then set the phone to video and entered the shop with his phone in hand and did some casual browsing just like any tourist and got the inside on film before he made his way outside again.

'Here, pal, feast your eyes on this,' Robbie said to me and handed me his phone. I watched the video he'd recorded inside the shop, and it was a pretty basic set up: one long display counter either side as you entered the shop and one display counter to the rear of the shop. Each display counter was caked with diamond necklaces, bracelets, rings and earrings along with a huge floor standing safe standing against the back wall.

'Very nice,' I remarked.

'Here, take a look at what's in the windows,' Robbie said.

I handed Robbie his phone back and he set it to pictures, then handed it back to me saying, 'Feast your eyes on these little beauties and don't forget to zoom in on the price tags, pal.'

I did as he asked and immediately I could see where Robbie was coming from as the prices on the gems were fucking enormous. I had seen enough and turned to the Jock asking him, 'How much are the diamonds worth in the windows?'

'In Sterling or Krones?' he asked.

'Sterling,' I replied.

'Eight hundred thousand with roughly a further one point six million in the display cabinets inside, plus whatever is inside the safe,' he said smugly with a cheesy grin on his face then took a large mouthful of his whiskey.

I smiled at him thinking he was just another crazy Rangers fan who liked too much alcohol, but this one was as bright as the ginger mop on his head.

'Well, I'll drink to that,' I said looking at Robbie, and took a sip of my pint.

'What do you think, Mac?' Jacques asked me.

'I'm never one to turn down a decent opportunity, Jacques, you know that.'

'Aye, that's the spirit, pal,' Robbie said.

'So as far as planning goes, gentlemen, how many hands do we need?' I asked.

'Us three and one more?' the Jock suggested.

'Are you thinking what I'm thinking?' Jacques asked.

'Who?... Mick?' I replied hesitantly.

'Sure, why not. He is a locksmith after all,' Jacques replied.

'Who the fuck is Mick!?' the Jock enquired. 'I hope this Mick is not some crazy Irishman,' he added breathing heavily through his nostrils.

'No, he's not. And Mick is kind of new to this game and may need some persuading,' Jacques pointed out.

'Would that be two by four persuading? Or money up front persuading?' the Jock asked with a puzzled look on his face.

I said, 'To tell you the truth, I'm not really sure.'

'And you got the balls to call me mad, pal. And furthermore, don't you have anyone to hand that you can rely on?' the Jock retorted.

We explained to Robbie about Mick being a locksmith and being used to opening safes.

'Aye, okay, I see your point, pal. Ask him if he is interested, I'm off back to my hotel to get some rest as I want to check the night life here in Cardiff as well as the fine Welsh women, 'Robbie stated rubbing his chubby hands together.

'Okay fine. Call me tomorrow, mate, and stay out of them strip clubs.'

'Not if I can help it, pal,' Robbie replied laughing.

With that agreed, we departed with handshakes and headed back to Barry to visit Mick and somehow persuade him to come in on the job with us. But will Mick join us?

On our way back to Barry Island, Jacques and I discussed our options on how best to approach Mick to come in on the job and we figured our only option was to ask Mick outright with no beating around the bush, just straight up front. I rang Mick on his mobile and arranged for me and Jacques to meet him at his apartment, which he agreed to, but Jacques suggested that we take Mick to the Water's Edge for a couple of drinks and pointed out that it would be more in more a relaxing surroundings to try soften the blow if possible.

We parked the car and buzzed Mick's intercom. 'Hello,' he replied.

'It's me and Jacques,' I responded. Mick buzzed us in through the security door and as we headed into the lift, Jacques asked, 'Are you sure you want to ask him, Mac, as I'm having second thoughts, mate.'

'Fuck it, Jacques. He can only say yes or no, can't he?' I replied.

We arrived at the sixth floor with a "ping", the lift doors opened. I knocked on the door and Mick opened it. 'Come on through. Nice to see you both again, make yourselves at home. Coffee, tea or maybe something a little stronger?' he asked jokingly.

'Not for me, thanks.'

'Me neither,' I added.

'Well, this is nice of you to drop in on me,' Mick said.

'Yes, um, we were wondering if you want to come and see Man U play this weekend? 'Jacques asked him with a tone of enthusiasm.

'Now you're fucking with me, boys. You're winding me up?' Mick replied feverishly.

I looked at Jacques stunned and confused as to where this was going and calmly replied, 'No, Mick, it's the truth, mate. Jacques has got three tickets coming for this Saturday's game via a friend of a friend, haven't you, Jacques?' I said enthusiastically, going along with Jacques and costing him a few quid at the same time. Jacques spun around and scowled at me before facing back to Mick, turning the conversation away from what I had in mind and spent the next half hour going on about Man U, which does my fucking head in, as I only like Cardiff City, and to make matters worse, I would have to go to Old Strafford and watch the fuckers play with these two. Mick went to the bathroom grinning from ear to ear, so I immediately tore into Jacques.

'What the fuck are you doing? 'I asked him in almost a whisper.

'No! What the fuck are you doing? Where did you get I'm getting three tickets from? Have you got any idea how much this is going to cost us? 'he whispered back.

'It's not going to cost us, it's going to cost you, mate, 'I whispered.

'Fuck you, Mac!'

'No, fuck you! We were supposed to lay it on him straight and you come out with this bullshit football sketch,' I told him keeping it to a whisper.

With his face screwed up, Jacques pointed at me and said, 'Half each as I was on about going to a boozer and watching it on a big screen whilst trying to break the ice at the same time.'

I pointed at him and was about to tell him it was his fuck-up and he should have to pay when we heard the lavatory flush; we both moved back off the edge of our seats to a more relaxed posture. The three of us talked some more and arranged a Saturday in Manchester and our means of transportation when suddenly Jacques said smiling, 'Hey, Mac, why don't you see that girl in the travel agents and see if she can get us some cheap return flights?' Now the bastard was getting his own back on me for the football tickets.

'Yes, I will, good thinking,' I replied with a fuck you look at him.

Mick thought it all too much and suggested we go by car or rail, but Jacques insisted we stick with the return flights and lapping it all up in the moment of his self-reviews. Mick by now was totally thrilled to bits with his weekend ahead as well as Jacques, as it had all turned out nice for those pair. We both said our goodbyes to Mick and as soon as we were both out the apartment block and in the car, I turned to Jacques and told him, 'You fucking knob jockey! Flights?! Where did you get that from for Christ's sake? Get out of the car, you're fucking walking home.'

Jacques burst out laughing which only infuriated me even more.

'What the fuck are you laughing at?'

'Us, Mac. We're like two kids again.'

'That's because you are a kid! You only got to buy the tickets to—' Jacques cut me off.

'Mac, lighten up, will you? It will be a good time to ask Mick to come in on the job with us,' he pointed out still chuckling to himself.

'Don't laugh, mate.'

'I'm not anymore,' he replied turning to look out of the car side window.

'What about the Jock, what's he going to do?'

'Party in Cardiff probably?'

'What, till Sunday?'

'He'll be fine. He's booked into the Big Easy Hotel for the week and no doubt emptying his man fluid inside some stuffers fuck hole.'

Laughing I said, 'Where you going to? I'll drop you off.'
After a slight pause for thought, Jacques said 'The White Horse. Fancy a beer on me?'

'Why not, it will give you time to think where you're getting them Man U tickets from and me the flights.'

Really speaking, we had both put our foot in it and now we were both going to pay a hefty penalty to get out of the situation; still, that's the way things go sometimes. Even today I think we should have asked Mick in on the job right there and then with no fucking about! Jacques managed to secure the tickets for the Man U game via a friend of Robbie (The Jock) who had been living in Manchester for a few years who is connected in the football scene. All we had to do was turn up a few hours before kick-off at a pub and we'd be sorted with the tickets for the match, and it would only cost us a phone call. That left me with the flights of course, which I got my sister working on and she reckoned they won't cost that much on an internal flight.

As it turned out, the flights only cost me sixty-four quid each for returns, so it wasn't all that bad after all. Saturday soon came around and it wasn't long before we arrived at Manchester from Cardiff International Airport some forty minutes later. Once we had come through arrivals to the outside, Jacques dialled the number that Robbie had given him and after a brief conversation, Jacques hailed a taxi and told the driver to take us to a pub called the Black Grape. The taxi pulled up outside the Black Grape and as I handed the money over for the fare, the driver bade us good luck and sped off rapidly. We went inside to a packed pub that was totally going fucking nuts with football songs and every fucker making a racket in a sea of red.

Jacques made his way through the crowd, closely followed by me and Mick to the bar and ordered three pints of beer. Mick insisted on paying for the beer out of courtesy for our efforts and handed the barman a tenner. At the same time, Jacques asked the barman where he could find Big Jimmy. The barman said something to one of his bar staff who disappeared and came back with a huge figure of a guy working his way through the chaotic crowd. The barman pointed at us three as the big guy made his way towards us, literally shovelling people out of his way and asked us, 'Are you three Robbie's pals?'

'That's right,' Jacques replied.

'I'm Jimmy, best you come follow me over here then, 'he roared.

We followed behind him as he opened up the crowd in his path, shouting, 'make way, numb nuts, make fucking way!' The crowd opened up for him like the parting of the Red Sea; we followed in his wake until he reached a crowd of guys that was sat around a few tables singing football songs.

'Right, you lot, shift your fucking asses and make some room for these three,' he demanded. Everyone seemed to want to catch our eye and poor old Mick was shitting himself.

'Come on, fucking move, you bunch of spunk necks,' Jimmy barked out.

Three guys instantly vanished, but on the account of the size of Jimmy, I'd have moved too. 'Sit down, pal, and chill out. You be okay with me here and take no notice of these fannies, you're in good company.' Looking at Mick, Big Jimmy said, 'What's the matter, pal, you ill or something?'

'No, no, I'm err fine.'

'Thought you were going to hurl on my floor,' he said smiling but continued, 'I'm Big Jimmy as you know, how are you all? And how's that fucker settling into that sheep shagging lark you lot get up to in Wales?' he asked giggling.

'We're good, Jimmy, but Robbie is having teething problems with the sheep shagging,' I replied.

'What the fucks you mean teething problems?'

'Well, he can't run in Wellingtons and he won't wear a ski-mask! Plus, he's fed up of shagging the sheep last,' I replied joking.

With that comment, Jimmy started laughing his bollocks off and when he could catch a breath, he pointed at us and said, 'Ski masks, eh. You're fucking sick, pal.' And off he went laughing hysterically again.

Jacques, Mick and I raised our eyebrows at each other and quickly glugged some beer down our necks and just smiled back at Jimmy.

'Here are your tickets. You can come to the ground with us if you like, but after the game me and my lads have got some unfinished business with them Arsenal fans and you're not invited as it's not your bother. Hope you're not too offended.'

'No offence taken, Jimmy,' I told him.

'Care for any more drinks?' Mick asked.

'Are you trying to chat me up, pal?' Jimmy asked Mick.

'I'm sorry, I err, have I said something wrong?' Mick asked Jimmy puzzled.

'Either you want to fuck me or you're gay, in which case it could be both. Now if you ask a man if he wants a drink then ask him manly like, pal,' Jimmy said staring wildly at Mick.

'What you having?' Mick tried, shitting himself.

'Double Jacks and Coke! It's my pub, pal, and you're a guest here so the drinks are on me,' he replied giggling.

Big Jimmy waved his hand in the air, beckoning the barman to come over which he did immediately; Jimmy told him to take our orders pronto.

We stuck with lagers, ordering three pints which the barman brought back minutes later, along with double Jacks and coke for Jimmy, who then put a bag of cocaine and a money bag full of ecstasy on the table and invited us to help ourselves saying, 'To help get into the swing of things before the match begins, lads.' We declined but thanked him for the invite to which he replied, 'Is you fucking lightweights from Cardiff or you Welsh Baptists that's been influenced by your half-sister Joan of Arc? For fuck's sake, pal, enjoy yourselves.'

With that thrown in our faces, I grabbed the cocaine, opened the bag and wet the tip of my finger, dabbing it in the white powder and sucked the coke off the end of it, likewise Jacques followed suit. As for Mick, he sucked the length of his finger and put it inside the bag of powder and took more than the average user does a day and sucked his finger clean and then said, 'What does it do?'

All of us around the table looked at him gobsmacked except Jimmy who said to Mick, 'Ay ay, pal, when was the last time you had fucking sherbets? You're not a barrister, are you? 'Cos let me tell you, pal, in ten minutes time you're going to fucking sound like one!'

Everyone around the table burst into fits of laughter including me and Jacques. Mick must have dabbed a good two grams and albeit was his first time on the shit with only fifty minutes left to kick off.

'Right, lads,' Jimmy shouts out. 'Finish your drinks and let's get to the ground and show these fuckers our new banners. 'The pub instantly erupted into cheers of hysteria with beer being thrown in the air and the odd skinny fan!

'Follow me,' Jimmy yelled as he opened a door that led into the car park out back and once outside, he ordered all those present to get into the four mini buses waiting. 'And don't forget to use the floor space. You three included,' Jimmy barked looking at me, Jacques and Mick.

Mick started to come up on the coke and wouldn't shut up about how good Man U were as the side door slid to a close with crates of Stella produced and everyone reached out for a can for the journey.

'Fuck, this feels good,' Mick says. 'Feels like I'm in heaven, what a sensation! I can't remember the last time I had a feeling like this,' he added smiling.

'Probably because you never had cocaine before,' I reminded him.

'Just try and keep it together, Mick, and you'll be fine, okay?' Jacques advised him.

'Feels like I'm here but I'm not, if that makes any sense to you 'coz you're not me, so you can't be feeling what I'm feeling, though you probably are? I mean 'coz we're going to the match together and we're in the same van, which is a first for me but of course you never knew that till I just told you. So you see, you now know you haven't missed anything on my behalf, which you all naturally understand, if you get my point?' Mick finished with everyone staring at him in stunned silence!

'What?' Mick said shrugging his shoulders.

'Thanks for your in-depth view of one's analogies and to draw comparisons, my Welsh friend, you're off your fucking head on coke and going to see the greatest team in the world. I just hope you can sing as well as you can gas! And by the way, pal, which planet in the solar system are you from, eh?!' Jimmy asked him, eyeing Mick cautiously.

'Earth,' Mick replied, pleased with his answer.

The mini bus erupted in fits of hysterical laughter at Mick's reply when suddenly the mini buses came to a screeching stop a few streets away from the football stadium and everyone bailed out. 'Get the banners, lads,' Jimmy yelled out.

We all went in on foot from here though the street was packed with fans and police in vans and on horses; they seemed to be directing the fans which way to go to the stadium gates. We arrived at the gates and within twenty minutes were inside, going up a staircase and out onto the terraces.

'Get the bloody banners out,' Jimmy cried out.

Already the ground was packed to capacity with songs being sung from both supporting fans. Mick had a huge grin on his face. 'It's electric in here, lads. I can't thank you enough, and if ever I can repay or make it up to you in some way, it'll be my pleasure,' Mick stated.

'It'll come sooner than he thinks,' Jacques said to me in an undertone.

'He's off his fucking head, mate.'

'It's like he's smiling for the whole world.'

'It's quite possible he'll be cracking one off at half time too, 'one of big Jimmy's boys remarked. Jacques and I had a quiet laugh on the side while Mick got used to his buzz of coke.

The match kicked off and at the end of the first half, Man U were 2-1 up on Arsenal, and the atmosphere in the stadium was electric with the hairs standing up on the backs of our necks. The queues for the toilets were enormous, so I pissed into a water bottle amongst the fans, as did a lot of them. The second half got under way with Arsenal kicking off and eight minutes later, they scored from a corner, levelling the match even. Both teams started to defend in a big way and the ball was not going near either goal posts until Arsenal played a long ball through the midfield and their striker ran the ball past Man U's defence just outside their box and struck the ball into the bottom left corner, past the goalie and into the back of the net; the Arsenal fans erupted into hysteria again.

And that's how the game finished: 3-2 Arsenal. Jimmy and his entourage bade us farewell before they went to sort out some unfinished business with the Arsenal fans somewhere. But in all, it was a great day even though Mick and Jacques' team had lost, they were in fine spirits and me too for that matter.

We stayed on the terraces for ten minutes as to let the stadium empty out a bit before we made our way out into the streets. We followed a couple of straddlers in the same direction they were heading and after about fifteen minutes of walking, we saw a cab and hailed it down.

'Where you going?' the cabbie asked.

'Take us to a hotel or a pub close to the airport,' I told him.

'Will do, climb in.'

We had the usual cabbie chat enroute. Where you from? How long you here for? How was the match? …etc, etc., etc. The cabbie parked outside a nice-looking pub and asked us if okay. We told him it would do and paid him thirty-five quid and went inside the pub to the bar area and ordered up three pints with three steak and chips from the menu and sat down next to the window to wait for our food to arrive.

'I feel like shit, guys, and tired too,' Mick said chewing his lips.

'That's the coke wearing off, mate,' I replied to him. 'But you'll survive.'

'Not sure his lips will,' Jacques said laughing.

'We'll get these steaks down our necks and then go to the airport, as our flight back to Cardiff is at ten and I don't want us to miss it,' I told them.

'Neither do I,' Jacques added.

Mick started probing both his cheeks with his tongue and touching his teeth with his fingers. He scratched his nose and played with his bottom lip a lot.

The steaks arrived and Mick struggled to eat his, but he did manage to chew half of his gum off whilst me and Jacques polished ours off in no time. We asked the barman to order us a taxi to take us to the airport and twenty minutes later we were in departures. We got back to Cardiff International Airport and shared a taxi back to town, each of us getting dropped off along the way with me being last. I paid the driver and got in to my apartment shutting the door behind me. I kicked off my shoes and went to the kitchen, and drank a pint of water then stripped off and jumped into bed, knackered. I lay awake a while thinking that we couldn't mention the job to Mick as he'd done too much cocaine and he wasn't in the right frame of mind to approach him.

Not only that, we had a great day, and Jacques and I didn't want to spoil it for Mick as he was having the time of his life to be honest, so it would have been inappropriate of us to ruin it for him. But tomorrow would be another day and the right time to ask him that his skills were needed; I wasn't sure how he was going to react to our proposition so to speak, but what I could guess, was that it's not going to be good only sour grapes.

And with that in mind, I turned my attention to all those lovely diamonds just sitting there calling me. And then there was the biggest upset to all this and that was getting them out of Norway safely and then turned into cash which can be hard of course, but I know a few Jews who like diamonds in a big way and they got the money and know a good deal when they see one. I fell off to sleep thinking of all possibilities on how to get them out of Norway, and sometimes the simplest ways are the best and are always overlooked. We were going a little more help…My thoughts drifted to Fox.

The next day I woke up at 11:00 am feeling shattered and drained, but there was only one thing on my mind and that was to convince Mick to come in on this job with us and to make it priority. I showered and made a mug of tea, and then sat down picking up the TV remote and turned on the news channel to see what'd been happening in the rest of the world, but it was the same stories with more suicide bombings in Afghanistan in the Helmand province, more troops dead again. Global warming issues and the housing market crashing leading us into a recession and unemployment rising etc.

I lit a cigarette and called Jacques on his mobile phone and went straight through to voicemail. I didn't leave a message and just hung up as I hate talking to machines myself.

I called Mick who answered immediately. 'I'm still fucked, mate,' he said groggily.

'Me too, but listen, try to recover from it and I'll call you around twelve thirty, mate.'

'Yeah okay, fine. See you later,' he replied, ending the call.

I was in the middle of making another cup of tea when my mobile rang; it was Jacques. 'Okay, mate, how are you feeling?'

'Not too bad now, but I felt shattered when I first woke up. I've had an overdose of caffeine and feel a tad better, thanks.'

'Listen, mate. I called Mick a few minutes ago and have arranged to meet with him at twelve thirty and you're going to be there too, okay?'

'So you're definitely going to ask him the sixty-four million dollar question then, Mac?'

'Something like that, mate, yes.'

'Are you sure it's wise to ask him, mate, it's just he might get the wrong impression of us?'

'Whatever the impression he gets, I know I can trust him to keep his mouth shut.'

'Fine then, mate, but I bet you it goes tits up and don't say I haven't warned you, Mac!

'I'll give you a ring around twelve-ish to let you know where we're at, ok?'

'Okay, do that and I'll be there, mate.' And with that the phone line went dead.

Jacques has been through some shit in his life as his parents got divorced when he was at a young age, sadly, he totally went off the rails mixing with bad company, which led to him going to jail at seventeen for smash and grabs on jewellers and electrical shops, whereby he would put a car through a shop window (or batter the shop window with a spade) and grab a load of electrical items or grab a hoard of gold, and be gone in two minutes.

At eighteen, Jacques was released from Portland Young Offenders Institution and came back to Barry Island for a few weeks, and wanting to stay clear of crime, he decided to travel to France and enlist in the French Foreign Legion where he stayed for three years. He spent two years in four jungles training for jungle warfare and spent eight weeks on Devil's Island in French Guiana (famous in *Papillon*) as a bonding session with another 11 Legionnaires in the Rep, as they had to spend the next two years trusting, living and watching each other's backs. From there, he went to Djibouti in Africa, playing his part in x-amount of missions into Somalia as a peace-keeping force, even though he was classed as a mercenary by the seldom few who do not understand the Legion is a modern day army and the roles the French Foreign Legion play around the world as a primary peace keeping force taking on duties that other world countries cannot take undertake due to their political ties and investments in those countries where hostilities have erupted.

All he ever said about Somalia was it's full of dead bodies, the majority being children and the minority being adults, and that there is no democracy in the country, and that the dictators that run it don't give a shit about their own people, and that the people don't give a shit about each other. He called it Badlands and that's as far as he would open up on the subject when he wanted to talk about it, that is not just to anyone, as you have to know Jacques a long time for him to open up, much the same as you and I.

But the Legion did teach him a trade before putting him back into society: welding.

At twenty-one, he returned to the U.K. and back to Barry Island and got a recognized apprenticeship with J. B. Engineering, a small local firm on the docks where he stayed until he got his papers and coding in welding, and with an apprenticeship under his belt, the world was his oyster. Jacques decided to go contracting around the U.K and the rest of the world. Though very much the gentleman, he comes across as a laid-back person. You can trust him with your life, even though he can kill a man with his bare hands in the blink of an eye if pressed hard enough.

Chapter 3

Curiosity Killed the Cat

I phoned Mick and Jacques just after midday asking them to meet me at the Water's Edge for that chat. I drove into the car park of the Water's Edge half an hour early (for a change) and parked up. I walked to the pebbles beach opposite and took in the view across the Bristol Channel which is not much to look at but it's better than being surrounded by concrete and car fumes. I lit a cigarette, inhaling deeply as I knew this chat with Mick was going to be traumatic for him. Still ... shit or bust, I guess, at a flip of a coin. I liked it there, a soft breeze blowing, and watching the exposed sand dance across the beach when the tides out with the faint sound of the sea breaking on the shoreline. My phone rang and I answered it; it was Mick. 'Where are you? Jacques and I are in the bar. We saw your car but can't see you anywhere?'

'I'll be there now, I'm just getting some sea air. You can order me a bottle of lager.'

I turned off the phone and made my way inside the bar and sat down at their table. 'Okay, lads?'

'I feel a little rough around the edges,' Jacques replied.

'Yesterday was awesome. I should not have taken the cocaine as it totally fucked me up. Though, I can't thank you both enough for a fantastic day.'

'You're welcome, Mick,' I told to him.

Jacques raised his eyebrows at me as if to say, 'Don't ask him,' when Mick handed me a bottle of lager. 'Cheers mate, thanks,'

I asked Mick if he'd thought about his future and had he any immediate plans.

'Not at this moment in time, I haven't given it much thought. But I will need to get a job soon though, as money don't last forever.'

'How would you like your own business again?' I asked eagerly.

'That isn't going to happen, Mac, as I don't have the money to start up again, and I can't see the bank lending me any money as I've been out the country for years, so I got no credit history here…'

I interrupted him, 'What if we could help you to get started again if the opportunity arose in your favour?'

'I'm confused, mate, I'm not sure if I follow. What … are you trying to lend me the money or something? I couldn't possibly accept.'

'Finish your beer, Mick, I'll get us three more bottles.' On my return back from the bar with the bottles of beer, I asked Mick and Jacques to join me for a stroll along the beach to which they both agreed. I lit up a cigarette as we took a slow stroll towards the end of the beach. Eventually, we arrived at some rocks near the end of the beach and suggested we sit down on them. Jacques shot me a look and shook his head (as if to say not now) but I took no notice.

'Mick, I have a problem and I need your help,' I blurted out.

'Sure, if I can help you, by all means. What is it?' he replied.

'I need you to open a safe for me and my friend.'

'I haven't got the tools to open a safe, but if I did, I'd be glad to. Why? Has he lost the key or combination?'

'Something of the sort, Mick.'

Jacques interrupted, 'And it's in Norway.'

'Norway?! What is it doing in Norway? I don't follow you. Why not get a locksmith in Norway to open it?' Mick asked puzzled.

I hesitated but said, 'Because we can't.'

'But why not, I still don't follow you?'

'Because it does not rightfully belong to us although what's inside it, does,' I told him.

'But if it's not rightfully yours, then how do you expect me to open it…' and that was the moment the penny dropped. Jacques and I looked at him with deep regret, but Jacques was right, Mick wasn't having any of it.

'Are you asking me to do what I think you're asking me to do? No! You can't be serious. Ha ha, you're joking, right?'

'No, we're not. We're serious, mate,' I replied sternly.

'But… you work. Come on, fellas, you don't do this sort of shit, you can't?'

'Oh, but we very much do, and have been doing this sort of shit occasionally for quite some time, mate, apart from working on refineries and oil rigs.'

'Fuck, hell no fucking way! And the going to Manchester to watch the match was to butter me up, I suppose, was it? You deliberately set out to gain my trust and then you come out with a ridiculous notion that I will rob a safe for you?'

Me and Jacques sat in silence and let him get it out of his system as Mick continued telling us, 'Have you thought what the consequences would be if we got caught and went to prison? I can just see it now in the showers in some foreign prison, being asked to pick up someone else's soap that has been dropped on purpose and no sooner have I bent down, I'm being bum fucked if not gang raped, fuck it! The answer's NO! Fuck You!! forget it,' he finished.

'Hear me out a little, mate,' I began but Mick cut me off.

'No. I don't want to hear you out if this is your answer to me getting my own business again. How fucked up is that I ask you? I got to steal it, no way, not for you, not for my grandmother, most of all not for fucking anyone! I need a drink, I think. I thought you were my friends, fuck!' With that said, he turned and stormed off back up the beach towards the Water's Edge.

'Told you not to ask him, mate,' Jacques said necking the rest of his beer and throwing the bottle into the sea.

'Come on, let's catch him up. He'll get over it, just you wait and see.' I lit a cigarette up and we started walking slowly back up the beach after Mick.

Back at the Water's Edge, we could see Mick stood at the bar. We walked in and stood either side of him, I turned to him and told him that we were sorry for asking him to do such a crazy thing and that we were bang out of order, and hoped this would not affect our friendship and that we can still be mates. Jacques apologised too and showed great remorse in his expression and ordered Mick a double vodka and coke, which he drank down in one go, so I ordered him another which he repeated drinking it down in one.

Then Mick turned to us and said, 'I got a question for you both.'

'Of course, ask anything,' I replied.

'Tell me you never took me to Manchester to sweeten me up? That's all I want to hear from you both and nothing else.'

'Mick, mate, how long have we known each other? I know you have only just met Jacques, but in all honesty to your question, no mate, we didn't take you to see United and try to use it as a sweetener. It's just this sort of work is your field and we're stuck, it just happens to be you're the closest person we could trust to ask, mate. If we could trust someone else, then we would have asked them, but there is no-one else. Even without you, we're going to do it anyway

39

and seeming you took those diamonds in Germany and took a beating for it, we kind of thought there might have been a chance you were not telling us everything, which is understandable under the circumstances.'

'I'm honest in what I told you, Mac. It was a one off and that's all,' he retorted.

'We have been totally honest with you, Mick. We haven't lied or deceived you in any way. Maybe a little up front but that's about all.'

'I was more shocked and angered to say the least after what happened to me in Germany. It just brought terrible memories flooding back and I over-reacted, that's all, guys.'

Jacques handed us both a Bacardi and Vodka and coke, and suggested we go outside away from the barman's big ears, to which I nodded in agreement. We sat at a table in the beer garden in silence when Mick asked us, 'What's inside the safe?'

'Why do you want to know?' Jacques asked him bluntly.

'Curiosity, of course,' Mick replied sharply.

'Diamonds,' I informed him bluntly.

'Oh no! Not those fucking things again,' he chuckled.

'Afraid so, mate.'

'How many?'

'To tell you the truth, we're not sure, but roughly over two point three million pounds worth,' Jacques replied.

'WHAT?!' Mick cried out.

'We know there's that amount roughly on show in the display counters and windows, so whatever's in the safe is a bonus,' I told him.

'Are you serious? That's like an incredible amount of money. Are you armed robbers then?' he asks inquisitively like a child.

'No, mate, if we were armed robbers, we wouldn't be asking you for your help, would we. No, we're not them sort of people. We go in after everyone has gone home from work to their creature comforts of their homes, which allows us a good eight hours to do what we want without causing any harm to anyone,' I told him.

'We can drill the safe ourselves with a magnetic drill, but if we fail to hit the pin in the locking mechanism then all the locking bars jam as you know, and we won't be able to open the door. Then we gotta piss around with oxyacetylene bottles and start burning, which takes longer. It all costs time when all we want is in and out as fast as possible,' Jacques kindly informed Mick.

'What about alarms?'

'Oh, they're not a problem. Nothing a can of filler foam for cavities in walls won't sort out and a heavy-duty pair of cable cutters for the telecom wires running underground,' I said, enlightening him.

'But how and where do you know where to find the cables?' he asked.

'Ah well, that's easy. The telecom companies have been generous for years by marking their drain lids on the ground with *Telecommunications* stamped on them. So, we look for them, lift up the cover, find the cable with *Telecommunications* stamped all over it and cut the cable in half. It won't kill you or even give you a shock, as there is no electricity running through the cable. Pick a telecom engineer's brains over a pint and you'd be surprised what you can find out, especially if he's been sacked or made redundant.

'Anyway, why do you want to know all this if you're not interested?' I reminded him.

'It just sounds exciting, that's all.'

'It is exciting, mate, and the rewards can be exciting too as can the lifestyle in the end.'

I left Mick and Jacques, and went to the bar and ordered more double Bacardi's and Vodka cokes along with burgers and chips, and couldn't help feel Mick was going to be coming with us after all, as he was too over-interested in what we had told him so far. Anyone who did not want a part in what we were planning, should have by now made their excuses and left Jacques and I on our lonesome as past experiences had taught me.

Carrying the drinks over, I could tell Mick was still picking Jacques's brains when I rudely interrupted them both saying, 'Ok, guys, that's more than enough small talk for one day, I reckon.'

'Yes, I agree. Tomorrow is another day,' Jacques said in agreement.

'But I was getting into it all,' Mick sighed.

I winked at Jacques who knew Mick was on the hook.

'Here is your order, sir, three burgers and chips,' said the barman as he set them down on our table and left.

Just then, Jacques' phone rang. 'Hello, Robbie, how's it going, mate? Yeah, everything's good, mate,' he babbled on for another two minutes before he finished the call and said to me, 'That was Robbie. He's been having the time of his life in Cardiff and he wants to see us tomorrow for a meet.'

'Fancy a few hours in Cardiff, Mick?' I asked.

'I'll go with the flow,' he replied before popping a chip in his mouth.

'Jacques, text Robbie and let him know Mick is coming in too.'

'Sure, Mac, I'll send it now.'

'Who's Robbie?' Mick asked.

'He's a very good friend of mine, 'Jacque's replied.

'You'll like him he's…well—'

Mick interrupted, 'Can I ask you something without going back on the subject?'

'Fire away, mate,' I said with a raised brow.

'Just out of curiosity, that's all, do you know what make and model the safe is?'

'No, but Robbie got it on video on his phone.'

'And you can see it for yourself tomorrow when you meet him,' Jacques added.

'I was thinking I might be able to help you after all. If I can identify the make and model of the safe, then I can tell you exactly where to drill through the locking mechanism.'

I smiled at Jacques and said, 'Problem solved.'

'Looks that way, but we'll find out for sure when Mick sees the video for himself.'

'Thanks, Mick, that would be a big help. Are you sure, as we don't want to get you to do something you're not comfortable with,' I told him.

'Not a problem as I'm not doing anything wrong… Am I? Well, not really,' he added.

'Right, I think the best thing we can do here then is call a taxi up to town and have a few more drinks, shoot a few games of pool and try get an early night,' I suggested to them both.

We took the taxi ride up town to the White Horse and switched back to lagers and shot a few games of pool, and had a laugh at the same time. It turned out Mick was a good pool player and whipped our butts and the regulars in there too. Even the landlord was impressed with Mick's performance and asked him to join the pool team – fancy that!

But Mick declined the landlord's offer for now and said he would think about it. A woman had taken an interest in Mick too, so me and Jacques urged him to buy her a drink which he did; she invited him to sit down next to her by patting the seat with her hand.

'Looks like they're getting on like a house on fire,' Jacques commented.

'Yes. Good on him, mate,' I replied.

We both left Mick to it with his lady friend and got taxis our separate ways home after we had been to the Chinese takeaway. Back in my apartment, I thought I couldn't wait for tomorrow to come, so that Mick could feast his eyes on the safe. And then there was the planning which always gave me a kick as I treated it like a safety briefing – safety first!

I thoroughly enjoyed going over the details of the crime we were going to commit and smoothing out the awkward technicalities that could jeopardise or inconvenience us. I made sure my analytical balances were fine-tuned and always at the fore-front of my mind, making sure nobody was a liability to themselves or to any other persons that were involved. And that there was a plan B to act upon if anything did go wrong.

Chapter 4

The Girl Next Door and Tapas

The next morning, I got woken up by banging on my front door. I got out of bed, put my shorts on and opened the door to see my next-door neighbour, Susan, looking distraught.

'Sorry to bother you this early, Mac, but I locked myself out and was wondering if I could wait here till the locksmith arrives? Nice body by the way, 'she added eyeing me up and down smiling.

'Yeah sure, come on in. What time is it?' I asked her yawning.

'Seven am. I was on my way to work and closed the door without thinking. I must have left my keys on the bureau.'

'Tea or coffee?' I asked her.

'Coffee please, black with one sugar.'

'You're sweet enough,' I told her suggestively.

'Thanks for the compliment, mind if I smoke,' she asked eyeing me up and down.

'Sure, go ahead, make yourself at home.'

'Do you work out, Mac?' She asked bluntly.

'Not really,' I replied eyeing her up and down as I lit my own cigarette.

'I do every day in my lunch hour except on Sundays,' she informed me.

'Here's your coffee, Sue, and the only time I get to work out is in the bedroom.'

'Ooh really?' she replied, sounding surprised.

I looked at her with a playful suggestive smile as she inhaled on her menthol cigarette and blew a smoke ring in the direction of my crotch, followed up with a cheeky eyeing. I was sat on the sofa opposite her and couldn't help thinking she was playfully cock teasing me. She was dressed in her office attire, wearing a fitted black suit jacket over her white open-collar shirt, with a tight-fitting black skirt cut a good few inches above her knees, over black seamed stockings with black court shoes on her feet. *I want to fuck her,* I thought to myself.

'Do you want to come over for dinner with me tonight, Mac?' she asked, partially parting her inner thighs so I got a quick flash of her suspenders and black knickers.

I broke a wide smile and said, 'I'd love to *cum* over.'

'Eight thirty fine for you?' she asked, playing the cum remark down.

'Sure, Sue,' I replied, loving her approach.

'What's that bulge in your shorts?' she blurted out, putting her finger between her lips.

'Why don't you come over here and find out for yourself?' I replied, staring at her lips relishing in her cock teasing act.

She stubbed out her cigarette hard in the ashtray and came over kneeling between my legs and pulled my shorts down to my ankles and spread my legs wide apart and said all too thrilled, 'Oh yes, nice juicy cock.'

She grabbed hold of my cock and put the rest in her mouth, sucking it long and hard, twisting her wrist at the same time. Once stiff, she gave my cock a few vigorous yanks whilst licking its thick shaft and slowly sucked each of my balls. Looking up at me wide eyed, pleased with herself, she stood up and threw herself over the kitchen work top and said, 'Come on, fuck me hard!!'

I complied with her wishes and walked slowly over to her and hitched her tight skirt up over her buttocks, revealing her suspenders and black thong. I pulled the thong to one side as she reached around with both her hands and pulled her rounded bum cheeks apart, allowing me to get a good eyeful of her partly shaved pouting wet pussy before I pushed my thick cock half way inside her hot wet breach. Sue laid her head down on the work top and gasped, 'Argh! Fuck!! That's a fat cock!!

I took a firm hold of her waistline and I thrust my cock deep inside her and slowly pulled its fat tip out to the edges of her inner breach, again, listening to her panting gasp, then slowly sank it back inside her and began rhythmically pounding her away. Sue grabbed hold of the tap faucet on the sink with both hands and cried out, 'Come on, that's it, fuck me harder!'

I lifted her leg off the floor and forced her knee up on top of the worktop and started pounding her pussy hard, my fat cock ramming in and out of her. 'You want this, you fucking want this?' I said through gritted teeth.

'Fuck yes, I want it!! Don't stop,' she begged.

45

'Yeah, yeah, yeah, yeah, yeah, yeah,' I said through gritted teeth, hearing my balls slap hard against her and every time they slapped against her my cock dug deeper inside her, she let out little hiccupping groans which turned me on even more, destroying my soul and wrecking my brain's stimulation. Sue thrust her buttocks backwards taking in the cock's length. I fucked her harder!

'Arghhhh God, I'm cumming! Fuck yes!! I'm gunna cum! Argh God, yes, yes, yes, yes, give me that fucking fat cock right there, you fucker!' she screamed out.

My cock went berserk, throbbing uncontrollably inside her as the spasms in my Achilles heel shot up through the backs of my legs to my balls, squeezing them tighter as they burst under her submission, exploding my hot fluid inside her soaking cunt. I pushed my cock down deeper to the delight of her magnificent groan. Her love juices exploded all over my magnanimous meaty cock and hot soaked balls, sending violent shudders through her collapsing body as her leg buckled from underneath her. I held her up by her waist and buttock, pushing her back over the work top, exhausted!!

'Fuck! You're fucking fantastic,' I gasped, playfully slapping her bum.

'God. Fuck yeah, that fucking cock is amazing,' she panted adding, 'Phew! We should do this more often.'

'Yeah, we should, you're the best fuck I've had in weeks.' I lied.

'Thanks, you're a top shag yourself,' she said between bated breaths adding, 'Mind if I use your bathroom to straighten myself up?'

'No, go ahead,' I replied, withdrawing my semi chunk of meat from her soaked pussy adding, 'Do you want more coffee?'

'Fuck yeah,' she hoarsely replied.

Five minutes later, Sue reappeared brand new again. She lit a cigarette and exhaled. 'I wanted to have hard sex like that with you for ages, but you're hardly home,' she said sipping her coffee adding, 'and when you're home, you're always out.'

'So, you've knocked on my door previously?'

'Yes, several times. I've so wanted to fuck you for ages,' she replied confidently then her phone rang. 'Okay, I'll let you in. It's the locksmith, can I buzz him in from here, Mac?'

I nodded to her and said, 'I'll take a shower and see you later then?'

'Too fucking right you will, you've had your starters honey so it'll be straight to the main course tonight. I'll see myself out, honey, and thanks for the coffee and the shag.' She opened the door turned and blew me a kiss and was gone.

What a way to start the day; that was rampant and horny as fuck, I thought to myself. I got a feeling all was going to go well today with me and the rest of the lads in Cardiff later on. And with that in mind, I took a long shower grinning from ear to ear.

I got dressed and took a taxi ride to the Water's Edge to collect my car from the car park. From there, I headed to the greasy spoon for a full breakfast and a flick through the morning papers when Jacques called me on my mobile phone.

'Okay, mate,' I answer.

'Yeah, good, mate. I tried calling Mick but he's not answering. He's probably shacked up with that woman from last night.'

'More than likely, mate, but he could be sleeping.'

'I'm going to call a taxi and get my car from the Water's Edge, so as soon as I pick it up, I'll come and get you to get yours.'

'I've already been over and got mine. Once I've finished my breakfast, I'll pick you up, mate, to get your car back.'

'Yeah, that'll be great, Mac, see you soon.'

I drove around to Jacques 'pad and beeped the horn and waited. A minute later, we were on our way to the Water's Edge. I turned to Jacques and told him of my morning with Susan (the girl next door) and filled him in on all the details.

'I wish the girl opposite me would give me an early morning call like that, you spunky bastard you,' he commented.

'She's invited me over tonight for the main course,' I told Jacques smugly.

'How long has she lived opposite you then?'

'She moved in about a year ago but we don't get to see each other that much because of our work.'

'What type of work does she do then?'

'I'm not sure. I've never asked her, mate, but she dresses professional, office type.'

'What, city worker type?'

'Yes, that type.'

'You fucking jammy bastard!!' Jacques replied sulking.

I drove into the car park of the Water's Edge. Jacques got out and said, 'I'll call Robbie for a time to meet and I'll try Mick again. As soon as I got something sorted, I'll give you both a bell and let you know where to.'

'Okay, no problem mate, catch you later.' I spun the car around, beeped and drove off.

Around eleven o'clock, I decide to call Mick on his landline but he did not pick up, so I tried calling him on his mobile but it went through to his voicemail.

I decide to go to the bookies and have a little flutter while I was waiting for Jacques to get back in touch with me. I parked opposite the bookies and made my way inside and as I entered, I picked up a betting slip and started looking at the race meetings that day pinned up on the wall. After a quick study of all the race meetings, I decide to try a Placepot. I picked my six horses and started marking the boxes when a voice said, 'Okay, Mac?'

I looked up and there was an old school friend. 'Alright, Daz.'

'What are you doing in here?' he asked.

'Oh, I just drop in once in a blue moon and try a Placepot.'

'My luck stinks! I haven't had a winner in weeks,' he confessed.

'I'm not a heavy gambler, mate. I only bet a fiver max as I can afford to lose that till next month.'

'Wish I could bet a fiver a month but I'm addicted to it. I can't walk past a bookies without going in.'

'You want to try and get some help, mate, if it's got a grip on you that bad.'

'I know… But I can't, it's hard. I've been betting for twenty years and haven't got a cockle to show for it.'

'Well, maybe one day you'll hit the big one, Daz. Look, I got to go as I have more important stuff to take care of.'

'Yeah okay, nice seeing you.'

'You too, Daz, and be lucky.'

I placed my bet and left but just couldn't help feel sorry for Daz having his life dominated by a horse and not only this, he didn't even own a fucking horse. Can you imagine what might happen when he gets to the pearly gates? The angels would tell him to turn around, pin a tail on his ass and kick him out the heavens, and he'd come back reincarnated as a fucking race horse. I got into my car and gave Mick a ring on his mobile.

'Hello, Mac.'

'At last, where have you been, Mick?'

'Ah, now that would be telling.'

'She tied you up or something, mate,' I chuckled.

'You won't believe what happened when you and Jacques left the White Horse last night.'

'What?'

'I'm chatting to Sara, that's her name by the way, and she invites me back to her place and no sooner has the door closed when she starts groping me and whips my dick out and starts giving me a blowjob in the hallway.'

'Was she good?' I interjected giggling.

'Listen will you, Mac. She leads me into her lounge and puts a porn film on and pushes me onto the sofa which happens to recline. She tears her kit off apart from her knickers and starts blowing me off again. When it's up again, she straddles me so her back's facing me and rams my dick inside her and fucks it hardcore. She jumps off my dick and pulls to my feet, she bends over and I start banging her from behind doggie style when she grabs my dick and pushes it into her bum! I've never done that before in my life,' he said excitedly.

'So you liked it then?' I asked trying to hide my laughter.

There was a slight pause of silence before Mick answered, 'I guess, yes.'

'What happened next?' I asked, loving the moment.

'I was shagging her up till fifteen minutes ago when her phone rang and she tells me to get the fuck out as her husband is on his way home from working away.'

'You're lucky he didn't walk in on you two, you might not be here now,' I said laughing.

'She even got my address so she could put it in her sat-nav to call round for more sex.'

'You made an impression then?'

'She wants me to slut fuck her and wants me to pull her hair so her head tilts all the way back. She's scary, mate, so I don't think I'll be going back to her house again.'

I'm laughing hysterically as I've been in the same situation in the past but managed to enjoy myself and get out of there rapidly.

'Jacques will be in touch today as we have to go meet Robbie,' I reminded him.

'I know, I'm going to scrub up, mate, and wait here until I hear from you. I'll give Jacques a bell as I got a missed call from him.'

'Yes, call him and tell him about your night with Sara and I'll see you later, okay.'

'Okay, Mac. See you later.'

'And make sure you give your cock a good scrub as you never know what you may catch from women like that, mate.'

'Fuck off,' he said and the line went dead.

I was in fits of laughter at Mick and lit up a cigarette and started the car and headed back to my apartment and waited for that all-important phone call. The call came in later that day from Jacques who told us we were to meet with Robbie at Miguel's Tapas Bar down the bay in Cardiff Docks at 6 pm; I favoured somewhere a bit more secluded and out of earshot of Joe public, but Jacques reassured me that all would be fine as business there didn't pick up till after 8.30pm and that there were a few closed booths that were basically for the romantics, but we would take one of them as the staff there leave you alone, which is very typical of the Spanish. Mick had offered to drive us in but Jacques insisted we take a taxi as we could have a quiet drink and something to eat while discussing a few points regarding the Norway job.

And more importantly, so Mick could feast his eyes on the safe and try to identify the make and model of it, so we know where to drill the locking mechanism, making life a lot easier for us.

At five thirty, my phone rang and Jacques informed me he and Mick were waiting outside in a taxi. I grabbed my wallet and jacket, and headed down to the taxi.

We chatted on the way to the tapas bar and had a laugh as Mick filled us in on a few more details regarding Sara, and we all agreed there was something lacking with her, and even the taxi driver agreed with us as they got big ears and don't miss a trick, as they're always listening to other people's conversations even when they pretend not to be taking any notice. I reminded Mick that he should go to an STD clinic to get his cock checked out, but Mick took it to heart and got the hump with me and Jacques, as we were both laughing, winding him up of course.

We apologised to Mick for ripping the piss out of him and promised him not another word would be mentioned on the subject that night.

We arrived at the bay which is predominantly made up of numerous restaurants, bars and night clubs that has a cobbled streets with lantern-lit alleys leading off the main thoroughfare which attracts a lot of interesting people on the weekends when you have to book days in advance to get a table in a restaurant, and you can expect to queue up outside one of the many bars and night clubs for up to an hour or two before you can get in, but in the week days it's a lot quieter. It was up one of these lantern-lit alleys that Jacques was leading us that we could hear Spanish music echoing down the alley, which gave you the feeling of authentication.

We rounded the bend in the middle of the alley and there was Miguel's, and sat outside was Robbie. He greeted us with a warm smile and handshakes as we introduced Mick. 'How'd yous enjoy the match, and did big Jimmy look after yous okay?' Robbie asked us.

We told him all went well and that the match was great, and Jimmy was ever the host and we thanked him again for sorting the tickets out.

'Neigh bother, pal,' he replied.

'Shall we go in and order some food as I'm starved,' Jacques suggested.

'Och I, pal I've been holding back till yous got here.'

We went inside and were immediately greeted by a waitress who showed us to a table, but Jacques asked her if we could have a booth instead. 'Of course, sir,' she replied and showed us to a booth that offered more privacy.

We sat down and she gave us all a menu each and asked us if we wanted drinks. 'Beer or wine, gents?' I asked the others.

'Go for the wine, pal, 'Robbie suggested, to which we all agreed.

The waitress brought back two bottles of Chardonnay and filled our glasses, and after we decided what we wanted to eat, I beckoned the waitress over and gave her our order of Mediterranean soups, salads, tortillas and various grilled meat and fish dishes.

I said to Robbie, 'How was your weekend?'

'Magic, pal. I went around a few clubs, as you do, and went in to a lap dancing bar and had a couple of private dances. Then I met two Scotch lassies in Luigi's Wine Bar, took them both back to my hotel with our kebabs from Chippy Lane and let me tell yous, that wasn't the only meat full of juice I ate that night,' he said and burst out laughing along with us.

'Can you show Mick the video on your phone so he can see the safe?' I asked Robbie.

'Sure, no problem, pal.'

He took out his phone and spent a few seconds playing with it before he handed it to Mick saying, 'Just press play, pal.'

Mick viewed the video with interest with the odd frown thrown in and then scowled before he looked up puzzled.

'Well, can you identify it?' Jacques asked him.

'I need you to send the video to me via Bluetooth so I can view it properly on my phone so I can zoom in a bit more.'

Robbie sent the video to Mick via Bluetooth and once received, Mick played the video again and kept saying to himself 'uh huh' and 'okay.'

We looked at him in silence shrugging our shoulders at each other as if to say, 'What's happening?'

Then Mick spoke, 'Right, got it.'

'Got what? 'we asked in unison.

'You found yourself a Weisman & Thomason Euro Vault, model VX-200,' he said smiling.

'It's no good smiling, pal, we haven't opened it yet,' .

'Tell us what model VX-200 means, can you Mick?'

'Okay, it's a grade nine safe, which is top of the range and better than a Hubbard in the UK, and can withstand some serious punishment.'

I leant forward and asked him, 'What type of serious punishment?'

'Well, if safes were into sadomasochism, then this is the one that likes to be punished. It can withstand a blast of ten grams of C4 plastic explosives, oxyacetylene won't touch it and neither will drill bits.'

'So how do we open it, pal? 'Robbie asked him with a puzzled look.

'You don't,' Mick replied.

'WHAT! Fuck, hell no…'

'Wait a minute. Who opens the damn thing then?' I asked.

'The safe does at an allocated time by the computer inside it and then you will need the combination too,' he giggled to himself.

'So what's so funny?' Jacques asked Mick.

'This is your nemesis, my friends, and mine too,' Mick replied smugly.

'Och no. Surely something can open it?' Robbie asked Mick.

Mick explained, 'The door is seven inches thick. The housing is six inches thick, made up of three-inch thick high tensile steel plate, then a one-inch thick stainless steel sheet and another two-inch thick H.T.S. plate, plus two five-mm sheets of glass either side of the stainless steel sheet. That's why you can't burn or drill it, not in the time limit you have.'

'So what do you suggest we do?' Jacques asked him inquisitively.

'Leave it alone and pass on it,' Mick replied, taking a sip of his wine.

Our orders arrived and the waitress laid them on the table, and none of us felt like eating except for Mick, who started picking his way through everything and placing it on his plate. We had a nibble here and there at the assortment of snacks and polished the wine off in silence. I called the waitress over and ordered another two bottles of Chardonnay.

'I know what we'll use to open the bastard thing,' Jacques announced.

'What?! A fucking fairy's magic wand and a sprinkle of unicorn dust?!' Robbie blurted out sarcastically.

'What you got in mind, Jacques?' I asked, paying no attention to Robbie's sarcasm.

'The cutter of all cutters; it's portable and don't need anything except air,' he said with a smug grin on his face.

I smiled and nodded in agreement, and said, 'It's a possibility?'

'What can you possibly use that has not been tested on it already?' Mick asked bewildered.

'That's simple to us, Mick,' I told him.

'Well, what is it then?

'Fuck I pal, you're right. Ne-bother with that on our side, 'the Jock agrees.

'What the hell are you three going on about? I just don't follow.'

'Jacques, do me and Robbie the honours here and explain to Mick about our terrestrial friend and what it can do.'

'Gladly. I should have thought about it when Mick was describing what the safe is made out of but I'll put it down to the wine.'

'Me tooz, pal. Strong stuff this wine, it's eleven percent, is it not?'

'Have you ever heard of a plasma cutter, Mick?' Jacques asked him with a raised eyebrow.

'Err…no! Can't say I have.'

'It will cut through a two-inch steel plate at a rate of two meters per minute. It will also cut through one-and-a-half-inch stainless steel at a rate of fifteen inches per minute, and it only uses air which gets sucked in and mixes with an electrode in the torch that gets turned into an inert gas that burns at two thousand eight hundred Fahrenheit. Also, you can attach a gouging nozzle to gouge out chunks instead of cutting, and it can remove ten kilograms of steel in one hour depending on what size nozzle you're using, and the width of the cut can be from half inch to an inch and a quarter. 'Jacques raised his glass as to toast and added, 'To our terrestrial friend!'

'To our terrestrial friend!' we all said, toasting with the clink of our glasses.

Except Mick, who was still clueless but said, 'Well, that all sounds good but you know why they put the glass and stainless between the steel plates, don't you?'

'Yes, mate, we do. Because when you burn through the plate, the glass melts and re-seals the cut line, and that's also why they fill some safes with a mixture of glass, marble and copper shards so they melt and fuse to each other,' I informed him smugly.

'But how did you know that?' Mick asked.

'Because we done our homework, pal,' Jock informed him smugly with a grin.

'It's going to take a while to get a plasma cutter in Norway and it's going to cost a lot more than in the U.K too, as everything is double the price and plasma cutters are six grand here, so it will cost twelve to fifteen grand over there easily,' I told them.

'Buy the plasma cutter here and drive over there with it? Also, we will need a transformer to plug it into, but we can buy the transformer in Norway,' Jacques suggested.

'Fuck I pal, road trip,' Jock grinned whilst shelling a prawn.

'Right, enough talk for now, gentlemen, I suggest we finish and enjoy the rest of our evening and tomorrow I'll start making preparations for our departure, and as you know, whatever gets planned, we stick to and all play their part without question or argument,' I reminded them.

'What about me?' Mick asked.

'Sorry, Mick, but your work is done here, and I'll tell you now you won't be coming to Norway with us, but thanks for your expertise and for enlightening us. Without your knowledge, we might have come a right cropper mate. But you will be rewarded for your time,' I told him.

But Mick didn't look too happy. He looked upset when he suggested sheepishly, 'I could do something.'

'I pal, like keep whoever drives the car company on the road as I feel two should go by car and the other one by plane, but if Mick goes in the car then two can go by plane. What yous guys think?' Jock asked.

'You got a good point, Robbie. Let's give it some more thought tomorrow when our heads are clearer,' Jacques suggested.

'I agree. Tomorrow with clearer heads,' I replied.

'I'm half cut and want to make love to that waitress, 'Robbie announced giggling away.

Mick seemed to know where he stood now, so he raised his glass to us and us to him, and from there we ate a little more of the grilled foods and polished off the wine. We paid for our order and left Miguel's. I lit up a cigarette as we walked back down the alley with the sound of the Spanish music fading away. We said goodbye to Robbie on the main thoroughfare, watching him walk slightly off-balance head towards Bar Metro happily singing away to himself. The three of us caught a taxi back to Barry Island with me being dropped off first. I said my goodbyes to Jacques and Mick and then headed up to my apartment, reminding myself that I had a date with Susan, the girl next door, which had almost slipped my mind. I got out of the lift on my floor and knocked on Susan's door but got no answer.

I knocked again but still no reply, so I went into my apartment opposite, leaving my door open to grab a pen to write her a note and slip it under her door when the door slammed hard behind me. I spun around startled and there stood Susan semi naked in black underwear, suspenders and stilettos with a naughty grin on her face and spoke suggestively, producing a can of cream from behind her back that she began to slowly shake before saying

'I thought you might like to have your main course and dessert here, Mac?'

'The starter was of excellent quality and I must thank the chef personally,' I mused as I admired her celestial body.

She walked slowly towards me exhibiting herself; I smiled in approval of her until we met and embraced with a slow unhurried kiss. We unlocked our lips and I slowly pulled her towards the bedroom by her free hand keeping eye contact with her.

'My, my, you're full of surprises,' I told her.

'I like to keep a man on his toes and give him the unexpected,' she replied with a look of mischievousness written all over her face as she backheeled the bedroom door shut with her stiletto and ordered me to strip naked and lay on the bed, as she shook the can of cream vigorously with a lustful naughty grin on her face as she eyed me strip naked and then lay on the bed. She walked teasingly up to the bed's end and slowly straddled her legs over both of mine, kneeing them to a close, resting her buttocks on both my knees before she leaned her head downwards and grabbing my cock with her free hand, lifted my cock over on to my stomach and sucked my balls in turn several times before stuffing my cock in her mouth, toying my tip with her lustred tongue whilst massaging my balls with the palm of her hand. With my cock growing in length and girth, she released it from her lips and sat upright smiling down at me as she popped the lid of the cream off, firstly squirting a little cream on two of her fingers and sucked it off hard then instinctively showered my balls and stiffened meat with cream for her to wildly feast upon before fucking it raw!!

I awoke the next morning to find Susan had gone and a note had been placed on the pillow next to me. It read

Thanks, stud, I had a great time, it was fun and it's nice to be with a man that don't snore. Gone to work to sort out other people's problems, you're tidy for a bachelor. Here's my mobile number, call me anytime you're free.

Sue -x-

I smiled to myself and got out of bed, and made my way to the kitchen. I flicked the switch down on the kettle and went in the bathroom and wrapped a towel around my waist. I came back in the kitchen and made a cup of tea and lit up a cigarette then slumped onto the sofa and thought about Sue and how wild she was and she was definitely the cwtchy type of woman that pulled a man in close to her when she was sleeping, keeping my arm firmly between her breasts. I shook myself out of it and put the news on the TV, the same old crap apart from the weather. Just after 8 am, I took a shower, washing Sue's love juices off me, and shaved as I don't like a stubble as it makes me feel unclean, and stripped the bed of its soiled linen and put it in the washing machine.

I decided to give Bernie a call in France to see how our little investment was coming along. We bought an old ten-bedroom farmhouse with a few out buildings along with four acres of land nestled between Agde and Gruissan near the Béziers region eighteen months ago and had been renovating it in between work, but Bernie practically lived there, making sure a couple of the local hands were getting the job done and that they were not sat on their backsides just taking our money.

Once it was renovated, we planned to rent the rooms out to backpackers. Also if we put two bunk beds in each room, then we could double our income, and the small revenue it would generate would be sunk back into the out buildings and the surrounding land. Then once up and running, we were to employ a local to run the place and we had even contemplated getting ten mountain bikes to rent to the backpackers for a small fee too so it added to our income. Bernie wanted to build a swimming pool even though we were only a ten-minute ride from the nearest beach. He liked the idea of girls splashing about and running around in their bikinis showing off their assets. Nice one, Bernie, but was it a good idea? We were in no rush as it was a long-term investment but the property was stunning and we didn't want to transform it overnight as that would have upset the locals a lot, but with the local hired labour, we were accepted easier as we were putting a couple of Euros in their pockets for which they have been very grateful at times.

I rang him on his mobile and after a short time he answered, 'Hello, Mac, how are you?'

'I'm fine, Bernie. How are you keeping over there?'

'Great, mate, everything is just great.'

'And how's the renovation coming along?'

'Slow but good, mate. All the outside pointing is finished, we got a new roof on, all the windows have been replaced and most of the internal doors fitted too. Oh, and I found an electrician to re-wire the whole house for a few Euro and a couple of glasses of red wine down at the local,' he laughed.

'That's fantastic news, mate. How are the locals looking after you?'

'I can't fault them, Mac. Especially Chantelle, the barmaid, good as ever and she's even better in bed.'

'What, mate, you're banging the barmaid in the local?'

'Yes, mate.'

'You'll be lynched by the locals if they find out and then they won't work for us, 'I stated.

'Nah, mate, the locals got a rough idea we're at it but they can't prove it.'

'Why not? 'I asked a little puzzled.

'Because she drives up here around 3 am and leaves at 5 am. She likes me cuddling and kissing her and picking her flowers. She's hot for me,' he said jubilantly.

'You pick her flowers? Why not just buy them?'

'Chantelle says more thought has gone into making the decision of what flowers I pick her.'

'Makes sense, but just be careful, Bernie, you don't get caught with your pants down.'

'They'd run a mile if they saw my ass, mate,' he giggled.

'They will shoot you if they catch you,' I giggled.

'Yeah, they look the type too! And with me being an alien here, best I don't crack any rugby jokes to them mate,' he giggled again.

'Best not, mate. Right, mate, it's been good talking to you, I got to catch up with Jacques later so I'll pass on your regards, okay?'

'Yes, by all means. Tell him to come over here with you the next time you come.'

'Will do, mate, take care.'

'You too, Mac.'

'Bye, mate.'

'See ya.' Bernie's phone went silent.

It was good to talk to Bernie even for a brief time as I didn't want to leave him alienated over there in France, it was also good to hear things are progressing with our little backpackers venture. But we'd be seeing each other in a matter of time as I needed him to do something for me before we went to Norway, and he had to collect it from us in Calais and take it back to Agde. I lit up a cigarette and started weighing the situation up with Mick coming with us and was still fifty-fifty whether to involve him any further, but to drive from the U.K to Bergen would be a feat in its own and to do it by one's self would be even harder, as tiredness would be a killer, and as for the route to Norway, we'd leave that to the AA and their route finder system as you don't want a sat-nav doing your head in over a few hundred miles.

I had to start making preparations on the equipment we were to use and tally up the cost too; even though we had the money to purchase just about anything we would require, it was just nice to know what our return was after our overheads. I knew the plasma cutter would cost six thousand pounds upwards as a definite, but it had got to be brand new to do the job and seeming Jacques would be doing most of the burning, it had to be to his taste. Then there was the heat shield for his face or his face would burn and peel, a leather gauntlet so he did not burn his hands, and also a leather sleeve to go over the loom of the cutting torch otherwise the loom would melt because of the amount of heat the plasma cutter generates – safety first!

Also, we had to take into account any textiles in the immediate vicinity of the plasma when cutting that they didn't melt either. Plus, all the usual tools which we'd need so one had to do a bit of B & Q'ing, all bought with cash as credit cards were so easily traceable and could hang you in an instant.

Then there were hotels, ferry tickets and plane tickets, and reasonable excuses to be thought out, as well as getting those diamonds back into the UK, which the Jewish community would take care of as they seldom do once in a blue moon.

First things first, the plasma cutter, and we were going to need the best we could get our hands on and that was to be my priority for today. So, thanks to the internet, I was able to find what I was looking for and portable too on wheels as they can be very heavy depending on its size, naturally. I spent a little over an hour searching various web addresses looking for the right cutter and eventually found what I was looking for in the form of a Sceptretherm 1850-X5 priced at £7,495. Inclusive of VAT and the best portable plasma cutter in the world to date, and it'd only been on the market for two months and all reviews proved excellent. I printed off all the relevant details, which were its dimensions, weight and cutting depths through various metals. In the UK, it was fine, but in Europe, it was a different voltage and I knew just the man who could help us. Bernie! As he was already there, but first I had to see Jacques sometime today as we needed to replicate the outer and inner wall of the safe for a little time trial before we hit the real safe. I picked up the phone and called Jacques who answered, 'Okay, Mac?'

'Yes, mate. Are you busy today?'

'No. Why's that?

'I need you to come here and have a look at something for me.'

'Sure, mate, give me half an hour and I'll be there.'

'Brilliant. See you soon.'

Half an hour later, my intercom buzzed. 'Who is it? I asked in a mild-mannered tone.

'It's me, Jacques.'

'Come on up, mate.' I buzzed him in and left my apartment door open for him and a few minutes later he came in grinning.

'What you grinning at?' I asked him.

'I'm just happy, Mac. That's all,'

'Why's that?

'I can't wait to hear what you got to tell me, mate.'

'Sit down and have a look at the paperwork on the table and tell me what you think.'

'Sure, but I'll need a coffee to go with it.'

'On its way.' I made myself a mug of tea and asked Jacques if he wanted a bacon and egg toasty to go with his coffee.

'Sure, mate. I'm Hank Marvin.' He then turned his attention to the paperwork on the coffee table that I had printed off earlier and started scanning over the pages.

'Looks like you've hit the nail on the head with this machine, Mac.'

'Not bad for under an hour's work.'

'Well, it certainly looks like it can do the job, Mac.'

I informed Jacques it was the best plasma cutter on the market at the moment and that it was only two months old with every global engineering company screaming about it, plus all the reviews had given it top marks and that it was easily portable and a lot lighter than previous models. Jacques was altogether pleased with its cutting capabilities along with its depths too. 'I've been thinking that maybe we should ask Bernie to see if he can find the plasma cutter in France and buy it there as it will have a European plug fitted, he can also purchase the transformer,' I suggested to Jacques.

'Good thinking, Mac. Should we call him or make the trip and see him personally?'

'What do you suggest we do?'

'I say we call him and email him the paperwork on the plasma and get him to purchase one asap along with the rest of the paraphernalia that we need to go with it.'

'And once he has got what we need, we'll meet him in Calais and we can offload it to his vehicle and we can also offload a safe to him to take back to Agde.'

'Safe? What do you want a safe for?'

'So we can hold passports and cash for our backpacker friends when we open it for business.'

'Right, good idea, Mac.'

'Here's your bacon and egg toasty, enjoy.'

'Thanks, got any ketchup, mate?'

'Yes, in the top left-hand cupboard.'

'But I'm the guest?'

'Get it yourself, I'm not your bitch,' I said smiling, an eggy bacon toasty smile.

'Okay, and shut your mouth, it's a disgusting sight,' Jacques said un-amused.

I told Jacques that we needed to replicate the thickness of the safe with all the materials included of the structure of the safe, as we could time trial ourselves and use that time as a guide when it came down to the real thing. Jacques approved naturally and we agreed that along with the make and model of the plasma cutter we were to send to Bernie, we'd also send him the materials and size of them (on a smaller scale of course) that we'd need, preferably one third in scale to the original. Also, we discussed Mick's involvement and we both agreed that he should not get involved, but then as the Jock pointed out Bergen was a long way to drive by one's self. I scanned the information on the shopping list and set it aside to be mailed it to Bernie.

'Has Robbie gone back up to Scotland?' I asked Jacques.

'Yes, Mac. He left this morning, why?'

'Just asking that's all. I'll want him to come to France with us when Bernie has sorted out the shopping list and see what he thinks of our equipment.'

'When the Bolt says all is good, I'll call Robbie and he'll be here quicker than an asylum seeker.'

Jacques left and I decided I needed some sea air. With that thought in mind, I dug out my fishing rods and tackle box, donned my fishing clothes and headed on down to the car. I drove down to the beach and stopped at a shop on the way and purchased some munchies and three small bottles of water. I parked the car up and collected my gear from the boot, and walked the small distance to the beach head and set up my fishing stand with two rods and baited up one with the sand eel and the other with the mackerel, and cast them out and sat back and waited to see if there were any rays out there. I love the sea air; it's fresh and helps me think clearly, and it's also a graceful form of solitude with the calm lapping of the sea on the rocks is tranquil in its own rights, if you listen to it, that is. I spent the next four hours baiting up and feeding crabs with the occasional rattle of the rod tip and after catching three thornback rays, the biggest being seven pounds on the button, along with a small conger eel, I decided it was time to go back home.

Back at my apartment, I scrubbed my hands and put my fishing gear away, then made myself a cup of tea and lit up a cigarette, opened the balcony door and sat back on the sofa and smoked and drank, and then checked my email and sure enough, one was from Bernie that simply read: *Waiting*. I rang Bernie.

'Hi, Mac, I got the email, what's up, mate?'

'I need you to buy that plasma and the list of accessories that go with it. Also the steel, stainless and glass to the exact spec, asap.'

'I'm on it straight away, mate.'

'As soon as you have everything, call me. Then me, Jacques and a friend Mick will be on our way over, okay.'

'Sure, mate, but who's Mick?'

'An old friend.'

'Do I know him?'

'No, mate, you don't.'

'Can he be trusted?'

'Yes.'

'Are you sure?'

'I'm sure.'

'Oh right, anything else I need to know or do?'

'Yes. Give our French pals the weekend off when we come but pay them a half day wage.'

'No need for that, Mac, as they love a little time off,' he chuckled.

'Right. Anything you want from us over here?'

'Erm…Yes. Can you bring me some Welsh sausages?'

'Fuck off, mate! You're not serious?' I asked laughing.

'What's funny about wanting Welsh sausages?' he asked.

'You can get sausages over there, mate.'

'Yeah, but the pork and leek ones I miss as they taste so scrummylicious.'

'Okay, mate, no problem. I'll get them locally from a farm.'

'That'll be grand, Mac. Then I can impress Chantelle with them.'

'Anything else, mate?'

'No, Mac, that's all I can think of for now.'

'I'm going to deposit ten grand into your account to cover what we need.'

'That's a hefty sum, Mac.'

'The plasma costs just over seven grand in the UK.'

'Fuck me, mate! It must be a tool at that price.'

'I hope it is. Well, I'm going to let you go and get on with it, and I won't forget your sausages.'

'Okay, Mac. You be safe and if you can't be safe, be careful,' he chuckled.

'You too, mate, see you soon.'

'Nice chatting again.'

'See you soon, bye.'

I decided to send Sue, the girl next door, a text message asking her if she was free tonight and would she like to go out to a restaurant in Cardiff after she finished work, and asked her if she preferred Thai or Italian food. I went over to my computer and logged in to global oil and gas jobs to see what work was available, typed in pipefitter in Europe and pressed search. 143 jobs were found and as I started scrolling down through the list of jobs, looking at their locations with the majority in the UK and the rest in Europe, and as luck would have it, eighteen were in Norway with one job near Bergen; bingo, I thought, just what we were looking for. I clicked open the details and it read: *Eighteen pipefitters required immediately for a shutdown at Mongstad Oil Refinery Nr Bergen. Candidates must be time-served and have a minimum of five years' experience of working in the power, oil and gas industry.* It then went on to state the hourly wage and rotation of shifts, that being two weeks on and one week off with sixty hours per week to be worked Monday to Saturday with Sunday off as a rest day. Now this could work to our advantage; if I or we could get a start on this oil refinery, we could be placed legitimately in Norway.

I looked up Biz maps and typed in Mongstad Norway; after a few seconds, I got a marker on the map along with the miles scale and calculated the distance from Mongstad to Bergen, which worked out at roughly ninety kilometres which should take a good hour to drive, so that's two hours there and back. Perfect, I thought to myself. I go back to the previous page (oil and gas jobs) and emailed my C.V. to the company in charge and added a footnote explaining that I was interested in the Mongstad job. I lit up a cigarette when my mobile beeped two times. It was a text message from Sue:

Hey stud. Would love to come out to dinner with you, but I got plenty of paperwork on my desk so I won't be home till eight-ish, and I need a nice soak in the bath, you can join me in it if you like? Order in a Thai and share a bottle of wine at mine. L&K's me.

I immediately sent her a message back asking her to give my door a knock when she arrived home and this time I was going to find out what she did for a living in a mild sociable way.

I rang Mick to see if he had anything on for the day and he said he got a text message from Sara saying she wanted to meet him again or she'd tell her husband about them both. We both laughed our livers out as she was trying to blackmail him into bed – the bitch! Mick on the other hand was going to play along with her and try to boost her power buzz to see how far she would take it. I asked Mick if he would be prepared to accompany the driver to Bergen to which he agreed somewhat ecstatically.

He stated that he had nothing else on that day except to get his haircut and make a few phone calls regarding him finding a job and getting a bit of shopping to fill his fridge up. Mick suggested we go for a drink later in the afternoon but I declined his offer and told him I was seeing the girl next door later that evening and wanted to stay out the pub that day. No sooner had I ended the call to Mick, it started ringing again.

'Hey, Jacques, what's up?'

'Bad news, mate.'

'What's happened?' I ask him concerned.

'It's Robbie. He had a crash in his car yesterday and he's in a bad way.'

'How bad is bad?'

'Intensive care bad.'

'Fuck! That's bad. How did you find out?'

'His wife called me less than twenty minutes ago.'

'How did it happen, did she say?'

'I didn't fucking ask her, mate. She just thought I should know and said to get in touch with any of the other lads he's worked with and let them know.'

'Christ, mate, I'm sorry, really.'

'I need a stiff drink, Mac. Do you want to join me?'

'Sure, Jacques, of course. Where to?'

'The White Horse as soon as you can.'

This is all we needed I thought. Don't get me wrong, I naturally felt concerned for Robbie but not as much as Jacques or Robbie's family, after all, I have only known him a little over a week and only met him twice which somehow made it easier for me to deal with. I arrived at the White Horse fully knowing that Jacques would already be hitting the top shelf on Bacardi. I walked in through the main entrance up to the bar where Jacques was stood drinking Bacardi and coke. I walked over to him and put my hand on his shoulder, and said, 'Hey, mate, sorry this has happened to Robbie.'

'It's not your fault, mate,' he replied.

I ordered a double Bacardi and coke for Jacques who was silently deep in thought, and a pint of lager for me. Finding his silence awkward yet understandable under the circumstances, I had to ask him, 'How bad is Robbie?'

'I don't know, mate. His wife only told me what I had told you earlier. She was sobbing, so I thought it best not to ask too much.'

'You've done the right thing, mate. It's fucking unbelievable to think we were having a beer with him the other day.'

'I know, Mac. I just hope whatever happened, he just pulls through it.'

'Me too, mate.'

'I'll call her back tomorrow to find out how he is.'

'Does he have any children?'

'Yes. Two daughters and a son, but I can't recollect if he said he had another child from a previous relationship.'

'Christ, mate, that's going to be hard going on them too.'

'You're damn right it is, Mac. I think the oldest is fourteen and the youngest six or seven.'

'They're old enough to understand the full extent of their father's situation then?'

'That's about the gist of it, mate.'

'Would it be okay if I asked Mick to join us?'

'Sure, Mac, go straight ahead.'

I rang Mick and told him that Robbie was in hospital in intensive care and that he'd been involved in a collision in his car. His reaction was of shock and then he fell into silence. I told him that we were at the White Horse and that he was more than welcome to join us if he wanted. He agreed and joined us half an hour later after he had his haircut. Jacques was reminiscing telling us of how he and Robbie had first met on a power station at King's North and from there they worked most of the UK, Europe and the Middle East on oil refineries. The subject changed from Robbie to us and Mick told Jacques that Sara had been in contact with him and threatened to tell her husband of there one night stand, to which Jacques rolled around laughing and agreed she was using blackmail tactics on him but also warned him to be careful as it could turn nasty for him, and the best thing to do was to ignore her. Mick thanked him for his advice and immediately deleted her number from his mobile phone and toasted good riddance to her.

I reminded myself not to drink anymore alcohol as I wanted to see Susan later in the evening. I informed Jacques of my pre-arranged plans with Susan to which he smiled and told me that I didn't have to stay on his account, though Mick agreed to keep Jacques company a while longer. I went back to my apartment and feeling sleepy from the beer I decided to take an afternoon nap but not before setting my alarm clock for 7 pm, that's if I didn't wake up before it went off.

I got undressed and slipped under the covers and shut my eyes, and thought about the unfortunate events of the day beginning with Robbie and hoping that he would pull through no matter the outcome. And then my thoughts turned to the job in Norway and all those lovely diamonds glistening away, crying out to be stolen and have some character stamped upon them with or without Robbie, bless him. I began to drift into the dark abyss of my subconscious and there was Fox smiling, twirling around and around but always looking over her shoulder at me, calling me and beckoning me to join her.

I was startled out of my sleep by a loud ringing, like a fire alarm going off, and as I opened my eyes confused by the sound, I realized it was only my alarm clock going off; I turned the damn thing off. I had slept solid for over three hours and if I had not set the alarm, I would be fast asleep there now in no man's land, dreaming away or wrestling with the subconscious mind. I went to the kitchen and drank a pint of water and then lit up a cigarette and put *The Jam* on the hi-fi and turned it down so I could hear it in the background. I finished my cigarette and checked my emails, and there it was, just what I had been hoping for. A message from the engineering company thanking me for my CV I had sent them, stating that they would be contacting me in due course regarding the job in Norway, but it had come at bad timing, or had it? I thought of calling Bernie to cancel the shopping list I had sent him via email but thought it better to let things ride for the time being and see what the outcome of Robbie's accident was, hopefully all was good and well.

My mobile beeped twice it was a text message from Susan that read:

Can you sort out a bottle of wine for tonight please? See you at eight thirty
x me

I decided to ring Mick on his mobile and find out how he and Jacques were getting on; he answered in slurred voice and said they was very drunk and intended going for a curry at the Taj Mahal restaurant, but added that Jacques was bearing up over Robbie. I reminded Mick to make sure that Jacques got home as well as himself in one piece. Mick assured me they would so I focused my attention on the evening ahead with Sue.

I shaved first and then took a shower, and put my shirt and jeans on, leaving my socks off as they were less to take off, and had a bottle of Chardonnay in the fridge that had been chilling for a few weeks. I splashed a little aftershave on but making sure it was not too over-powering and checked myself in the mirror, looking good, I thought. I glanced at my wrist watch that showed five past eight when there came a knock on my door; I opened it and standing there in front of me was Susan with that naughty smile on her face.

She said, 'Hey there, stud muffin.'

I smiled back at her and said, 'Hey there, gorgeous.'

'Do you want to grab the wine and come over?'

'I'm right behind you.' I grabbed the wine from the fridge and went across the hallway to her apartment.

She kicked her shoes off and said, 'Make yourself comfy.'

I closed her door behind me and complimented, 'Nice place you have here.'

'Thanks, Mac. It's manageable and it's mine.'

'Shall I put the wine in your fridge?'

'Sure, I need to take a long soak. Do you want to order the food while I run the bath?'

'What do you like Thai style?'

'Just order away, hun. I spent two months in Thailand and love the food as well as the culture, so anything with ginger and lemon grass will be fine,' she said whilst running the bath and taking her clothes off but retaining her underwear.

'Did you go to Ko Samui when you were there?'

'I take it you've been to Thailand too, you naughty boy?'

'I've been to Bangkok, Ko Samui and spent a few days in Pattaya.'

'Ah! The world-famous Sin City,' she said laughing.

'That's the place, but I had to get away from the whore bars and all the pissheads.'

'Bangkok's full of them too, hun. But Pattaya or Sin City is a little on top, so I take it you coped with Bangkok okay then?'

'Yeah, I liked the hustle and bustle of Bangkok.'

She looked me straight in the eye and asked, 'Have you ever fucked a whore or lady boy, hun?'

'No! Have I, fuck! Have you?' I replied angrily.

'I was joking with you, Mac,' she replied giggling.

'The Thai women don't appeal to me, they're too clingy. Anyhow, I was spoilt for choice by all the European, Australian and Israeli women taking in the culture like you, and the whores were the last thing on my mind!'

'I believe you, hun. You're too decent for that stuff and when you're done ordering, you can join me in the bath for a soak. Oh, and make the order for an hour's time.'

'Just what I was thinking. Would you like a glass of wine to accompany you in the bath?'

'No thanks, hun, all I need for now is you and your company.'

I placed the Thai order and then joined Sue in the bath; sitting behind her I began to gently massage her shoulders. 'Oh, that feels sooo good,' she said relaxing a little more adding, 'I haven't done this in a long time.'

Silently, I carried on massaging her shoulders, neck and her upper arms when she moved my hands down to her firm breasts, her nipples were already hard, I stroked them gently with my fingers before I moved one hand down over her stomach, making slow figure of eights downwards towards the tease of her partly shaven pussy and then back up over her stomach again, eventually back to her firm breasts, occasionally butterfly kissing her neck and ear while playing with her rock-hard nipples.

'Don't stop, Mac, don't stop. Keep touching them,' she whispered through deep panting gasps.

Keeping one hand stroking her breasts, my other hand ironed over her hips, gradually delving down towards the depth of her partly shaven pussy. I gently stroked around her inner thighs as my fingers slowly crept closer towards her chastity, teasing it. She parted her shaking legs a little wider, inviting my fingers to enter her inner chaste. I felt her chest bloom outwards as her breaths suddenly became deeper as my fingertips delicately teased the fleshy boundaries of her modest pussy every now and again making her body judder, till I gently parted the soft lips of her cunt which made her gasp and quiver ever more as the tips of my fingers slowly seduced her inner chaste, exciting her thrilled cavern walls. My fingertips brushed across the crest of her dimpled succubus that made her body stiffen with grunted groan!

I kept on kissing her neck and shoulders all over with heavy breaths when she forcefully took hold of my hand and directed it to her protruding pinnacle, which I began to stimulate in an unhurried circular motion. Her body stiffened again, forcing herself hard back against my growing cock as she pushed one leg out over the side of the bath. She began to writhe slowly at first then increased into a gyrating rhythm, lifting her buttocks up and down as I rubbed her bulbous pinnacle up and down harder. She bit the sides of her index finger hard before letting out a deep moan as she grabbed hard at my thigh, digging her nails in deep as I slipped two neat fingers inside her sobriety of exploration. Her panting gasps grew aggressively hardened as I increased the pace of my working two fingers, fucking her hot fuck hole as my insane thumb vigorously worked hard on her bulbous pinnacle. Her nails dug deeper into my thigh. 'Oh fuck! fuck!' she huffed out, adding, 'Don't you fucking stop! Fuck it harder!! Mmm*mmm*. *URGH! GOD, FUCK! I'M… I'M GUNNA CUM!!*

Her legs began to thrash about wildly in her metaphoric extravagance as I drove my fingers in fast, probing her inner chiffon, hitting her epiphany! She let out a squeal as her body jerked up out of the water and then collapsed back into the bath, panting hard. With her body trembling, she threw her head backwards and yanked my head downwards to meet her succulent wet lips and kissed me rapturously, teasing her tongue inside my mouth. She eventually pulled away saying, 'You're so fucking perfect, I wish I met you years ago.'

'Did you enjoy it?' I asked knowing she had.

'Enjoy it? I fucking loved it, Mac. Where have you been all my life?'

'Across the hallway,' I replied to which we both started laughing wildly.

Later on, we talked during the course of the meal of my work and of her profession, which turned out that she was in investment trusts for a major company in Cardiff City. We finished the wine off and cleared the table after which both of us smoked a cigarette naked and went on to her bedroom only this time I backheeled the bedroom door shut! In all, neither of us got much sleep that night, except for a few cat naps here and there when we finally fell asleep in each other's arms for the last few hours before her alarm went off at 6 am. I unlocked from our embrace but Susan quietly said, 'Shhhh, hun.'

'Do you want me to get up with you?' I asked croakily.

'No, lover boy. You just go back to sleep,' she whispered and kissed me on the cheek.

'Thanks,' I replied and closed my eyes again.

Chapter 5

A Series of Events

I was woken up by the sound of a hammer drill ringing outside of the apartment block. I glanced at my wrist watch; it showed 8 am on the button – how typical of the civil engineering departments, I thought. I got out of bed and went into the lounge, but as Susan had already left for work, I got half-dressed, only putting my jeans on and carrying my shoes and shirt. I opened her apartment door and peeked out looking left and right to make sure I did not bump into any of the other residents whilst leaving and closed her door behind me, and quickly opened my door opposite. I stripped off and showered for ten minutes, shaved and made a cup of tea, lit a cigarette and laid back on the sofa thinking how Susan knew how to keep a man happy, and I wouldn't like to be in her shoes in work today, considering the hours she worked; I don't know where she gets all her energy from. Maybe that's why she made the most of it when she was feeling up for it, but I had to remind myself not to get attached and let my emotions take over, as Fox was back on the scene and I didn't know where she'd got to since she came out of prison, but it won't be long before she reappeared, and the sooner the better, for me.

I finished my cigarette and tea, and grabbed my car keys and headed for a greasy spoon for a cooked breakfast. After that I drove into Cardiff to a security specialist who dealt in new and used safes. After ten minutes of looking around inside the shop, I found a second-hand safe and asked the owner if he could hang onto the safe for a week or two, to which he agreed if I was paying him in cash. I told him to give me thirty minutes and I would return with the cash and with that, I drove to the nearest bank and went inside. I withdrew five hundred pounds and returned to the security specialist and handed the money over and pocketed the receipt and bade him good day. I then drove back to Barry and back to my apartment, picking my mail up on my way in out of the post box. I went up to my apartment and checked my emails and there was one from Bernie stating that he can go shopping when I'm ready as all items on the list are available. Bernie has always been efficient when it comes to work and I guess that's why he's got such a good name in the engineering business, much like all of those who count. I emailed Bernie back and told him to go shopping and to email me when the shopping list was completed.

I phoned Mick who answered after two rings, 'Hello,' he said groggily.

'It's Mac. Guess you had a good session last night?'

'Yeah, you can say that again, mate.'

'Listen, Mick, remember when we were in Cardiff at the tapas bar with Robbie and he sent you the pictures and the video to your phone from his?'

'Of course I do, Mac. Why?'

'Do you still have it all on your phone?'

'Yes. Why?'

'Thank fuck for that. Do not delete it, okay, as we're going to need it, so guard it with your life.'

'Is that all, Mac?' he grumbled.

'For the time being, Mick.'

'Good. Now fuck off and let me go back to sleep.' Then the line went dead.

I sat back on the sofa and smiled as I lit up another cigarette and thought to myself that even if Robbie did not pull through, I would ask Bernie to come in on the job.

That's if he would leave his beloved Chantelle for a few days. I decided to ring Jacques. 'How're you feeling today?'

'I feel like shit, mate,' he replied sighing.

'I just got off the phone to Mick and he's feeling rough too,' I told him.

'I just got off the phone to Robbie's wife and it's not good news.'

'Okay, mate, hit me with it.'

'Are you ready for this?

'Sure. Go on.'

'The doctors have scanned his brain and they seriously think he'll be brain damaged for the rest of his life.'

'Christ, mate, that's devastating news.'

'Too right, mate, and just when everything was going good for us.'

I paused slightly before I told him, 'It still can, mate, if we sort it out for Robbie and drop his family a few quid ...if you get my drift.'

'I know where you're coming from, Mac, but now isn't the right time for us to be discussing that stuff.'

'But we need to stay focused too, Jacques, even more so if what you say is right.'

There was a pause from Jacques and then he said, 'I guess you're right, Mac.'

'You do realise that Bernie is at this very moment shopping for everything on the list and has no doubt already bought the majority of the essentials.'

'I understand totally but we can't leave here at the moment, mate.'

'Jacques, I know you are a good friend to Robbie and you have a history together, but if you think about it, we've been through worse than this, especially you. After all, you did see a lot of shit in Djibouti and Somalia, and lost many friends and comrades there. At least if the worst comes to the worst, with Robbie you can still look at him and think of the good times, like the rest of us.'

'I don't need to be reminded of that business over there in Djibouti, but you are right. I'm going up to see Robbie and his family, and you don't have to come as I would rather go by myself as I think it will be easier for me to deal with the situation.'

'You do what you think is best for you mate, and I'll sort things out at this end, but if I can help in any way, you know where I am.'

'Thanks, Mac. I'll keep that in mind. You are a true friend.'

'You are to me. When do you plan on going?'

'Today, mate. I'll call you when I get there, but think nothing of it if you don't hear from me for a day or two.'

'I understand, just take your time on the way up there.'

'Will do, and keep Mick away from Sara as we don't want anything to happen to him.'

'In fact, I was thinking of sending him to France to give Bernie a hand as they can have a little bonding session together.'

'Good idea, mate. I got to pack a few things here and then I'll be off. So don't do anything I wouldn't do and I'll see you in a few days. And give my regards to the Bolt.'

'Of course, mate.'

I needed to call Mick just to finalise a few things with him and most of all for him to upload the video from Robbie to the computer so we could see it in a bit more detail and Mick was going to need some tools of his own, but then again maybe not. I was still feeling hungry and that was coming in the form of a big fuck off steak at a little inn on the outskirts of Barry town called the Captain's Wife, which is renowned for its great menu but most of all its steaks. I called Mick thinking it would be far better if he joined me for a nice succulent steak and inform him of Robbie's bad health and discuss his role in Bergen, and also to ask him if he was prepared to go to France and join Bernie at our little hotel for backpackers and help the Bolt out with a few things for our journey into Scandinavia. I asked Mick if he wanted lunch on me, to which he said yes, so I picked him up at 1 pm and drove us both out to the Captain's Wife in Sully.

The Captain's Wife is a seventeenth century inn which is situated less than 25 meters from the shoreline, now guarded by a high wall the inn was first a blacksmiths and a coach house with accommodation for people travelling the coastal routes across South Wales. The inn is also said to be haunted by many a ghost and back in its day, the smugglers used to drink in the back room out of sight from the travellers, though the smugglers laughter could be heard in the main bar and sometimes their laughter can still be heard today on occasions. Since its coach house days, it has mainly been used as a public house though twice in the eighteenth century, it was razed to the ground by fire due to its thatched roof now replaced with slates. So there's plenty of history in this old place which authenticates itself for its charm and a somewhat eerie presence inside.

We entered the pub through the main doors, both of us having to duck as the doorways were low but the ceilings were higher, which only added to the inn's character. We were shown to a table next to the large leaded window overlooking the beer garden and across the scraggy shoreline. The waitress took our order of two ten-ounce sirloin steaks with thick cut chips and mushrooms. and two pints of smugglers – a local ale brewed more for the authenticity of the inn than anything else, but it was only right to order such a drink with the pub's history and original stone walls giving it ambience with bits of livery and nautical antiquities lining the walls and ceiling here and there.

I informed Mick of Robbie's brain scan and that the doctors think he may have permanent brain damage. To this Mick exclaimed his shock and devastation on the matter, and seemed to be more choked by the news than I was, which clearly showed in the sorrowful expression written all over his face. The ale arrived and Mick was quick to take a few good gulps of it in succession but then pulled a face in disgust of the strong taste of the ale now grappling his tonsils. All I could do was laugh but said to Mick, 'You're better off sipping it, mate.'

'This smuggler tastes like piss and mud mixed together.'

'I know, mate,' I said still laughing.

'Whatever made you order the damn crap?'

'Oh, I just thought that it would go with the setting. But if you sip the ale to begin with, you will get to like it as you have to let your taste buds get used to it first,' I stated.

'Fuck that, I'm not drinking it, mate,' he said still pulling a face.

'Go on, you'll be fine.'

'No chance, Mac.'

'Do you want a different drink?'

'Too right, Mac. This stuff is poison, mate.'

'Well, you'll have to go to the bar and order yourself one as I'm sticking to the smugglers, mate,' I told him still laughing.

'Not a problem,' he said and stormed off to the bar to order a different drink.

When I was younger, I used to come here to the Captain's Wife with a crowd of mates every Sunday with our girlfriends for a Sunday lunch or a carvery nowadays, and that was first time I drank smugglers, and we'd all done exactly the same as Mick, swearing never to touch the stuff again until the barman told us how to drink it and once you had a few sips of smugglers, it turned out to be quite a nice flavoursome ale, even though you could taste a hint of wood from the wooden keg which soon disappeared after a few sips. Of course, the girls would never touch the stuff, not after seeing our reactions, they would only settle for bottles of wine or double vodkas.

Mick returned with a pint of lager in hand and looking very much happier than a few minutes earlier. He sat down just as the steaks arrived with an assortment of condiments along with a peppercorn sauce thrown in at no extra charge as the steaks came in at eighteen quid each, so to charge for the sauce would be a little bit cheeky.

'I hope the steaks are better than the ale,' Mick asked.

'You'll love it, mate. Tuck in and enjoy.'

'So how long will it be before we definitely find out about Robbie's brain scan?'

'Jacques is going up there today to find out more details and to pay his respects to Robbie's family. I'll know in a few days' time when he phones me.'

'This steak is good, very nice, mate.'

'I was wondering, Mick, if you feel like going away for a few days if you have nothing on your agenda?'

'I have nothing on and could do with a change of scene.'

'How would you like a few days in France with a very good mate of mine, Bernie, to give him a hand with most of the stuff we are going to need in Bergen?'

'Sure, but you will have to give me a few days' notice and not just put me on the spot, Mac.'

'Of course not, Mick, I wouldn't do it any other way,' I replied smiling.

Mick beamed back and said, 'Great. I will get to have a look at your investment property too?'

'Naturally, as that's where you will be staying.'

'But I thought it wasn't ready yet?'

'It's not but it is habitable as Bernie has made good progress lately and you may even meet a lovely French woman there too.'

'But I thought they didn't like us?'

'Not exactly as history should have taught you that the Welsh and French are more like cousins.'

'I never knew that, Mac, when and where did you find that out?'

'Many moons ago from an old French teacher in school and more than likely your French teacher too, seeming we both went to the same school together.'

'Which teacher would that be then and in what year?' Mick asked.

'Well, if you think second and third year comprehensive, you would come up with…'

'Not Pudner, is it?' Mick interjected.

'You've hit the nail on the head,' I replied between chewing through my steak.

'He was a crazy teacher at times, though he always made sense but always looked confused.'

'So would you after working half your life there and putting up with some of the kids that went through that school.'

'Guess what you're saying is right. I wonder if Pudner ever had a nervous breakdown?'

'Probably, or he retired happily. Who cares, we got what we wanted though.'

'True, Mac. Fancy another a beer, mate?'

'No, you go ahead, I'm driving and I'm still sipping my smugglers,' I reminded him.

The waitress came and cleared our table, and asked if everything was okay with the meal as they always do (company policy) with a smile on her face. I told her that the steak was by far the best I had tasted, to which her smile broadened a little more. She asked if I would like dessert, to which I remarked only if she was on the menu, which made her blush and giggle before she scuttled off a little embarrassed. Mick returned and asked, 'What's the plan once we are in Norway?

'Let's not worry about that for now, but what I need to ask you is how would you open the front door and what type of tools would you use being a locksmith?'

'It depends on what locks are involved really, but usually a twenty-four-volt cordless drill along with a selection of drill bits and a barrel puller should be enough.'

'Barrel puller? What's that?' I asked puzzled.

'It's a length of round solid steel with a heavy weight that slides up and down with a stop on the end to stop the weight coming off. Then there's a screw attached to the end which screws into the lock and then you simply pull the weight towards you two or three times with a degree of force and the barrel pops out exposing the inside of the lock. Put a screwdriver in and turn, bingo, it's open,' he replied smiling.

'Hmmm, I see. So, what about deadlocks, how would you deal with them?'

'Oh, they're easy too. There are several keys available to the locksmith trade or you can drill the frame and lock in one and simply refill the hole, similar to drilling a safe.'

I summoned the waitress and asked her for the bill. Five minutes later, she came back and produced the bill. I gave her my credit card and she ran it through her handheld scanner and handed my credit card back along with the receipt; I tipped her five pounds in cash for which she thanked me. I drove us back to his apartment and once inside, I asked him to hook his phone up to his computer and upload the video of the jewellers along with the photos Robbie had taken. On completion, I viewed the pictures again but couldn't find anything of any use to us.

I then watched the video from inside the shop and pressed pause as it was showing the inside of the door and asked Mick to take a look to see what he could make out. Mick looked with interest and zoomed in on the door.

'It's pretty much straightforward, Mac. There is one Vale type lock and two deadlocks as far as I can make out.'

'How long will it take to get through all three locks?'

'Oh, no more than fifteen minutes down to about eight in a rush.'

'Good. That's what I needed to hear.'

'And the door and frame is made of timber, if that helps at all.'

'Yes, it does, now delete the pictures and video from your phone, or on second thought, keep them on there for now, mate, as we may need to show someone else.'

'Sure, Mac. Do you want me to save them on the computer?'

'No, Mick. That won't be necessary.'

'Anything else you want me to do, Mac?'

'Not for the time being, mate. You just chill out and go about your daily routines and if I need you, I'll call you and you can expect to be in France in a few days' time. It will be a nice break for the two of us, or three if Jacques comes with us,' I said smiling.

'I'm looking forward to it, Mac,' he replied excited.

'Good, so am I.'

'Guess that's it for now?'

'For now, at least, Mick, but you could pack a bag ready for the trip if you like so as to save time on the day.'

'I've already thought of that, Mac, and will have one ready to go by morning, mate.'

'So, I'm not the only one who likes to think ahead then?'

'I guess you're not,' he smiled.

'Well, I'll leave you to it then, mate, and give you a ring if there are any sudden changes but you'll probably hear from me tomorrow, okay.'

'Sure, Mac. You go ahead and do what you got to do.'

At 4:30 pm, I left Mick and drove back to my apartment and thought I'd give Susan a ring and see if she was free for the night. I thought about Mick and how he seemed to have come out of his shell, being around a few different guys for a couple of weeks, and thought was that progress on his behalf or mine? Still, what the fuck, he was a good friend and seemed to have settled quite well with us, and I thought Bernie would like him too once he got to know him. I thought of Jacques and what his reaction might be when he saw Robbie lying there with all the wires and God knows whatever other attachments the doctors might have plugged into him.

And then I thought of Fox and what she had been up to since her release from prison, and why she had not been in contact or shown up somewhere in the town.

Every time I thought of her, I felt an ache in my heart but I have to let nature run its course and wait for her to come to me when she is ready. I parked outside my apartment block and entered the building. I got out the lift and went into my pad, kicked off my shoes and lay out on the sofa, lit up a cigarette and called Bernie.

'Okay, Mac, how the devil are you?' he answered.

'I'm good, Bernie. Is it okay for you to talk?'

'Not at the moment as I'm out shopping, just buying some plates, and the rest of the ingredients are all in the basket but need preparation, if you get my drift.'

'Sure, I do, Bernie. I'll call you in an hour or two, okay?'

'Yes, fine, my friend, and the same to you. Have a good day, 'and with that he cut me off.

Obviously, Bernie was being totally cautious and portraying his character to be of good faith in front of whoever he was with. Nonetheless, better to be safe than sorry in this game as well as inconspicuous to the best of our ability as we don't want to stand out, and that's why none of us are over five foot ten too as you'll stand out a mile in other people's eyes, as it's a natural habit to notice things out of place psychologically.

I rang the girl next door, Susan, on her mobile and got her voicemail, expected as she was in work but left her a message asking her if she fancied spending the night at mine and that I would cook her an Italian dish with a nice glass of crisp Chardonnay. I thought I might as well go to the supermarket and get the ingredients for dinner that night and pick up a nice bottle of Chardonnay, and if she said no then I'd simply eat out along with Mick if he wasn't busy. I hate shopping but someone has to do it, so to me it's just another detested chore any bachelor has to do, even though I am quite good in the kitchen and find following recipes a piece of cake! I spent ten minutes filling one of them shallow trolleys (beats carrying a basket) and then stood in a queue for twenty minutes waiting to get served! I take my ear buds/phones shopping with me, so I don't have to listen to the store's "drive you insane melodies" that for some reason turn the public into zombie shoppers that aimlessly wander up and down the aisles, bumping into each other and knocking things off shelves and squabbling over the last special offer in the meat section.

Back at my apartment I quickly put the shopping away and the Chardonnay in the fridge to chill when Susan rang me on my mobile phone.

'Hey, hun, what's on the menu?'

'Well, for starters I was thinking tomato and mozzarella toasts followed by cannelloni, and for dessert, an Italian ricotta pudding.'

'My, my, you're quite the chef as well as a good fuck. It all sounds delicious and the dessert is mouth-watering, like you, hun.'

'You're very tasty yourself.' I mindfully told her.

'Hey, Mac, stop it. You know this thing between us is not going to end up in a relationship, right?'

'Ease up, love, I'm not going in that direction as we're both professional here so let's keep it simple but good.' and thought thank fuck for that!

'Sorry, I thought you were going off the track there for a minute.'

'Not at all, Sue.'

'Now there's a good boy. See you at nine then, stud, and no sex, only cuddles as it's off limits till next week,' she stated abruptly ending the call.

I thought she's on her monthly period and that explained her little bark at me as well. Still, cuddles are good, I thought smiling to myself.

I lit up a cigarette and put the five o'clock news on, and got a beer from the fridge and chilled for half hour listening to all the atrocities going on around the globe, which somehow makes my life better as there are far worse places to live in the world. But there's no escaping global warming.

I called Bernie in France. 'Okay, Mac, sorry about earlier, I was in the process of buying the stainless plates and I got some six-inch steel plate to make a frame to hold the rest together.'

'Great. So is everything on the list sorted?'

'Of course it is, Mac. Are you doubting my ability?' he giggled.

'Not at all, Bernie, you've done a fine job, mate.'

'It's nothing, Mac. So when are you thinking of coming over here?'

'Within the next few days, but it will be very short notice and more than likely on the day we depart here.'

'Not a problem, Mac, I'm not going anywhere,' he giggled again.

'You didn't use your credit card to buy the plasma cutter, did you?'

'How dare you insult my intelligence?!' he said with an ironic tone.

'I'm not trying to insult you, mate, I just don't want any comebacks on you.'

'Your perspicacious never ceases, does it, Mac?'

'Hey, I do have days off from being a perfectionist, mate.'

'I know, that's why you're single, mate, but I understand.'

'Understand what?' I retorted.

'You, Mac, as you won't let a woman tell you what to do.'

'You need to check your crystal ball, mate, because I think it's cracked. And you bought it from duty free, so it's fucked.'

'Anyway, we'll continue this discussion when you get here. So how is Jacques?'

'He's travelled up to Glasgow to visit a friend that's had a serious car accident that has left him with possible brain damage. He's visiting the man's family too.'

'Christ, that is bad, Mac. How long did he know the guy?'

'About eight years if I remember correctly. We'll talk of this when we come over, okay?'

'Sure thing, Mac. So Jacques may not be coming with you?'

'It looks that way at the moment, but we'll have to wait and see.'

'So what of your friend Mick, will he be coming?'

'Yes, he will and he's looking forward to meeting you, mate.'

'Same here, Mac, in fact I can't wait. He's mellow, right?'

'Of course he is, and you'll like him, I think.'

'Time will tell, Mac.'

'How's your lady Chantelle? Hope she's looking after you over there?'

'She's my Joan of Arc, mate. She can't get enough of me and I can't get enough of her, but on the whole we're fine, thanks. What about Fox, Mac, have you seen her lately?'

'No, Bernie, and I haven't a clue where she's at either.'

'She'll surface when she is ready to be seen, mate, don't worry.'

'Good to know you got it all sorted, so we'll see you in a few days, okay?'

'Can't wait, Mac, and don't forget my sausages, pork and leek please, mate.'

'Trust me, I won't forget. You and Chantelle make sure you don't get caught before we get there by the villagers.'

'Not a chance, mate.'

'See you soon, mate.'

'Okay, take care.'

'Bye.'

I got a lot of time for Bernie as he has taken care of our project mostly on his own, with me only being there for limited periods, and Bernie has let it all go over his head and not once has he called in anger for assistance like most would in our position. On the whole, I rather think he likes it in France by himself, especially with Chantelle. All I need now is for Jacques to get in contact with me so I know what direction to go in, but if he doesn't, then I would do what I think is necessary for all of us, and Jacques will have to join in wherever we are at whatever stage in whatever country we are in, and me knowing Jacques' full potential, he can be anywhere within twenty four hours in the world.

I focused my attention to the evening ahead with Susan and thought the only thing I was missing was candles, not that I class myself as a big romantic but we all try in our own humble way. So, with that in mind, I went out and bought four large scented candles, two red and two white, as they can lighten anyone's mood and seeming it was her time of the month, I didn't want her biting my head off like earlier.

My phone rang and I said hello. The voice on the other end introduced himself as Philip Browning from M.A.T. Resources, the company I had emailed my C.V to regarding the oil refinery job in Mongstad, Norway. He asked me for my passport details which I gave him and what is the nearest airport to me; I told him that it was Cardiff International. He then informed me that I should be in Norway within the next week, if not before. I told him that was fine with me so long as it wasn't in the next four days as I was in the process of moving house. I asked him if he needed any more skilled men and he said not at the moment, but he was looking for coded TIG-welders, so I gave him Jacques' mobile number and said he would call me with a definite date and ended the call on that note.

This phone call I was banking on to get us into Norway and it couldn't have come at a worse time with Robbie in hospital and Jacques on his way up to see him, and me and Mick on our way to France, but I can always work around this as you have to be versatile in this business but still it was good news. I then prepared dinner for the evening with Susan but not cooking it apart from the desserts, which I made up and put in the fridge to chill and the rest could be done when she arrived at 9 pm, if not before.

Sue arrived smack bang on 9 pm in her black silk pyjamas and black fluffy mules with a matching black headband. 'Hi, Mac, missed me? 'she asked.

'Oh, so-so, but glad you could make it and I love your jim-jams.'

'Thanks, I feel more comfortable in them. I would have come sooner, but I had to take a shower first. I hope dinner is ready because I'm starved.'

'Make yourself at home. I'll get the wine.'

'Great. I could do with a glass after the day I've had.'

'You had a bad day, have you?'

'Bad is not the word, Mac.' I handed her a glass of wine. 'Thanks,' she replied continuing, 'Some stupid office junior mislaid an important document which meant that I couldn't assess a claim without it and I had my boss on my case over it until another assessor found it at the bottom of his files on his desk, which meant that I had to work through lunch and catch up on the two hours it was mislaid.'

'Did the junior get told off or reprimanded in some way?' I asked.

'No, she didn't. I think Ashton has got his eye on her as he pervs on all the new young girls, the freak.'

'Who's Ashton?' I asked her whilst putting the tomato and mozzarella toasties on a large plate.'

'Ashton is the boss's son. Also a director in the company and a right prick most of the time. He asked me to go for a meal with him once when I first started working there. but I refused. telling him I had a boyfriend, and he wouldn't take too kindly to the idea of me having dinner with another man if he found out. The prick kept pestering me, asked me to go out with him until I lied to him saying my boyfriend was a rugby player for the Cardiff Blues, which sent a shiver down his spine which kept him off my back,' she snapped.

'Good thinking,' I said, placing the starter on the table and topped up our wine glasses, turning the conversation around to my day.

I told her that I had lunch with Mick and was going to France to meet Bernie and show Mick our little property investment. I told Susan of our venture to turn it into a bed and breakfast type accommodation for backpackers who were travelling around Europe just to add a little extra income for me and Bernie. She inquired to what part of France we were in and I told her near Carcassonne (though we are actually miles away from there) and explained we were far from renovating it before she got any ideas about coming with us to visit. We ate dinner followed by dessert, and Susan complimented me on my cooking skills and even shamefully went so far as to look in the bin for some sort of packaging as she didn't believe I had cooked it myself with me being a bachelor and all. Satisfied with her findings, I opened another bottle of Chardonnay and joined her on the sofa, to which she slipped an arm around me and cuddled into me whilst she watched some girlie show on my television. Half way through her girlie show she said through a long yawn "I need sleep". I turned the television off with the remote control to which she smiled tiredly, then led her to the bedroom where again she confessed she was worn out. We got into bed and she put her arms around me and said, 'Hold me, hun.'

I responded and put my arms around her and gently pulled her in closer to me kissing her on the lips. She responded with a long slow passionate kiss then quickly withdrew telling me not to make her horny as she was too tired to even suck dick. She turned her back to me and placed my arm between her small cleavage and within five minutes she was fast asleep. I stayed with her until her breathing was sufficient enough for me to know she was now in a deep sleep before I slipped out of the bed and went back to my lounge, lit up a cigarette and poured out the remainder of the wine left in the bottle.

I picked up the phone and dialled Mick's number and waited for him to answers, 'Mac, what's up?' he whispered.

'Hi, Mick, sorry it's late. I'm going to see if I can book us to France for tomorrow, okay?'

'Well… err, yes, but what time?'

'I'll try to get us on an afternoon flight but it may be earlier so I suggest you get some sleep now.'

'That's going to be hard as Sara's in the bedroom making herself horny for me,' he said still whispering.

'So that's why you're whispering 'cos Sara's there?'

'Yeah.'

'Not to worry, mate. Do what you have to do and then make sure she's gone by the morning. Make some sort of excuse like you have an appointment that you forgot about.'

'Mac, it's not going to be that easy as she's brought a bag full of toys with her and she's pretty much the dominant type.'

'Look, I'm going to try and book the flights now online, so as soon as I have us booked, I'll call you back so keep your phone close at hand even if you're in the middle of something.'

'Not sure if she'd appreciate that, Mac, as she's a little psychotic when it comes to stopping. I should have taken yours and Jacques' advice and had nothing to do with her again, but the sex is pure nymphomaniac stuff and I found out she only comes when she's on top.'

'Spare me the details and just do your best, okay.'

'Right, okay then. But try not to call in the next thirty minutes.'

'I won't, over and out.' I ended the call laughing and drank the glass of wine and began looking online to book us flight.

I wasn't really worried about the expense of the flight so long as I could get us to Toulouse from Bristol airport. As it happened, I managed to get us on an Air France flight at 1:40 pm the next day. So I smoked a cigarette while I waited till twelve o'clock and then phoned Mick. He answered breathing heavily and I could tell she was giving him a blowjob at the same time.

'Arghhhh ahh, yes, mate? 'he grunted out.

'We fly out at 1:40 tomorrow afternoon. Call me when she's left.'

'Ugh yes, right, ugh, OUTCH!!' and the line went dead.

I couldn't help but laugh and after my fit of giggles stopped, I went back to Susan in the bedroom who was still fast asleep. I nestled in beside her and cuddled her in, and I wished this was Fox instead, but I'll enjoy Susan's company for now, and closed my eyes and fell into a sombre sleep with her. The night passed and we awoke at 6 am to Susan's alarm on her phone. We drank our indifferences, mine being tea and hers being coffee, and thanked each other for each other's company with a kiss before she went off to work. I phoned Mick and let it ring three times and then ended the call as if a signal to remind him to hurry up and get rid of Sara.

Not too long after, he phoned me and said, 'Thank fuck for that. She's gone.'

'I'll come and pick you up at eleven-ish, so make sure you're ready, mate.'

'See you at eleven-ish then. I'll be outside waiting with my bag.'

'Great, see you soon.'

'I'm looking forward to it.'

I picked Mick up as agreed and on the way out the town, I visited a farm that only sold local produce and bought four packs of eight pork and leek sausages for ten pounds.

'What's in the bag?' Mick asked.

'Pork and leek sausages.'

'Sausages! What the hell for?'

'They're for Bernie, he asked me to bring some over with me,' I told him.

'But why not just buy them in France?'

'Because these are Welsh-made pork and leek sausages.'

'Oh right,' he replied bewildered.

I drove out onto the M4 motorway and headed for Bristol Airport, cruising at a mellow 80mph and halfway into our journey, we were on the Second Severn

Bridge spanning the River Severn which connects Wales to England, and five minutes later, we were taking the slip road onto the M49 and heading towards Avonmouth Docks. We passed through the docklands and industrial estates, and continued our route along the A4 and up the A38, finally reaching Bristol Airport. I drove into the long stay car parks and parked amongst the many hundreds of other cars. I opened the boot of my BMW series 3 and wrapped the sausages in scented nappy sacks I bought previously and placed them back inside my hold-all. Mick looked on with interest and raised eyebrows.

I zipped the hold-all up and placed a small padlock through the two zippers and placed it on the floor. 'Wait here a minute while a get the parking ticket,' I told him.

'Why did you put the sausages in nappy sacks?' Mick asked puzzled.

'Because if I don't, the sniffer dogs inside will smell the sausages and go berserk, and then I'll have them taken off me by customs as some food substances are banned and I don't want to disappoint, Bernie,' I said smiling at Mick and went to the nearest ticket machine, collected the ticket and placed it on the dashboard and locked the car.

Once we were inside the terminal and checked our bags in with Air France and collected our tickets after queuing for a short time. We bought a hot beverage each and went outside so I could have a cigarette. The time now was getting on for 12:30 am, leaving us just over an hour to wait before our departure.

'I'm going to have another smoke, mate, before I go back inside,' I informed him.

'Well, I'm going through to departures, Mac, so I'll see you up there.'

'Okay, mate, see you in a bit.'

I smoked half the cigarette and threw the rest on the floor before I joined Mick in departures. I got through customs with the sausages okay, except for a mild pat-down, and headed into the departure lounge and was unable to see Mick so I sat at the bar, an easy-to-notice place. Mick appeared clutching a duty-free bag. He had bought a pair of Ralph Lauren sunglasses and a Paul Cardinal shirt for a little under two hundred quid. Mick ordered us two bottles of Stella and with them in hand, we moved to a more comfortable seating area away from the bar. We talked about day-to-day stuff and admired a few women in short skirts and tight shorts showing off their pert arses and legs as they always do at airports. We kept spotting them in between watching *MTV* on a big screen and drinking our bottles of Stella.

Our flight was announced over the tannoy, asking all passengers to make their way to Gate 2. I told Mick to hang back a minute while I went and got us another two bottles of Stella. A while later, the last call was announced for Toulouse so we drained our bottles and made our way to Gate 2 with our passports and tickets, and once checked, we boarded the plane. After all the passengers were accounted for, the plane's door was closed and we soon taxied off to the runway, and after a short wait, the plane's engines began to roar suddenly catapulting us forward down the runway with ever-increasing speed our plane tilted back and began climbing into the air as the roar of the engines turned to a drone the higher we climbed.

The plane levelled out and a few minutes later. The seat belt signs went off with a ping-ping sound as they do. As always, there were those persons who make a mad dash for the toilets as soon as the seat belt signs go off and for the life of me I have not been able to work out whether they are wetting their pants drinking too much or they have shat their pants from taking off. At least I know who the lightweights were. I idly thought to myself, it's surprising that the majority of the toilet rushers are men.

'Will Bernie be there to meet us when we arrive?'

'Well, if he isn't, he can kiss his sausages goodbye,' I chuckled.

'How long will it take to drive to your house?'

'Not long, Mick, only about an hour and half, maybe a tad more, mate.'

'So what's your place actually like then?'

'In a nutshell, Mick. It's idyllic.'

'In what way?'

'You'll see soon enough for yourself, mate,' I replied closing my eyes and pictured the little town and smiled at the mere thought of it.

'I can't wait to see it and meet Bernie.'

'He's looking forward to meeting you too, Mick, but do be careful when we are in the town, especially if you see Chantelle, as the locals don't know of her and Bernie's affair, so it's important you don't let anything slip or we'll all be lynched, mate.'

'No worries, Mac. You can all count on me.'

'Just take a step back and go with the flow and you'll be fine.'

'What about the language barrier, as I know very little French?'

'Don't worry about it as most locals understand a little English, but they make out they don't as they think we've invaded their space and more of us will come and fuck up their quiet lifestyle, but they're not as bad as when we first bought the place though they are still wary of us. Apart from that, they leave us alone.'

Chapter 6

Agde, France

Thirty minutes into our flight, the air hostess brought us a light snack consisting of a pack of sandwiches with a choice of chicken tikka or lamb and mint, with a hot beverage and a two-pack of chocolate Bourbons. We both passed on the sandwiches but accepted a tea for me and a coffee for Mick, along with the chocolate Bourbons which we both dunked in our hot drinks. Ten minutes later, they came up the aisle with a trolley collecting everyone's cups and sandwich wrappers. Our conversation turned to Robbie and his well-being, and we both hoped that he would eventually recover, fingers crossed. Also, I had sent Jacques a text message before we left the UK to inform him that we Were on our way to Agde to visit Bernie, but he knew the real reason why we were going to France to visit him.

Everything will be grand tonight when we arrive, especially when we go down to the town for a little stroll and to see it all lit up with their different coloured little lanterns here and there illuminating the cobbled streets. There is only one bar-come-restaurant that can accommodate about fifty customers comfortably then outside there is a flagstone terrace that can easily seat one hundred people that overlooks the picturesque little marina and under a moon-lit sky it's very enchanting.

The captain announced that we would be making our descent in due course as the seat belt signs illuminated. The hostesses came around asking people to put their belts on and made sure that everything was in order before we landed. The plane descended and shortly afterwards we hit the runway with the softest of landings before we taxied off the runway until the plane finally came to a halt at the terminal. After disembarking, we collected our luggage from for the carousel and passed through customs without a hitch, and out to arrivals where Bernie was standing waiting for us with a huge grin on his face.

'Hello, Mac mate, it's great to see you.'

'It's damn good to see you, Bernie. This is a very old friend of mine, Mick. And Mick, this old man is Bernie,' I said jokingly.

'Hey, Mac, less of the old man stuff. And Mick, it's a pleasure to meet you, mate. So if it's okay with you two, shall we jump in the jeep and head for home?'

'After you, Bernie,' I gestured with a sweep of the hand.

We crossed over into the short stay car park and followed Bernie to his jeep. 'Here we are, just put your bags in the back,' he said.

'Bernie, have you got your fucking head screwed on, mate? I said in disbelief. 'What the hell is this piece of junk?'

'Don't start now, Mac, you only just got here and you're not doing the driving, so shut the fuck up and just get in. Come on, Mick, let's go,' he stammered.

Mick and I looked at each other gobsmacked and then I turned to Bernie and said, 'I'm not going in that piece of shit, mate, look at the state of it. It's a scrapper, mate! It's fucked!!'

'Mick, what do you see?' Bernie asked him.

'Well…err… I have to agree with Mac, Bernie, it's kinda fucked!'

'Right, the pair of you can walk or get a flight to Montpellier and then a taxi. There's nowt wrong with her apart from a few cosmetics,' he said whilst stroking the bonnet and wing of his jeep.

'Cos-fucking-metics! It looks like it's been crushed and then someone had a go a straightening it out.'

'Well, it wasn't that bad to begin with, but it did take a bit of a beating out, but I had to light roll it to get it into this condition, mate, and originally it was white but I sprayed matt black just to blend in.'

'Blend in? Blend in to what?'

'The town of course, otherwise they would have thought I was being stuck up, posh like a snob, standing out from the crowd, that sort of thing, if you follow my drift, Mac,' Bernie explained smiling.

'You've lost me, Bolt! It's more noticeable than a Ferrari in a car park on its own in that state.'

'I tend to agree,' Mick piped in.

'Well, you know how the locals don't like change, right?'

'Yes. Go on,'

'I bought it for six grand, full service history with one owner, but then I thought the locals will really give me the silent treatment as it looked so pristine so I … did the damage on purpose,' he confessed. 'And let me tell you, it drives like a dream. I've checked everything twice for any severe damage, trust me, I'm a mechanic, remember?'

'So why not just go and buy a scrapper?'

'Believe me when I tell you that the engine and gearbox is better in this one.'

'Fucking unbelievable,' I said, thinking aloud.

'It has full leather too and a CD multi changer as well as every conceivable extra. Cool, huh?' he said grinning.

'So what did the locals think when they saw the jeep?' I asked him.

'They pissed themselves laughing and point every time I go past them, but the plus side is that I get the odd free beers in the bar now and again as they tell me I need to save money and buy a better car,' he said giggling his balls off.

Mick couldn't believe his ears and was rolling around on the floor pissing himself laughing. I was doubled over laughing too. Even Bernie joined us in a fit of laughter. 'So, you see, there's method to the madness. So get in the jeep and let's go introduce Mick to them.' We got inside the vehicle and everything was like new; he started the car and the engine just purred.

'Do you know what, lads?' he asked.

'What?' we replied in unison.

'This jeep is like the Phantom of the Opera.' We just stared at him silently as he went on. 'It's ugly as fuck on the outside but underneath, it is all heart,' and with that statement he drove away from the airport for Agde.

'Did you forget my sausages?' Bernie asked grimly.

'No, not at all, mate, they're in my holdall.'

'Will you do me a big favour and take them out and put them in the cooler box in the back?'

'Why's that, mate?'

'To keep them fresh, as you don't know how the altitude has affected them.'

'You're not serious.'

'Just take them out and put them in the cooler, will you, mate,' he said frowning.

I handed Mick, who was trying hard not to laugh, the key to the lock; he took out the sausages and placed them in the cooler and handed me back the key.

'They're not squashed, are they, Mick?' Bernie asked him anxiously.

'Well, they seemed alright to me,' he replied grinning.

'Nice,' Bernie muttered and then asked Mick, 'Have you ever been to the Ville Rose before?'

'I don't know what you mean, Bernie.'

'You know, the Pink City, Toulouse, mate.'

'Can't say I have, but it looks very nice from where I'm sitting.'

'Do I detect a note of sarcasm back there?'

'On the contrary, Bernie, I'm just enjoying the scenery.'

'Good, we don't want you upsetting the locals with negative thoughts as they're mad to lynch us, aren't they, Mac?'

'Something along those lines, yes, but don't you think you're over-reacting in terms of the Agde people?'

'Are you trying to say something here that I can't follow?

'No, far from it. But you don't seem like your normal self, mate, what's up?'

'Nothing, nothing at all. Why, does it seem that way?'

'Don't worry, everything's under control.'

'What do you mean "under control"?'

'I've been getting a bad vibe off the locals lately but I can't work it out, Mac.'

'What's happened, what have you done?'

'I haven't done nothing wrong as far as I know, apart from Chantelle that is,' he said grinning from ear to ear.

'Have you upset her in any way, Bernie?'

'Hell no. We're madly in love, mate,' he stated.

'We'll try to figure it all out when we get there, mate.'

'You'll be surprised at the change of the house. There's been a fair amount of work done.'

'How come, you haven't emailed me some pictures of its progress?'

'Well ... I wanted to surprise you, Mac. You won't recognize the old place as the front wall has had another foot built on top of the existing wall as well as it all being re-painted. And the entrance has been widened by eighteen inches to accommodate the new gates.'

'What do you mean new gates? There was nothing wrong with the old ones. They looked fine to me.'

'The old ones were shot and too much welding needed doing. I saw these lovely oak gates in a type of reclaim yard, so I had a deal with the guy. I showed him our gates which he liked and swapped him along with three hundred Euros.

But I think I tucked him up in the process as these gates would cost over five grand to be made.'

'So the wall is now five foot high as the gates are?'

'Seven foot exactly, and six inches thick.'

'So where did you get the stones from to go on top of the front wall?'

'From one of the out buildings out back as it was falling down anyway. Wait till you see it before you criticize me for it.'

'I'm not criticizing you, Bernie, but we can't see out.'

A smile spread across Bernie's face. 'Yes, I know, mate, but now nobody can see in either which also means they can't see Chantelle. But it does add character to the place.'

'Right, I see, but what about the rest of the surrounding walls?'

'For fuck sake, Mac, one wall at a time and one out building at a time.'

'Anything else I should know about that I don't?' I asked getting a little irate.

'Yeah.'

'Well... Spit it out then,' I urged him.

'The value of the property has increased,' he said grinning at me.

'Result, mate,' I said continuing to ask, 'Where are the labourers to now?'

'Down in the town having a few cold beers no doubt.'

'Anything changed around the old town?'

'Nah, naff all, mate. It's still as quiet and beautiful as ever. Hey, Mick?'

'Yes, Bernie?'

'If you dig around over the back there, you might find a few odd bottles of lager, if you and Mac fancy one, mate?'

'What do you say, Mac?' Mick asked.

'Why not,' I replied lighting up a cigarette.

'They might be a bit warm though, guys,' Bernie warned us.

Mick found us a bottle each but Bernie declined, seeming he was driving and stuck to his bottle of water instead. Mick opened the bottles but like Bernie had said, they were too warm so they got thrown out the window on Bernie's orders and ended up in some hedge along the way. We left Toulouse behind us and started winding in to the country roads which passed the odd little village and the occasional farmhouses spread out along the way. Bernie decided to take the coastal road to give Mick a look at the Mediterranean coast line as we eventually came to the outskirts of Narbonne and drove down a narrow lane after taking another turn, only this time it led us down a steep country lane and even before we got to the bottom, we could see our little town and its marina.

Bernie turned to Mick and said, 'Can you see that big house surrounded by buildings over to your left above the rest of the town?'

'Err… Yes, I can.'

'That's home, mate,' Bernie grinned.

'It looks big from here,' Mick replied.

'It is. It's got ten bedrooms,' I reminded him.

Our house is ideally positioned being set back from the main part of the old town perched on a small hill. Its dominating presence manipulates the rest of the little town and houses as if it was watching over them, for it looks out of place and draws attention to itself by its vast awkwardness emulating on the horizon. It stares down across the town's red-tiled rooftops and the tiny marina with nothing more than a couple of small open fishing boats. The entrance or the inlet to this hidden place can only take such small boats as the narrow channel will not allow anything bigger to pass through without becoming wedged between the rocky cliff walls. The town has a laid-back idleness where everything is done at a slow pace apart from the food. Even on a hot summer's day, the only sounds to be heard are the bees bumbling around pots filled with lavender and the chug of a boat's engine coming or going in or out of the marina, along with the occasional fizzing of a Citroen Dolly engine slowly making its way through the narrow sublime cobbled streets.

Even the townsfolk just tend to bask in the heat of the day without so much as a murmur from their lips, only a nod of their head or a simple smile as to acknowledge your presence, but as the light of day fades, the town yawns and stirs, and by nightfall, the town awakes with numerous different coloured lanterns suspended from building to building illuminating the dimly-lit streets, where a majority of the townsfolk gather at the bar and restaurant to chat away usually till past midnight before they disperse to their dwellings.

Bernie drove the jeep steadily through the town and up the little hill to the house and stopped outside the big wooden gates of the house. 'Check this out,' he said and pressed a tiny remote. The gates swung slowly open as we proceeded through them.

'Wow! You're a fucking star, mate,' I said to Bernie.

'I thought you might like it. I wired them myself but aren't they class, Mac?'

'I think they're damn right impressive. You've done a grand job here, mate, and I take my hat off to you,' I replied joyfully.

We drove around to the rear of the house and went inside with our hold-alls into the kitchen. 'What do you reckon of the makeover, Mac?' he asked me.

'I don't even recognize the old place, Bernie, and as for the kitchen, it's marvellous. And I like the island in the middle, mate, it's fucking stunning, wouldn't you say, Mick?'

'I have to agree, it's better than I imagined from the outside,' he replied.

Bernie put the sausages in the fridge then he turned to us and said smiling, 'Come on, I'll show you the main reception room.'

We followed Bernie through a large empty room and then into an even larger room that had furnishings in with a huge grand fire place. The walls were as smooth as a baby's bum and untouched by colour apart from the fresh pale plaster with a chandelier hanging in the centre of the ceiling. Even the furnishings seemed apt with three large dark brown leather three-seater sofas and a chaise lounge. An 80-inch plasma hung on the wall opposite the grand fireplace with suitable items of other furniture to match. Over the windows draped marl curtains that fell to the floor which was now covered with old flagstones.

'I'm afraid from here on in around the rest of the house, is all three star as are the bedrooms, but what you will appreciate, Mick, is that we are still renovating the old place.'

'Old place, old place,' he repeated, adding, 'it's like a fucking palace, guys.'

'Well, I wouldn't go that far,' I said and winked at Bernie.

'Shall one show ones to their private quarters,' Bernie said jokingly.

We left the lounge behind and entered into a vast hall with a very wide staircase that you could drive a car up, that arced round to the left. Bernie was now relishing the moment and proceeded with his grand tour. 'You'll notice this fine staircase has been renovated to its former glory no less than six weeks ago, hence it's covered in polythene so as not to mark it.'

The bedrooms did feel three star, but in more than satisfactory order (I'd quite happily live here now if I hadn't other things to do first), but Mick was totally overwhelmed with the whole place and stated that he would never want to see the U.K again if he had a place like this to live in. We reminded him that that was our intention too. We put our bags in our allocated rooms and then met Bernie downstairs by the front door. 'Follow me, guys,' he asked us.

We followed him across what we call the driveway and over to an old barn, and went in via the side door. Bernie switched the lights on and there was building materials everywhere. 'Over here,' he said. We followed him to the far wall where a large canvas sheet was covering something he pulled the canvas off. Underneath were all the items on the shopping list, and there was our plasma cutter. 'I've put the wheels on it so you can feel the weight. Go ahead and move it.'

'Is it heavy?' I asked him.

'Not as heavy as I thought it might be,' he replied.

I grasped the handles and took the weight, and then wheeled it around and surprisingly, it wasn't that heavy to manoeuvre. 'Well, I imagined it to be a lot heavier myself. You've done a good job and where are all the plates?'

'You picked it, Mac, so the credit goes to you, and the plates are over here, I've taken the liberty of stitch welding them together in the order you suggested, mate.'

'Very nice and tomorrow we shall put the plasma cutter to the test,' I told them.

'I bought six nozzles of each type just in case some get fucked in the cutting process.'

'Good on you, Bolt. What do you think, Mick?'

'I'm at a loss, Mac, it just looks like a metal box on wheels to me.'

'That's what it is, Mick. You're a fast learner and I take my hat off to you,' Bernie said grinning.

'He'd make a great fitter or welder,' I said.

'That he would, Mac.'

'Are you two having a laugh at my expense?' Mick asked annoyed.

'Who, us? No, Mick, we wouldn't dream of it, mate, would we, Bernie?'

'No, not at all. Who does he take us for?'

'It feels like you're taking the piss,' Mick scowled.

'Is he paranoid, Mac, or am I taking things the wrong way?'

'I think it's open for discussion over a few beers, Bernie. What say you?'

Bernie turned to Mick and said, 'Fancy a few beers down the local?'

'Sure. But stop ripping the piss, will you, guys?'

'Touchy for a locksmith, isn't he, Mac?' Bernie said winking at me.

'Stop picking on him,' I said jokingly.

Bernie said, 'Okay, enough joking. Let's get back to the house and freshen up a little, and then we'll go down into town for a few drinks and a bite to eat.'

We changed into suitable clothing to accommodate the Mediterranean climate and headed down to the town in the beaten-up jeep and parked it next to the little marina.

Mick was totally taken aback by this gem of a place and like us wondered how it had managed to stay hidden for so long without some sort of property tycoon ruining the place by development.

We strolled over to the edge of the marina and again Mick was taken aback. 'Who put the steps down to the water?' he asked.

'Ahh... now they've been there for a few centuries, my friend,' Bernie informed him.

'They don't look that old.'

'If you take a greater look, you will see that they have been carved out of the bare rock either side of the slipway.'

'How far down under the water do they go then?' Mick asked inquisitively.

'I think no more than another ten or twelve feet as the tides here don't drop that much compared to back home. Quite a unique place, don't you agree?' Bernie asked.

'Totally, guys,' he replied in awe.

'And to your left overlooking here is the bar we're going to,' I pointed out.

The three of us walked along the marina's edge and up to the bar and entered through the main entrance. We walked past a few locals seated around tables and followed Bernie out onto the terrace looking out over the marina and sat at one of the many unoccupied tables. A waitress appeared, a soft gentle smile on her face. 'Bonjour, Bernie.'

'Bonjour, Chantelle,' Bernie said, smiling like a Cheshire cat at her.

'What would you like to order some food or perhaps drinks? 'she asked softly.

'First let me introduce you to my good friends, this is Mac.'

'Salut, Mac,' she said smiling.

'Bonjour,' I replied.

'And this is Mick.'

'Salut, Mick,' she said smiling.

'These are the two I said were coming to visit for a couple of days,' Bernie whispered to her.

'Yes, I gathered that, 'she whispered back at him. 'It's very nice to meet you both and I think your first drink will be on the house.'

'That's very kind of you, Chantelle,' I said.

'You're welcome, Mick.'

'I'm Mac, he's Mick.'

'Forgive me, Mac. Bernie, what drinks would you like?'

'I think three beers, love.'

'Quiet, my love, others may hear and then trouble on you.'

'Oops, I forgot,' Bernie whispered.

Chantelle left us and went for our beers.

'Bernie, I take my hat off to you, she is an absolute stunner, mate.'

'I know,' he said grinning.

'Has she got any sisters?' Mick asked.

'Unfortunately, no, Mick.'

'Damn. Are they all like her around here?'

'Not like Chantelle, but there are others.'

'They still use the guillotine in these parts, Mick, so be careful, mate,' I said playfully.

'Now I know you're having me on,' he said laughing.

Chantelle came back with our beers still smiling, 'The old folk think you have brought your friends to stay and more crap cars will follow,' she said giggling to Bernie whilst placing the beers on the table.

'Merci, Chantelle, and you can reassure the old folk no more crap cars will be coming,' he said laughing.

'I have to go back in the bar and serve, but will see you all after, okay?'

'Okay, see you later,' Bernie replied. And she disappeared back inside.

'Looks like you're not popular with the jeep from the black lagoon,' Mick said laughing.

'Nah, they're just jealous that's all.'

'Have you thought about a boat yet, Bernie?'

'I have but it can't be bigger than old Pierre's, the fisherman, as that would upset him as his boat is his pride and joy. The jeep's enough for now, so I think I should let them get used to that first.'

'You're probably right,' I said.

'Anyhow, the inlet to the marina is too narrow and wouldn't take a sport cruiser,' Bernie grinned.

We sat down and chatted about the past and present, and told Bernie of Robbie (The Jock) and his accident. I filled Bernie in on Jacques' activities and whereabouts, and Mick gave him some of his history and up to the present day. I told him of our intentions in Norway and he nodded as he listened intently and raised his eyebrows at the sum of money involved and sipped his beer slowly.

Bernie spoke saying, 'Now I get the full picture and why you need the plasma cutter.'

'There's a problem though.'

'What sort of problem?'

'We're a man down due to Robbie's crash,' I reminded him.

'Don't beat around the bush, spit it out, Mac.'

'Do you want in with us?'

'I thought you would never ask,' he said laughing and raised his glass in the air.

We all touched glasses and finished off the beer and the overall details I would fill him in on up at the house. Bernie went inside and ordered us lamb and pork steaks with vegetables, and brought back three more beers. Chantelle came out to us and placed three bowls of onion and celery soup with a lightly toasted French stick on the side as an appetizer.

'To tie you over till your dinners are ready, it's good. You'll like it, I hope,' she said.

We all thanked her with a merci and a smile. She smiled back and returned back inside to the other customers again.

The soup was absolutely delicious and went down well with all three of us heartedly. The lamb and pork steaks arrived and we totally devoured them along with the most delicious sauce that accompanied them, which topped it off for me and Mick, as Bernie had tasted it before.

'More beers, monsieurs?' Chantelle called out to us from the terrace doorway.

'Oui, mademoiselle. Trois biers,' Bernie called back.

'What was that you said?'

'Three beers, but I'm not that good at the lingo, Mick, just bits and pieces,' Bernie replied.

'Stay here long enough and you'll be as fluent as Jacques, Mick,' I added.

'Yeah, Jacques can talk the talk as well as walk the walk,' Bernie informed him.

'When do you think we'll hear from him, Mac?'

'As and when he's ready, Mick, but hopefully soon, mate.'

'Yes. He has a way of just appearing sometimes,' Bernie added.

'Does anything exciting happen around these parts?'

'Mick, if you want excitement, you'll have to go to Montpellier or Sète.'

'Monaco. How far is it from here?'

'What would you say, Mac?'

'About 4 hours away. And no, we're not going there at all on this trip but maybe some other day we will, Mick.'

'I didn't mean for us to go, I was just asking out of curiosity, that's all.'

'This is the life for me; nice, quiet and very, very laid back. Absolutely magic it is,' Bernie remarked.

'I tend to agree, mate, and that's why we bought the old place, Mick, as we can step in and step out when it takes our fancy.'

'How much do properties go for around here?' Mick asked.

'Ah, that would be telling,' Bernie giggled.

'What about another couple of beers, chaps?' I asked changing the subject.

'I'm in,' Mick said.

'Me too,' said Bernie.

And that's how the night continued, sat out on the terrace drinking beer and chatting away till past midnight when we were more than merrily drunk and talked on about anything and nothing. Chantelle came out and said the others had all gone but we could stay and drink more if we wished to do so. Bernie got us one more beer for the road and paid the bill for all of us and reminded us we had to walk up to the house as he was incapable of driving. Before we left the bar and Chantelle told Bernie she may possibly see him later, he smiled at her and blew her a kiss and then zig-zagged away along with me and Mick. The house, normally a ten-minute walk, took us a good half hour, and on top of that Bernie had left the remote for the gates in the jeep, which meant we had to walk down the side of the house and fall over the wall, which we all did bursting out laughing as we did so. Bernie wanted to play with the plasma cutter, but I managed to persuade him not to. We got inside the house after a good door scratching with the key and Bernie got us a nice chilled beer which we drank and then retired to our rooms and into our individual comas.

I awoke to the annoying sound of cockerels and their disturbing cries. I got up off the bed still fully dressed from a few hours earlier and drew back the curtains and in the dawn light I could see two cockerels walking around the yard when suddenly there was a thunderous BANG!! A cloud of feathers was strewn into the air. I thought what the fuck and opened the window and peered around and saw Bernie with a huge grin on his face, quickly tip-toeing bare foot across the yard only in his yellow Y-fronts carrying a shotgun. He bent down, picked up the now dead cockerel off the floor and shook it a few times just to make sure it was dead.

'What the fuck are you doing?' I called down to him.

'Shhhh! Not so loud, Mac, you might scare the other one off,' he said frowning as he tip-toed off and vanished through a doorway in one of the out buildings. Stunned, I shut the window lit a cigarette up and made my way downstairs to the kitchen for a cup of coffee.

As I got to the top of the staircase, Mick came out of his bedroom all goggle-eyed in his boxers and asked me, 'What's going on? I thought I heard a loud bang?'

'You did, mate. Bernie's on safari out back.'

'What?

'I'm off to the kitchen, you coming?'

'Might as well, I'm awake now,' Mick said yawning.

'Oh, by the way, we slept in the wrong bedrooms last night.'

'Did we? I hadn't noticed, Mac.'

'Neither did I until a few minutes ago,' I replied walking down the staircase.

We were both sat in the kitchen drinking our cuppa's and eating toast when BANG!!! Mick and I both jumped instantly, startled by the unexpected loud bang.

'What's he up to?' Mick asked gruffly.

'I think you'll find out soon enough,' I told him and carried on sipping my tea.

'What about the neighbours, Mac? It's just gone 6 am.'

'It's private property, mate. There's nothing they can do, I think.'

The back door flew open and Bernie came bouncing in beaming from ear to ear, carrying two dead black cockerels and a shotgun, he said, 'Morning, mates. Fucking noisy cockerel bastards no more. These two little fuckers have been doing my head in for weeks! Every morning they've been making a bastard racket. Some days it's nice to have a lay in bed, if you know what I mean.'

'Yeah! I know what you mean,' I said sarcastically.

'Me too,' Mick added.

'I see you found the kettle and toaster then. So you two want some fine Welsh sausages, bacon and eggs?

'Sure we do, isn't that right, Mick,' I said smiling but not really giving a flying fuck.

'Sure thing, Mac,' Mick replied sarcastically.

'Well, the frying pan's over there and everything else is in the fridge, I'll have three eggs with mine,' Bernie said grinning.

'Why do I have to cook?' I asked.

'Okay, you pluck these little fuckers and I'll do us breakfast then?' Bernie barked back.

'Nah, you can pluck them and we'll sort the breakfast.'

'Deal,' Bernie replied.

'Is there going to be anymore shooting today, Bernie?'

'Not anymore, Mick. Why's that, mate?'

'Good, I'm going back to bed.'

'What for, the sun's coming up,' Bernie exclaimed.

'Sleep,' Mick replied, necking the last of the tea in his cup.

'Lightweight!!' Bernie said, teasing Mick.

'Catch you both a lot later,' Mick said and went back to the land of nod, leaving me and Bernie to sort out the chores.

I cooked the breakfast while Bernie took great delight in plucking the two cockerels outside, sat on the kitchen door step talking to them as he plucked away.

'Whose cockerels are they?' I asked him.

'Dunno, but there ours now, mate,' he replied laughing.

'You mean you just shot someone else's birds?'

'Proper free range these are, mate. Unlike that supermarket rubbish, these are quality birds.'

'Breakfast's ready.'

'Coming, mum.'

'Don't start that crap with me, it's too early in the morning, mate,' I told him.

We sat down at the table and tucked in to the breakfast and after another mug of tea for me and a coffee for Bernie, I asked him, 'What time did you wake up?'

'Four thirty when Chantelle left.'

'Oh, she came here last night?'

'Of course she did, mate. She complained that you or Mick snore too loud.'

'I woke up in Mick's room and Mick in mine.'

'That'll be the beer, mate. Still, it was a good night, eh?'

'Yeah, but I could have done without the shooting this morning.'

Bernie laughed and said, 'Those cockerels needed fucking shooting, Mac, and you'll thank me for it in the morning.'

'Probably, mate, nice sausages by the way.'

'I know,' Bernie said chewing away on one.

We finished our breakfasts and whilst I washed up, Bernie gutted and washed the two cockerels and put them in the freezer. After I showered, feeling the better for it, and put a shirt, shorts and shoes on and came back downstairs to where Bernie was waiting, he said, 'You're going to need more than that on if you're going to use the plasma, Mac.'

'I know, but let's get it rigged up first, then take it from there,' I suggested.

We went over to the out building and Bernie opened the double doors whilst I wheeled the cutter near the doorway while Bernie brought the loom and leather sleeves to cover it. He connected the loom to the cutter and fitted a cutting nozzle. He produced a couple of scrap metal plates which he placed on top of a few stones to raise them from the floor.

'Here, put these on first,' he said and handed me a pair of overalls and a pair of his old boots.

'Thanks,' I replied.

'Ready to rumble, mate?' he asked.

'Let's do it,' I replied, putting on the leather gauntlets and head screen but not before Bernie gave me a flame-proof balaclava to put on too. I picked up the plasma's cutting torch and moved forward towards the plates and knelt down next to them.

'Ready, mate?'

'Ready,' Bernie replied.

I held the cutting torch close to the plates and pulled my shield down over my face and squeezed on the trigger. Immediately on arcing, the flame appeared and I began to cut through the metal plate like a knife through butter, as the flame cut through an inch and half of metal in seconds. I let go of the trigger and the flame disappeared. I removed the shield and balaclava, and breathed in the air.

'Fuck! That gives off some heat, mate.'

'I know. I could feel it from here.'

'Not sure how we'll stand up to this in such a small space as it might affect us all.'

'Well, that's what water's for, Mac.'

'I'm thinking oxygen and fumes, mate.'

'You'll be okay, it's just you got to get used to it first,' he replied reassuringly.

I spent a few minutes using the cutter and again the results were superb. I gave the screen and balaclava to Bernie, who with eagerness donned it and cut through the plates a few times. He stopped cutting and removed the head gear.

'Fuck! That is one fast cutter, mate.'

'I wish Jacques was here to test it though.'

'No worries, Mac, he'll sort it on the job.'

'Right, let's make some space inside and try it on the test piece.'

Bernie's face lit up instantly on hearing my suggestion. We made a big clearing and threw all the other materials well out the way and wheeled the cutter further back inside and closed the double doors.

'Now we'll know what we're up against and what to expect in Norway, 'I told him.

We dragged the test piece into the middle of the clearing we made and stood it upright. I put the head gear back on and got the torch going again, and began to cut at an angle, slowly working the flame into its cutting depth. I cut about four inches when I got a blow back and got showered in molten metal that burnt through the overalls to my chest.

'Fuck, bastard, twat,' I screamed dancing around.

'Are you okay, mate?' Bernie asked concerned.

'Shit! That was fucking hot.'

'Come on, let's get you up to the house.'

'No, I'll be alright,' I replied.

'Well, let's see how bad it is first.'

I removed the head screen and opened my overalls, and sure enough I had a few burn marks on my chest. I switched off the plasma cutter and headed to the house with Bernie to bathe the burns and have a cup of tea. I lit up a cigarette and held a damp cloth on my chest when Mick appeared and asked, 'What is that on your chest, Mac?'

'Blow back from the plasma cutter, mate.'

'What's a blow back?'

'To put it mildly, Mick, he burnt himself whilst using the plasma cutter,' Bernie informed him.

'Oh. How badly?' he asked whilst pouring himself a cuppa.

'It's nothing really, Mick. It can happen to anyone.'

'So I guess you'll be going for the gouging nozzle next?' Bernie asked me.

'Straight after I've finished a cuppa, mate,' I said smiling.

'That's my man,' Bernie said grinning.

All three of us went back to the out building and inspected the previous cutting. The depth was fine but where we had cut at a depth of one-half inches. The glass and stainless plate had melted into one thus re-sealing the cut. I changed the cutting nozzle for the gouger and started the plasma up.

'Here goes everything,' I said.

'Let's hope so,' Bernie added.

Mick just raised an eyebrow in silence.

I squeezed the trigger of the torch and the flame shot out and with a minor adjustment, I began to gouge the metal plates away at an alarming rate but good on our behalf. Bernie started the stopwatch to time me. The hot molten slag dropped onto the floor and with various bits of debris laying there, it wasn't long before we had a small fire on our hands. I stopped the gouging process and Bernie extinguished the fire, but the building had filled with smoke too, so we opened the double doors and waited till the smoke had disappeared and closed the doors again. Bernie swept the area around the template as clean as he could and then laid down a double sheet of fire blanket.

'Wouldn't it be better to leave the doors open to let the smoke and fumes out?' Mick asked.

'In an ideal world, yes, but you can't leave the jeweller's doors open when burning the real safe, mate,' I said.

'And in these closed conditions, we'll know what we are in for on the real job and can make adjustments to plans accordingly,' Bernie added.

'Makes sense, I suppose,' Mick replied.

I went back at it, gouging away and again the metal plate was being stripped away with chunks falling on the floor, and the heat from the plasma cutter was tremendous, but after a while I hardly felt it apart from the dampness of my clothes. After a while, I stopped, marking the time elapsed. I told Bernie and Mick I needed a break and a drink to which they agreed, following me outside into the shade out of the heat of the day. I smoked a cigarette and we all went back inside to inspect how much damage had been done in those couple of minutes before we were smoked off the job, so to speak.

The gouging had made an awful amount of progress compared to the cutting we tried earlier and there was no repeat of a blowback. Bernie shovelled the now cooling metal outside out of the way and on closer inspection, I had gouged through the outer plate, stainless plate and the glass. The hole was only about six inches square, but there was still the same to gouge through again before we would actually be inside the safe. But that was far from our main goal as we had to practically gouge the whole side of the safe away to gain access to every shelf inside the main safe in Norway to remove all the diamonds. The clock continued to tick against us for now.

'What's the sketch then, Mac?' Mick asked inquisitively.

'We need to keep gouging away,' I replied.

'I'll go and get us some liquid refreshment from the house I think, anyone interested?' Bernie asked.

'Good idea. I'll have a bottle of water, mate, thanks,' I replied.

'That's all you were getting or you'll get the sack for drinking on the job,' he said laughing whilst walking away to the house.

I made my way over to a large box and dug around inside it for the head screen with a fixed filter attached and two face masks with toxic filters fitted for Mick and Bernie. Once again, I donned the equipment and told Mick to put his mask on which I adjusted for him and told him to close the doors, and once they were closed, I started gouging away again, asking Mick to make a mental note of the time. This time I started at the top left-hand side and worked my way down to the bottom, gouging at roughly a three-inch width, washing away the metal, glass and the first stainless steel plate.

I came back up to the top and started from left to right, gouging the same width, and by now I was soaked from head to toe with sweat from the heat of the plasma cutter, only stopping when I had cut all the way across the top. I removed the head gear and Mick his mask.

Bernie had already removed his and said, 'Wow, you certainly went for it then, mate,' he handed me and Mick a bottle of water each.

I drank it quicker than a camel at the oasis and said, 'Fuck, that was hot work.' Bernie handed me another bottle of water which went down equally as fast as the first.

'Be careful, you'll drown yourself, Mac,' he said.

'Not in a hurry, mate. How long did that take to gouge out, Mick?' I asked.

'Just over an hour, Mac,' he replied.

'Right … so in theory then, by the time we gouge the other side and bottom, that'll be another hour, that means two hours in total and another two hours for the inner part. In all, roughly four hours in total,' I informed them.

'Ah, just look at it, some price work, we can shave a good few minutes off,' Bernie stated.

I turned to him and said, 'that was price work mode.'

'Well, its four hours gouging time then, shall we break for lunch?' Bernie suggested.

'Sounds good to me,' Mick said.

'No. Let's get these plates out the way and then break,' I told them.

'Late lunch it is then,' Bernie said.

'Do you think I might be able to have a go at gouging?'

'No!' we both called out, cutting Mick short of finishing what he had to say.

We went back to work on the steel plates, only this time it was Bernie who was going to have to do the gouging, so once again the double doors were closed and the gouging continued as did the clock. Bernie eventually gave us the signal that he was done, so we pushed the doors open and Bernie took the head gear off and stated that the plasma was one of the best toys he had played with in years. He had managed to gouge the other side and bottom in forty-five minutes but he wasn't happy with how much heat it gave off and tore his overalls and t-shirt off him, as they were soaked through with sweat. Mick handed him two bottles of water which didn't even touch the sides and then Bernie stormed off to the house and reappeared several minutes later with three bottles of beer in his hand; well, me and Mick could only accept his kind gesture and join him in his quenching thirst after which we shovelled the cooling metal out into the yard and shut the doors.

We all headed down into town after cleaning ourselves up a bit for a late and well-deserved lunch .The day had heated up and even for a weekend, the town seemed deserted apart from an old man sat on the harbour wall, who looked to be making or repairing his fishing nets with a pipe hanging out of his mouth, blowing out the occasional puff of smoke through the side of his mouth.

His black and white dog that resembled a border collie got up on its feet and slowly made its way into a shaded area of a derelict boat lying clumsily on its side with its timbers scorched to a pale white from year upon year of the sun before the dog laid down clumsily on its side as if the scorching sun had finally beaten the dog into submission. The dog licked its paw as it curled up in a snug ball on the boats shaded side and closed its old weary eyes.

'Penny for your thoughts, Mac?' Bernie asked me.

'Oh, nothing, mate.'

'What's on your mind? You were deep in thought there.'

'I was just wondering about that old man over their mending his nets.'

'Who? Old Pierre?'

'If that is his name. I thought, would that be me in many years to come.'

'Far from it, Mac, you got more going for you than Old Pierre,' he said reassuringly.

'You got a lifetime to get to his age,' Mick reminded me.

'Come on, let's finish up here and get back on with the job at hand,' I told them.

'You're determined to get this out the way today, aren't you?'

'I sure am, Bernie, as we fly back tomorrow night, mate.'

'Oh yes, I almost forgot about that, Mac.'

'Me too,' Mick added.

'Let's make hay while the sun shines,' I said laughing.

'And there's plenty of that left,' said Mick.

Bernie frowned and asked Mick, 'Plenty of what left?'

'Sunshine,' Mick replied.

We finished our lunch and went back up to the house. I started gouging out the inner plates and eventually I broke through the other side, but I kept going until the top and side was completely clear of any slag that might still be joining the plates together. Forty minutes in total for my work and then Bernie ripped into the remainder but not before we drunk another two bottles of water each and I had smoked a cigarette. Bernie took the same time as me and then with a crash, the template fell out of the frame and onto the floor. Mick raced to the house and came back with three cold bottles of beer which quenched our thirst for the whole of five minutes before Bernie went to the house and came back clutching another half dozen bottles.

'Thank fuck that's over and done with,' he said relieved.

'Yes, thank fuck,' Mick said in agreement.

'For now, that is,' I reminded them both.

'So, what's it like on a Saturday night in the town?' Mick asked us.

'It's great, mate,' Bernie replied, and continued, 'so make yourself look pretty for the women and careful they don't tear the clothes of your back,' Bernie told him whilst keeping a straight face.

'I hope I meet a cracker.'

'Plenty of cologne should entice them, Mick,' I told him.

'So plenty of cologne does the trick for them?'

'That's what he just said, didn't he, mate? And don't forget to wash behind your ears,' Bernie said joking.

Mick was deep in his own thoughts after that little piece of harmless information and you could see he had already worked his evening out while Bernie raised an eyebrow and I smiled as if to say to each other, he's fallen for it. We finished off the beers and went inside the out building and packed everything away, then we removed all traces of our activities so Bernie didn't have to answer any unnecessary questions when the locals came back to work on Monday after me and Mick had returned to the UK. We went into the house and I decided to go to bed for a couple of hours feeling tired from all the heat and with the beers on top of it all, leaving Mick and Bernie to it. I awoke with the alarm going off on my phone at 7:30 pm and headed for the shower and then got into fresh clothes and headed downstairs just after 8 pm, but there was no sign of Bernie or Mick. I called out to them but there was no reply; the house was empty.

Then I happened to notice a note on the kitchen table which read: *Gone sightseeing with Mick. Back later.*

I made a mug of tea and smoked a cigarette, and thought what the hell I'll just leave them a note back. I used the pen left on the table and wrote on the reverse side of their note: *Sleeping beauty's gone down to the bar, hurry up, I'm lonely.* And then I heard the jeep pull up outside, then Bernie and Mick came in.

'Where did you two get to?'

'Down to the beach for a swim.'

'Yeah, and there were a few girls there too who were teasing us in there bikinis,' Mick said grinning from ear to ear.

'Only Mick scared them off,' Bernie said laughing.

'No, I didn't, you did!'

'Like fuck did I, mate, you did as you kept grabbing hold of your balls when you were trying to converse with them, so they probably thought you had a dose.'

Laughing I asked them both, 'What you going to do now?'

'Simple, get cleaned up and go to the bar, so Mick can see these lovely women.'

'Yeah, I can't wait,' Mick said eagerly.

'I'll hang five here for you while you sort yourselves out.'

As soon as they headed upstairs, I threw the note on the table in the bin and went out to the jeep and started the beast up and drove down to the bar and parked up opposite the little marina and went inside. I ordered a nice cold beer and went out back and thought that Bernie and Mick had only got a ten-minute walk here and Mick could take in the scenery along the way, and if he's lucky, he might even get a history lesson from Bernie too. I lit a cigarette and smiled at the mere thought of them being irate having to walk the short distance, lucky for them. Old Pierre was still in his spot next to the marina with his faithful dog at his side mending his fishing nets and puffing away on his pipe under the light from the lamp nearby. I took a sip of beer and reflected on the past couple of hours hacking away at the template with the plasma cutter.

True enough, the plasma cutter stood up to its review and was by far an awesome piece of kit that any engineering company would love to have on board, and when Jacques gets to grips with it, things should go a lot smoother than what me and Bernie had accomplished today. I glanced across the marina at Old Pierre, who had stopped working on his nets and was now walking along the edge of the marina with his dog, both of them tiredly ambling as if their legs would buckle from beneath them at any moment and collapse to the ground. *Shame,* I thought.

Chantelle came out and said hello, and asked where Bernie and Mick were with a slightly worried look on her face, but I reassured her that they would be here shortly which put a smile on her face. She told me she had two friends coming later that she would like for us to meet. I told her that would be brilliant and even more so if she could join us too.

'I have arranged to work till 10 pm,' she informed me so that she can spend time with her friends and Bernie too.

'What about your folks around here seeing you with Bernie?' I asked her.

'I don't care anymore as it's gone on too long for us hiding our feelings from everyone,' she stated smiling.

'Bernie thinks they'll shoot him if they find out about you two,' I told her.

Chantelle giggled and said, 'I think tonight is a good time for all to know.'

'Why are you giggling? Bernie's petrified on the quiet.'

'Because I love him and his ways, but they will not shoot him,' she reassured me.

'Will you get married to him?'

'Of course,' she said smiling even more. 'He has to make me proper, is how you say?'

'That's about the gist of it.'

'Gist, what is gist mean?' she asked with a confused look on her face.

'That you are correct,' I said and gave her a smile.

'Oh okay, good.' She smiled and then added, 'I go back for now, Mac, another beer, perhaps?'

'Merci, Chantelle.'

She turned on her heel and strode into the bar with a class of elegance in her steps.

Bernie was in for a big shock tonight at some point, but I wasn't going to tell him, I was just going to sit back and enjoy the show, and giggled at the mere thought of what was coming. I lit up another cigarette and giggled to myself some more.

'Here is your beer.' I looked up and smiled at Chantelle, not forgetting to thank her of course.

She left me to my own devices out on the terrace when Bernie growled, 'I suppose you think making me and Mick walk down was funny, do you, Mac?'

'On the contrary, mate, I thought you could with the exercise,' I replied laughing.

'Like fuck we do. Anyway, what you trying to say that I'm overweight?'

'Don't take it to heart.'

'I'm on Bernie's side on this one, Mac,' Mick said.

'Sit down and take the weight off your legs,' I said smiling.

I offered them a drink but Bernie said Chantelle already had it covered. They sat down and just to ease things after their little walk, I got them both to tell me a bit more about their day together which was quite fun on their behalf, especially from Mick's point of view, frolicking with the girls on the beach. Chantelle brought out their beers and left us all to it as the locals started to turn up, though most of them eyed me and Mick with curiosity, except for those who had already seen us, so I guess we made good table talk for them at least.

'I have to inform you both that I will be having a session tonight to see you both off and I hope you will join me,' Bernie told us.

'Drink what you like, mate, just don't upset the locals or they might shoot you,' I replied.

'I'll take it easy,' Mick said.

'They will shoot you for wearing all that cologne, mate.'

'But you said the women love it,' Mick replied.

'Never mind what I said, you're an alien to them, so you won't get this close to them,' Bernie told Mick, pinching his thumb and forefinger together.

'Never know your luck, Mick, they might throw you in a basket and use you as potpourri,' I said laughing.

'Stay away from the candles as you might go up in flames,' Bernie remarked.

'Okay, you two, pack it in. I've been around you long enough to know when you're having a go at me or ripping the piss,' said Mick grinning and drinking his beer.

'Salut,' Bernie announced.

We joined in with him and said, 'Salut,' back.

'I'd like to stay here if I can,' Mick asked.

'I'm afraid that will not be possible just yet as I need you to bring a safe here from the UK, which I happened to have purchased last week,' I told him.

'I thought you robbed them, not bought them.'

'I was just thinking that myself, Mick,' Bernie added.

'It's for the house here.'

'Why's that then?' Bernie asked puzzled.

'Because we're going to need it when we open for business eventually,' I informed them.

'So how do I get it here?' Mick asked.

'That's an easy one, Mick, you drive it, I guess. Right, Mac?'

'That's right. Are you comfortable with driving it over here, Mick?' I asked him.

'Sure, not a problem, guys,' he answered.

'And then you can join Bernie on the road trip.'

'More sightseeing for us, Mick,' Bernie mused.

'Happy days,' Mick replied smiling.

The next morning after breakfast, we said our goodbyes to the girls with a few departing kisses and then Bernie drove us to the airport, and after a firm handshake, we watched him drive off in his battered jeep! Our flight departed and landed on time with no hiccups, though customs searched Mick's bag and found nothing except dirty laundry. After that, we were on our way back home.

Chapter 7

Gone Shopping

Back in Barry, I dropped Mick off at his pad and then headed round to my apartment, collecting my mail on the way in from my pigeon (post box) hole. I closed my apartment door behind me and dropped my hold-all on the floor and kicked off my shoes. I proceeded to the kitchen where I got a bottle of beer from the fridge and lit a cigarette and sat on the sofa going through my mail, bills mainly, but then I opened a letter from a Phil Browning from M.A.T. Resources with my flight information, stating that I was due to fly out to Norway on the coming Friday and that there would be an e-ticket waiting for me at the check-in desk at Cardiff International Airport. Great, I thought, just what I had been expecting, though in principle, it would have been better to have departed on the Sunday, but beggars can't be choosers. I opened another beer and went over our time in France and smiled, pleased that all had gone well especially with the plasma cutter. I finished off the beer and went to bed, as in the morning I had to go and do some shopping.

The following morning at 10 am, I drove out to Cardiff to a second-hand car dealer to buy a small van and after some negotiating with him, I was now the owner of a Ford with a full M.O.T for £1800 cash, nothing fancy as its use was only to transport a few things and then its life would be over. I drove back to Barry Island to Mick's place and pressed the intercom, and after a few seconds had passed, a hello came out the speaker. I told Mick it was me and got buzzed in. Once inside his apartment, I asked him to accompany me into Cardiff to purchase a few items that we were going to need and also to drive the van back. We picked up the van first and then headed over to Taylor Tools, where I picked out a pair of heavy-duty cable cutters and told Mick to pick himself a 24-volt cordless drill and the drill bits that he would need to sort the locks out.

'Don't they have barrel pullers?' He asked.

'How should I know?'

'Can I ask them if they got any?'

'Why don't you look through the catalogue first and see if they have what you need in there,' I suggested to him.

'Good thinking.'

Mick looked in the index of the catalogue and said, 'Ah, maybe.'

'Maybe what?' I asked him.

'It's not listed as a barrel puller but they got something listed as a lock puller.'

'Will it work?'

'Possibly, I'm finding the page now,' he replied whilst flicking through the pages of the catalogue.

Mick found the page he was looking for and told me it was the same tool and assured me it will do the job.

Once all the tools were purchased, I thanked the salesman for his efforts in helping us to load the van up, after which he smiled and said, 'Have a good day.'

'We will,' I assured him grinning from ear to ear.

From there I set off with Mick in tow in the van and drove to the security specialist to collect the safe I had previously purchased the week before and with the aid of a forklift truck, it was loaded into the back of the van. I turned to Mick and said, 'You head on back to Barry and I'll catch up with you in short while.'

'Where are you going?

'I have to email the Bolt,' I replied.

'Right, see you later then.'

'Here's the combination to the safe, so when you get home, put the tools inside the safe and cover the safe over with a sheet or something.'

'Will do, Mac.'

I found an internet café and bought a caramel latte and sat in an empty booth and sent Bernie an email, asking him to find a suitable vehicle for the road trip, also that Mick would be joining him within the next few days. I told him I had confirmation with a start date on the oil refinery in Norway and would chat soon regarding the matter. I finished my latte and drove to Mick's apartment. Once inside, I asked him if it was okay to smoke; he said yes, but I would have to smoke it out on his balcony adding he had already covered the safe with a spare bedding sheet and locked the tools inside the safe. I told him that he would be back in France within the next few days and that he would have to drive down to Poole in Dorset to catch the ferry to St Malo in Brittany and then drive to Bernie in Agde and help him to get the safe inside the house and to help him load the other vehicle up with the plasma cutter and the other items we were to need for Norway. Mick said he would gladly leave for France today, but I told him that would be fine but not wise just yet, as I had to make sure that I had treble-checked that we have everything on both shopping lists for the job as it would be better to find out now rather than later.

It was now late in the afternoon and I asked Mick to follow me down to the van and once there, I asked him to pop the bonnet open on the van. I got a small adjustable wrench from the tool kit in the boot of my car and proceeded to remove the positive terminal from the battery just in case some car thief decided to steal it and not only make off with the van but also the safe in the back. I told Mick that I would be in the White Horse roughly around 6:30 if he hadn't anything else planned he could join me to which he agreed but reminded him to catch a taxi as we could both have a few drinks.

In the meantime, I went back to my apartment to go over everything in mind for a good hour and checked the shopping lists three times for all the items in the shopping basket, and as far as I could tell, everything was accounted for. If we needed anything else, we would have to improvise on the job because sometimes you never know, the unexpected will crop up when you least expect it. When I arrived at the White Horse, Mick was already there.

'You're early, mate,' I told him.

'Yes, I know, Mac. I was bored stupid so I thought what the hell, I may as well have a pint.'

'Fancy another?' I asked him.

'I'll order these, mate, same as usual, is it, or perhaps something off the top shelf?'

'A pint will be fine, thanks.'

When Mick came back from the bar, I asked him if he felt nervous at all and what he thought was in store for him now that things were moving a little faster with the job looming ever nearer. Mick said he'd never felt so calm and couldn't work out why he had a lack of nerves, but I reassured him all would be well and panicking only escalates into paranoia and panic attacks. He laughed at this but I told him that was how people lose their bottle on jobs and when people lose their bottle on jobs that's when everything goes wrong and mistakes are made, which can lead to being caught. I told him that at any time he felt he was not feeling up for it or nervous to let us know immediately, so we could pull him out of the job all together and that would be the end of it for him.

'I'm not afraid or panicking, but if I get any of those feelings, you'll be the first to know,' he said smiling.

'I think it's all the fun you've had lately and that's why you're not worried.'

'What about you, Mac?'

'What about me?' I replied.

'Are you worried?'

'Like fuck am I! I'm more worried about you,' I replied laughing.

'No need, I'm cool,' he said reassuringly.

We were on our second pint when in walked Fox, more elegant and more beautiful looking than ever. She clocked me and Mick, and then headed to the bar.

'Care for some champagne?' I said to Mick.

'Nah, let's stay on the lagers,' he replied, not noticing Fox had come in.

'Look who's at the bar with her back to us,' I nodded in her direction.

Mick turned around and said, 'Who, which one?'

'The tall brunette.'

'Now I know what you mean with the champagne,' he replied laughing.

'It's okay for you, she didn't throw champagne over you.'

'Yeah, I know, but at least I get to finish the bottle off,' he replied laughing again adding, 'Not tonight you won't, she just got herself a proper girlie drink, don't turn around, she's heading this way.'

'Really?' I replied, trying to sound surprised. A warm feeling started to make its way through my veins.

Mick quickly glanced up and said, 'Here she comes.'

'Okay, boys. How are tricks?' she asked smiling.

'Better than the last time we met,' I replied smiling back.

'What about you, Mike?'

'It's Mick, not Mike, and all is good,' he informed her frowning.

'Sorry, Mick. I was going to offer you boys a drink but from our last meeting, I gather you'd decline,' she remarked.

'How right you are, love,' I replied sarcastically.

'Can we put that little incident behind us and start again?'

'Only if you promise me you won't throw your drink over me?' I replied.

'Scout's honour, Mac, I promise,' she replied displaying her fingers scout style.

'Well in that case, why don't you sit down. And it's real good to see you out,' I said.

'Not now, Mac, we'll talk about that later, but for now tell me how you've been keeping,'

'So-so,' I replied.

'Aw, poor baby got the hump with me,' she jested.

'I haven't got the hump with you, I'm furious with you,' I retorted.

'And why is that, oh mighty Mac?' she said sarcastically.

'Because you didn't tell me when you were getting released, that's why!'

'Don't worry yourself, Mac, I've done a lot of growing up in that hell hole of a place, but like I said, we'll talk about it later, love, okay?' she said and broke her perfect smile.

'Should I be going before this gets out of hand?' Mick asked innocently.

'No!' we both answered together.

'Fine, just stop bickering, you're both making me feel uncomfortable,' he stated.

'Sorry, Mick,' Fox said eyeing him with contempt.

The mood softened and once past a few awkward silences. We got back on track of things in general and had time to fill Fox in on mine and Mick's last two years of her being banged up in prison. Mick made his excuses to leave as time was ticking on and left me and Fox together, though Fox and I asked him to stay, he said he was tired.

'Would you like another drink?' I asked her.

'Yes, I would, Mac. Have you anything at your place?'

'I have a bottle of white wine in the fridge if that's okay?'

'Of course it's okay,' she said taking hold of my hand. Fox squeezed it gently adding, 'Come on, Mac. Let's leave these drinks and get a taxi back to your place.'

'Are you sure that's what you want?'

Fox shot me a look that could kill and said through a dry hoarse whispers, 'I haven't had a man in two years, only a few women, and to put your mind at rest, I only had sex with six. After all, we all have needs, haven't we?' She finished her drink off in a long foul gulp.

'That we do,' I replied finishing my drink off as well.

When we got to my apartment, Fox complimented me on my neatness and then she got undressed and took a long shower, leaving me to my own thoughts and when she emerged from the shower with a towel wrapped high around her torso, she asked where my wardrobe was.

Two minutes, later she returned wearing one of my shirts with her hair tied back and smiling softly.

'Can I put some music on?' she asked tenderly.

'Sure you can, love, help yourself,' I replied admiring her.

'You still got this *Chade* CD,' she said excitedly.

'It's yours, remember?'

She let out a giggle and said, 'Of course I do.'

'I keep it to remind me of you,' I confessed.

'In that case, I'll put it on for old time's sake.'

'Would you like that glass of wine?'

'Yes, that would be nice,' she replied smiling.

I poured the wine and handed Fox her glass; she took a small sip of the wine and then placed the glass down on the table. Fox stood there in all her magnificence, looking at me with those hypnotic jade green eyes then slowly walked towards me and wrapped her arms around me, saying how much she had missed me. I embraced her and told her how much I had missed her too. She cupped the back of my head and pulled me towards her soft lips. Only to stop an inch away as if hesitating before our lips met and kissed me passionately. Her fingernails dug impulsively into the back of my neck while her other hand pulled me in even closer to her. I responded to her every move with my hand running gently through her long damp hair as the other hand softly squeezed her firm buttock. I moved away from her delicate lips, kissing her across the cheek then moving to her neck with her little gasps becoming more apparent. Her nails dug firmly deeper as I pulled lightly downwards on her hair, pulling her head back, perversely exposing her larynx, displaying itself in full bloom; I kissed it softly. I moved back up to her lips that were now dually wet and even more delightful to mine. She started slowing the moment down, killing the passion with a decreasing en garde, withdrawing her lips and eased her nails out of my neck.

'Christ, I've missed you so much, Mac,' she whispered in my ear.

'I've missed you so much as well,' I whispered back in her ear.

'Maybe,' she replied, her warm breath cascading across my ear and neck.

'I have loved you from the moment we first met,' I confessed, raising my glass of wine to her. Fox raised her wine glass to me and wrapped her arm around mine so we both drank from each other's glasses whilst keeping eye contact with each other.

Fox told me of her explorations whilst in prison along with the pressures and hardships of the penal reform. Twice Fox reduced herself to tears saying prison had taught her a lot more than she expected with regards to her outlook on life and the battles she would have to win over other prisoners by whatever means deemed necessary. She explained the reason why she had thrown the champagne over me saying that she needed someone not to blame as such, but more of a release of inner anger that had built up inside her whilst in prison and had to vent it at someone. She apologised for the incident and understandingly I reassured her everything was forgotten about and nothing was taken to heart. Relaxing, she nestled herself in beside me. I kissed her softly on top of her head.

'I'm feeling tired, Mac,' she whispered.

'Let's get you to bed, love.'

Fox squeezed me tightly around the waist and in a tone of insecurity, she asked, 'Are you coming with me, Mac?'

'Yes, love,' I replied warmly.

'Good,' she said through a yawn.

We went to bed and lightly kissed and stroked each other when I asked Fox to turn over and close her eyes. I put my arm around her waist and pulled her into my body. I gently stroked the soft silk skin of her back and hips with my fingertips, kissing her occasionally on her shoulders until her rhythmic breathing became shallow, and it wasn't long before she was in a deep sleep. I continued for a while longer with a smile upon my face. I watched her thinking how beautiful she looked laying there sleeping, her curves cascading from head to toe. I slipped out from underneath the bed covers and quietly made my way to the lounge and opened the balcony doors and stepped out into the moonlight and lit up a cigarette. I thought if I had really wanted to have sex with her, she would have obliged me, but there is one thing I have never done with Fox and that was to make her feel obligated. I inhaled deeply on my cigarette and blew the smoke out thinking that maybe…just maybe, she had finally come home for good.

I stubbed out my cigarette, brushed my teeth and then got back into bed. She hadn't moved a muscle and as I lay next to her bringing my right leg over the backs of her legs, I closed my eyes as I slipped my arm around her torso and snuggled in to her warm body. I felt at peace knowing she was here safe next to me and with that thought I could sleep easy…at least for tonight that is, if she hadn't gone by the morning when I awoke.

I felt her next to me before I opened my eyes and kept them closed as she softly stroked my chest with her head resting on my shoulder and snuggling herself into me. Her emanating warmth and her touch immemorially seductive, as her fingernails glided slowly down my ribs and across my torso to my pubic region where she rested them all the while kissing my shoulder and chest, her hot breath torturing me. I responded by gently easing her on top of me. She looked down at me, piercing my soul with those jade green eyes. She smiled at me as she put her finger on my lips to stop me saying anything. I lay there submissively and smiled back at her. Keeping her finger on my lips, she leant forward and whispered in my ear, 'Be gentle with me, my love, it's been a long time for me.'

She began kissing my ear and my neck, moving onto my lips, eventually working her way down my torso to my ever-growing length until she put it in her mouth and slowly sucked it to its metaphor, caressing my balls in unison as her dominance heightened as did my body in correspondence to her every touch, kiss and stroke. She straddled my body, brushing her hardened nipples across my chest as her hand slid between her legs, grabbing hold of my now full cock and painfully pushed her tight wet pussy down, grimacing as she forced every inch of my throbbing cock inside her, stopping half way as she emitted cries of anguish as she gently lowered herself down engulfing my girth into submission until she had fully taken my cock inside her. Already panting, she began to slowly rock her hips gently back and forth before she gently raised herself up and down my shaft, gasping and panting, her nails dug in deeper and deeper. I, too, slowly began to thrust in her rhythmically to her melodic downward stroke until she closed her eyes and threw her head back and began slowly gyrating back and forth as her nails tore deep into my chest.

She urged me on. 'Don't fuck me,' she gasped as she increased her rhythm thrusting herself harder on me, her panting was now growing faster with deeper groans of pleasure coming from her mouth. The more she increased her rhythm, the more I wanted to increase mine until we were both panting and gasping hard. I held her by the waist and thrust my cock deep inside her. 'Argh fuck!' she cried out. She down at me with flustered anguish and panted out 'Don't stop… harder.' I took the dominant role and started thrusting harder and deeper into her now soaking wet pussy as my fingers locked into her hips. Her nails had dug in so deep into me she was now drawing blood from my chest to my lower abdomen. I grimaced with both pain and pleasure, and kept fucking her as our panting and gasps became even louder when she cried out, 'Now Mac! Fuck me hard now!'

I fucked her hard and fast inside her tight imprisoned wet pussy to her cries, moans and painful gasps reminiscent of a woman being tortured that echoed around the bedroom in pure ecstasy when I felt myself coming, my fingers dug into her hips and hers into my heart and ribs. Then in our final moments, her whole body slammed down on my cock as my fluid tore out of me and inside her, her love juice flooded out of her basting my stiff cock and balls as Fox collapsed onto my chest, our bodies shuddering when our lips so beautifully met that the electric tingling sensation from the orgasmic rush now flowing through both of us erupted into what was a long lustrous hybrid passionate kiss, only dying in the ebb of our fading orgasms. When our heavy breathing returned to normality Fox raised her perspired body up and stared wildly at me. I looked back at her and was about to say I love you when she put her finger on my lips and softly said, 'Shh, shh, shhhhh.'

She kissed me on the lips and softly whispered in my ear, 'I love you too…hold me, just hold me.'

I did as she asked without replying and figured this was her moment and if this was the way she wanted to do it after two years in prison, then so be it. Inside, I was ecstatic and overwhelmed as she lay on top of me, still panting every now and then, her arms wrapped around my neck. I stroked her moist back delicately when she slowly eased herself off me to my right side and pulled me in closer to her, keeping my one arm across both her breasts, I moved her long dampened hair to one side exposing the back of her neck. Instantly I began to gently blow my hot breath across it and butterfly kiss the nape of her neck whilst lightly stroking her breasts around her nipples. Gently, she moved my stroking fingers from her breasts down to her naval and put her hand over the top of mine holding it firmly in place so it couldn't go wandering anymore. Her breathing eased more and more until eventually she was fast asleep. I kept hold of her, enjoying the warmth of her body, wishing I too could fall back to sleep but I couldn't and never have been able to, so I went into the kitchen and drank a bottle of water, and lit a cigarette up on my balcony after which I joined Fox again who was still comfortably sleeping, and before I knew it, fortunately for me so was I, thanks to Fox.

I felt her stirring from her sleep and pulled her in closer to me. 'Mm nice,' she whispered and then turned on her side to face me whilst wrapping her arms around me.

'You've slept well, love,' I told her.

'No thanks to you. How come you're still here, you were never one to stay in bed.'

'I guess that's down to you,' I replied smiling at her.

'Mac love, I have something to ask you?'

'Sure, Fox, what's on your mind?'

'I've been thinking this for a long time and having time to work things out more clearly in that hellhole of a prison...'

'Okay, you sound serious. What is it?'

She spoke softly, 'I know I've been a little wild in the past, but in prison, all I could think about was you and I came to realise that you're the man for me.'

'So are you trying to say you're back for good?'

'Sometimes you just don't get it, do you,' she exclaimed whilst propping herself up on her elbows and smiling glamorously.

'So you are back for good?' I asked again.

She let out a little giggle and then said, 'Of course I am, silly,' and nudged me in the ribs and then quickly leant forward and gave me a sly kiss on the lips.

'You've made me the happiest man alive,' I told her and pulled her to my lips, giving her a lingering kiss of my own.

She playfully pushed me away beaming from ear to ear and said, 'Well, come on then!'

'Well, come on what?' I asked puzzled.

'Christ almighty! Have I got to spell it out for you?' she said smiling.

'I love you and always will,' I replied, thinking that's what she wanted to hear.

'I know that, love! You know, the other one?' she said rolling her eyes in her head, but still smiling.

'What, the big one?'

'Finally, Mac! Well, come on then, ask me,' she said excitedly, springing to her knees and put her hands up to her lips.

'What! Marry me?

'Ooh! Say it properly,' she asked, playfully punching me in the chest.

The penny dropped and in my best composure whilst looking her in those jade green eyes, I paused holding her gaze, looking for her devotion and commitment and found it there in an instant. 'Will you do me the honour in making me the happiest man alive and marry me?' I asked her sincerely.

'Yes, yes, yes! 'she screamed out ecstatically, throwing herself on top of me and kissing me till I almost suffocated.

Not that I minded of course and after some serious passionate love-making between us, we both emerged from the bedroom with a new sense of vigour and a new goal in life.

Fox told me of her commitments to the probation office and that was one of the reasons why she had been out of sight for a while, even though she was living back at her parents' house in Wenvoe on the outskirts of Barry and had been staying in keeping a close watch over her shoulder everywhere she went, as the police had only recovered just under £800,000 of the money she stole from the bank that landed her in prison and feared that they would be following her, but she was convinced that the police were not on her tail. Suddenly, paranoia hit me like a hammer blow to the head! What if they were following her? What if she had led them to me to us?

'Mac?'

What if they were watching us?

'Mac?'

Maybe they already knew about our plans for the Norway job?

'Mac?'

What if they were watching Jacques and Mick?

'Mac!'

Maybe they got phone taps on us?

'Mac!'

Wait a minute, I thought to myself, *Norway is out of the UK's jurisdiction which means Interpol would be on our backs! We're fucked!!*

'Oh shit! Mac!!'

Slow this shit down, I thought to myself, *don't let it get out of hand.*

'For Christ's sake, Mac! Answer me! What's wrong with you!!' Fox screamed at me.

'What's wrong?' I asked her, snapping out of it.

'You weren't responding when I was talking to you. You went pale and started sweating, love. Are you okay?

'Why yes of course, love.'

'Well, you don't bloody look okay. Are you on medication? I'll get you a glass of water, love. Just stay there and relax.'

'No, no, no. I am not…on… medication,' I replied but it was too late, Fox was already out the bed and running to the kitchen. I slumped back into the bed and put a pillow over my face, embarrassed!

Fox came back with the glass of water. 'What you doing?

'Hiding,' I replied.

'From who?'

'You.'

'What? From me?!'

'Yes!'

'Well, you're not doing a very good job hiding are you? And you're not making any sense either, Mac. You're scaring me, babe!'

I sat up fast and pulled the pillow from my face and shouted out, 'BOO!'

Fox threw the glass of water in my face adding, 'That's it! I'm fucking out of here. I'm not putting up with this weird shit!!'

'Don't go please,' I begged her.

'Then tell me what the fuck is going on?

'Okay, okay, I will, but all in good time.'

'NO MAC! I WANT TO KNOW NOW OR I'M LEAVING!!

'Cool it, will you?'

'COOL IT?! YOU SCARED THE LIFE OUT OF ME!!

'I'm sorry, love, come back to bed.'

'GET YOUR ASS OUT OF THAT BED RIGHT NOW AND TELL ME!'

Fox's tone softened, adding composure she said 'I'll make us a cuppa and you can tell me all about it. You've got 10 seconds to haul your ass onto the sofa, honey, or I'm out of here!'

'I still want to marry you,' I called out after her trying to sound normal.

'That's currently on hold! Now get your sorry ass in here on that bastard sofa!!,

I told Fox that I was going to Norway to work and was due to fly out on Friday, and that's what caused my little moment back there in the bedroom and that I was thinking how much I was going to miss her seeming we just got back together (ish), and pointed out that I had just proposed to her which made me feel guilty telling her at the right opportunity. Fox bit her bottom lip for a moment then smiled and said it was typical of us in life how one minute we were together and the next we were parted by misfortunate events. I laughed and nodded in agreement, and gave her a big comfy hug only for her to shrug me off and take a sip of her tea and say, 'It's not funny.'

She asked if I was on any sort of medication again, to which I reassured her that I wasn't, which brought a smile to her face and then she gave me a quick kiss on the cheek, took another sip of her tea and asked about Bernie and Jacques. I lit up a cigarette and told her of their whereabouts and gave her a tiny history lesson on Mick and his misfortune with the diamonds, to which she laughed her head off but at the same time she felt sorry for him and said he should have taken all the diamonds, stating that's what she would have done given the chance. A thought crossed my mind.

She made us Spanish omelettes and toast accompanied by two more mugs of tea and then we took a long shower together. It was getting late into the afternoon when I decided to turn the phones back on and it wasn't long before my mobile started popping up three missed calls from Jacques and one from Phil Browning from M.A.T. Resources who had left voicemail. Browning asked me to give him a call to finalise details. I called him first confirming that I was still available to fly out on Friday and then he gave me all the contact information I would need once I reached the camp on the oil refinery in Norway and who was going to pick me up from the airport on arrival. I lit a cigarette and Fox lit one too.

'I thought you had given up?

'I like one every now and then in good company,' she replied giving me a wink.

I called Jacques who was in fine spirits and he told me Phil Browning had been onto him too and had sent him confirmation that he was going to Norway too which was a result on our behalf. Fox held her hand out for the phone to speak to him, so I told him there was an old friend here who wanted to speak to him and handed her the phone. After her brief chat with Jacques informing him that I had proposed to her and she had accepted, she handed the phone back to me. Jacques congratulated me after I informed him he was to be my best man at our wedding. Jacques said he felt honoured and would do his best as best man keeping the conversation brief we agreed to meet up if I weren't preoccupied with Fox.

Fox asked if I could give her a lift to her parent's house in Wenvoe, so we got dressed and drove out there.

'Do you want to come in with me and help me break the good news to them? She asked smiling.

'Of course I will, love,'

'Thought you were going to make a poor excuse and not come in?'

'I tried to but couldn't come up with one,' I answered laughing.

'You cruel bastard!' she replied laughing.

When we got to her parents' house, they were not at home to which she said I had gotten away with it for now but we can tell them another day together. We reluctantly kissed each other goodbye but Fox insisted I call her later after I had seen Jacques. Though I invited her to come with me, she smiled and said no as it was probably boys stuff and told me to get in the car or I'd be late giving me a wink, I winked back at her.

I called Jacques who was at home so I drove over to his apartment, stopping at a drive-through along the way and picked us up burgers and fries. We stuffed our faces with them and Jacques gave me the run-down on Robbie in the hospital which still hadn't changed with him lying there in a coma, though his wife was a little less distraught with the amount of comfort she had received from family and friends along with Robbie's work mates. Jacques too had got a phone call from M.A.T. Resources confirming that he too was going to Norway and would be on the same flight as me on Friday which made us both jubilant. I told him how our terrestrial friend had performed along with other parts of the plan and what parts Bernie and Mick would play. Jacques was eager to get the job over and done with and sort out Robbie's family with his share of the diamonds once turned into cash. He was delighted that I was back with Fox and with the prospect of marriage looming in the not-too-distant future, Jacques asked if I was doing the right thing by taking this job on.

I told him it was on before Fox came back on the scene and that the money was needed anyway to which he laughed and left the subject at that. I left Jacques and got hold of Mick, who was happy to just sit back and chill out, mentally preparing himself for what lay ahead, so I jested he go get some joss sticks and crystals. The rest of the week went fine with me and Fox, though she was sad to see me go on the Friday. I had given Mick instructions to leave for France on the Monday and emailed Bernie to let him know that we were on our way to Norway and that Mick should be with him late on Monday evening or early Tuesday depending how his map reading went.

Chapter 8

The Norwegian Diamond Heist

I gave Fox the keys to my apartment when she dropped me and Jacques off at Cardiff International Airport in my car, and after a lovers farewell kiss and cwtch (Welsh for cuddle) from each other, Fox drove away with tears running down her cheeks. Two hours later, we were airborne on the first leg of our journey to Schiphol Airport, in Amsterdam. After waiting three hours in Schiphol for our connecting flight for our second leg of the journey to Bergen in Norway, we were airborne once again. We touched down at Bergen Airport and after collecting our luggage, we passed through arrivals and out of the terminal where we had to locate the taxi firm stated in the itinerary waiting to take us to Mongstad Oil Refinery some 90 kilometres away. I approached a car with the taxi's company name written on the side and informed the driver that we were expected and that one of the company's taxis was to take us to Mongstad Oil Refinery. The driver called his office and after a brief conversation with whoever he was talking to in Norwegian, he said, 'It's okay, I will take you.' The driver stepped out of the taxi and placed our luggage in the boot space, and then ushered us inside the taxi and asked us had we been to Norway before.

'No, it's our first time,' I replied.

'It's a very beautiful country.'

'Really?' Jacques commented.

'Yes, really, as you will see. Please put your safety belt on, the roads to Mongstad can be harsh this time of year.'

I asked the driver, 'How long would it take to reach the refinery?'

'Oh, maybe something like one and half hours,' he replied smiling.

'That long, eh?'

'For sure, it's Norway.'

Like all taxi drivers, the banter continued for a while longer and then eased off apart from him pointing out places he thought we may be interested in along the way.

Jacques and I took in the scenery along the way to the refinery, consisting mostly of wooden houses painted in various pastel colours with a few stone ones dotted here and there, shrouded by mountains and rocky hills with many roofs covered in what appeared to be a moss-like substance, with pine and fir trees scattered around them. The traffic was surprisingly light, but maybe it was due to the time of day and within an hour, we could see the flare stack of the oil refinery, its orange flame burning fiercely in the distance ahead lighting up the skyline as darkness fell. Twenty minutes later, we were driving up a long wide road and at the crest we looked down and could see the sheer magnitude of the refinery and the huge camp that had been constructed of wooden two-story buildings that were to accommodate the workers and us. The sheer scale of the camp reminded me of the chalets at Butlin's that had once existed on Barry Island's headland, but to Jacques it reminded him of the barracks in Orange in France and Djibouti in Africa. The taxi driver continued down the hill as the whole site engulfed us and continued his way through the camp eventually stopping outside a building signed reception.

'You have to go in now and show your passport,' he told us. He took our luggage out of the vehicle's boot space and asked Jacques to sign the receipt for the taxi fare for the sum of 168,000 Krone (equivalent to £168 Sterling), so that he could claim it back from our company. With the receipt signed, the driver said enjoy your stay in Norway and bade us goodbye, then jumped in his taxi and drove off not even waiting for a tip from us. I looked at Jacques who shrugged his shoulders so I shrugged my shoulders back at Jacques.

We picked up our luggage bags and hauled them up the steps to the reception counter in front of us to be greeted by a really good-looking blonde woman in her mid-20s who smiled and said something in Norwegian. I told her we were English to which she said, 'Yes, okay.' I then told her that we were there on behalf of M.A.T Resources to which she said, 'I know.' She then asked to see our passports which we handed over to her. The blonde fiddled around on her computer for a while and then asked us, 'Are you two friends?'

'Yes, we are,' I replied.

'Then I will try and place you together in the same rig,' she said smiling.

'That would be very kind,' I replied smiling back.

Two minutes later, she said, 'Yes, okay, you will be in housing block A22 rooms 23 and 28,' and handed us our keys along with our passports.

We thanked her kindly to which she replied not a problem and then gave us directions to our housing block, telling us to look for our number on the outside of the building and added, 'Enjoy yourselves.'

'We'll try,' replied Jacques.

It took us a good ten minutes to find housing block A22 and having to haul our luggage up to A22, even though our luggage had wheels, we both still found it a bit of a drag! We located our rooms on the first floor that consisted of a single bed with en-suite bathroom with a small heater on the wall, a single three-shelved wardrobe next to a writing desk with a medium-sized electric heater underneath it with a curtained window above. Opposite the bed on the opposite wall was a 30-inch LCD TV, basic but functional, I thought. I unpacked my case and made best of the space available for my clothes and took a long hot shower after which I went and got Jacques, deciding we both needed to do a little recon and get our bearings. The housing block comprised of two floors; the ground floor which had accommodation and a laundry room with 4 washers and 4 dryers, plus a sauna room, while on the 1st floor there were two TV rooms, smoking and non-smoking, with tea and coffee facilities in both plus the accommodation. With the housing block done, we ventured outside and made our way back to the reception area where Jacques had pointed out there was a bar on the camp, so we thought we would go and mingle. The bar was pretty much packed and I was shocked to find that two pints of lager was costing us £10, but we laughed it off and analysed what was going on around us and after spending £30 on six pints. Finishing off our third pint each, we decided to go back to A22 and get an early night in as we had to meet our company rep in the morning for our placement with supervisors and get through our trade tests and site inductions, and all the rest of the usual bullshit. We could not get the price on the beer out of our heads and laughed all the way back to A22, and after we said our goodnights to each other, we got the much-needed shut-eye after our long day of travelling from the UK.

The following morning, we both headed to the canteen for breakfast after which we met our rep Bjonar in his office who issued us with our PPE (Protective Personal Equipment) and then went and sat a 3-hour induction course, which at the end of it we had our photograph taken and were issued with our security passes that were to be kept on display around our necks at all times. Just when we thought it was all over, Jacques and I along with 10 other new starters were put on a bus and taken to a large corrugated shed and given our trade tests that lasted just over an hour which we both passed with flying colours. Then we were all taken back to the camp by bus and again made our way back to the office to see our rep; Bjonar, who asked us to get into our PPE and follow him to a waiting mini bus to take us on the refinery to our place of work, and for us to get our bearings around the oil refinery for when we start work in the morning.

Then Bjonar showed us M.A.T Resources' offices on site and where we were to meet our supervisors and general foreman who would show us our work places. We were taken back to the camp by bus and told that work started at 7 am and finished at 5 pm unless we were asked to work overtime. We checked the camp map and got our bearings there too, and were amazed to find that they had a sports centre there with a full gymnasium, steam room, tanning rooms, football, badminton, basketball as well as a fitness trainer, so we were well catered for regarding keeping fit if not spoilt rotten as far as past-times went, but Jacques was naturally in his element and could proudly show off his physique. We found the internet room which was free but the only drawback was you had to book in advance. Luckily for us, we had both brought a laptop each and with the whole camp being free wireless internet we could use whenever we liked though it did have its restrictions attached for security reasons. All in all it was a fantastic setup all round with most of the leisure facilities available to us free of charge.

We spent our time just acquainting ourselves with our surroundings but keeping focused on our work as well as the workforce around us, and spent our evenings in the gym keeping fit with 10 minutes in the solarium building up a tan and then finish off with a sauna, followed by a quick shower before heading back to A22 for a few cold bottles of beer either in my room or Jacques' room that we bought from the camp shop. I received an e-mail from Bernie that said he was on the road and all was well, though the hotels in the region were fully booked but he would try to sort out a hotel once he got here and that he had picked up a travelling companion who was good company, namely Mick. Jacques was pissing himself laughing at Bernie's coded message and cracked open another bottle of beer each for us, then he sent something back in morse code (dot dash dot dot dash stuff) saying have a safe journey. Not that Bernie can read morse code but he would know that it came from Jacques. The time was getting on nearing midnight, leaving us with just over five and half hours' sleep before we would get up and get into work fifteen minutes before we were due to start and have a quick cuppa and then get on the job on the refinery so we both went asleep.

It was our third night at Mongstad so we decided to go to the bar on the camp, and arrived around 9 pm and again the bar was full to capacity. When unexpectedly a Norwegian woman next to us started getting hassled by three Turkish scaffolders who had drank too much and began harassing her grabbing her bum, to which she told them to fuck off but the Turks didn't like her retort and grabbed her by her arm, calling her a whore and slapped her across the face, making her burst into tears. In the blink of an eye, Jacques had grabbed the guy's lower arm, twisting it so that the Turk instantly let go of the woman along with a cry of pain, and kneed the Turk in the bollocks which doubled the Turk over instantly, Jacques released his grip on the Turk's arm and let him fall to the floor. Next thing, the other two Turks lunged forwards at Jacques, wrong move I thought and gently pulled the woman out the way to one side. Jacques grabbed the two of them by their throats and kneed one in the balls, dropping him to the floor. Then there was a shining object in the last Turk's hand and remarkably, Jacques took one step backwards and kicked the Turk in the side of the face and took the object out of the Turk's hand, which was a knife and that Turk too dropped to the floor like a sack of shit knocked out cold. The whole incident was over in less than ten seconds. Jacques turned to the woman and asked her, 'Are you okay?'

'Thank you, yes,' she replied trembling.

'I don't think they will trouble you again,' Jacques reassured her.

'I think it is best we go as security will be here and you will be in trouble,' she stated.

'Don't worry, I'll handle them,' Jacques replied casually.

'My friend, she is here, back from the bathroom,' she said beckoning her friend to come quickly and explained what just happened to her. Her friend looked at Jacques and then at the three Turks on the floor, and then at me gobsmacked. I just smiled at her.

'We should leave right away,' she said taking hold of her friend's hand and pulling her away adding, 'you two must follow.'

'Right behind you,' Jacques replied.

We followed them outside and around the nearest corner, stopping in the shadows.

'We wait here to see if security comes,' she said, lighting up a cigarette for herself and her friend.

'My name is Jacques, and this is my friend Mac,' Jacques told them.

'Good to meet you. I'm Janika, and this is Mariann,' she replied smiling.

'How long have you girls been here?' I asked them.

'Two rotations, and how long have you been here?' she nervously replied, blowing her smoke out.

'This is our third night,' I said smiling.

'I think it is okay, no security coming. Would you like a drink with us?' Janika asked.

'Yes, but it would be mad to go back in the bar,' Jacques replied.

'Not in the bar, in our room. You like brandy?' she asked eyeing us both.

'Yes, we do, occasionally,' I replied.

'Good. Then you will follow us to our room,' she said turning and nudging Mariann to move off.

As fortune would have it, Mariann and Janika were housed in A camp too, right opposite us in Rig A23, and they too like us were on the first floor. Once inside Mariann's room, with the door locked behind us, the two women relaxed and got out a half bottle of brandy and poured it into four paper cups, topped off with coke. We told them a little of ourselves and a lot about Wales, and in return we got the same back from both of them. I showed my honesty by telling them both that I was involved with a woman back home which seemed to relax Mariann a lot more, but when Jacques stated that he was single, a huge smile spread across Janika's face and looking straight at Jacques, she told him that she was single too, which seemed to perk her up quite a bit along with Jacques too, as the chemistry started to grow between them while me and Mariann felt relieved knowing that we could just be ourselves and that neither me or her was going to attempt to hit on each other and sabotage each other's loyalties and ethical principles.

We stayed for another cup of brandy, but as it was getting late, we decided it was time for us to leave but not before we said our goodnights. Janika gave Jacques a quick kiss on his lips and eyed him up in the most besotted girlish manner, which Jacques relished in telling her that they must meet again for a quiet drink only to leave Janika blushing, and with that in place, we made our way back to our A22.

'It looks like Janika has got an eye for you.'

'I got an eye for her too, she's fucking stunning,' Jacques replied emphatically.

'I know and if I wasn't single, I'd be trying my hardest to get into Mariann, I can assure you of that, mate,' I stated.

'I'll have to be careful she doesn't get in the way of business.'

'Good point, but she seems a little laid back for that.'

'I can't wait to get her laid back,' he said laughing.

'I bet you can't,' I replied laughing.

'The first opportunity I get, I'm fucking her,' he said.

'That looks to be on the cards very soon.'

'The sooner the better, my balls are full and need emptying, mate.'

'The boys and girls giving you a hard time down there, are they?' I said laughing.

'Not for much fucking longer, rest assured,' he replied laughing as we strode into A22 and up the stairs to my door, where we parted saying see you in the morning.

We stuck to our routine round the camp, only changing it when Mariann and Janika accompanied us to the gym to play doubles at badminton for two hours, and after we had all showered (separately), we all met up outside and slowly made our way to our housing blocks. One night I invited them both back to A22 for a few beers with us which they dually accepted. At around 11 pm, Janika and Jacques left me and Mariann alone together; she lit up a cigarette along with me and prudently asked, 'Would it be okay if I stayed here in your bed with you tonight?'

Quite stunned, I replied, 'Don't you think it may change things between us and our partners?'

'I'm not looking for sex, just male company and to be held,' she said smiling.

'What if things escalate beyond company?'

'Then temptation will overcome us, making us weak,' she replied, looking me straight in the eye.

'Then I can assure you weakness will not prevail,' I told her assertively.

She smiled and then said, 'You can trust temptation will not prevail over me also, Mac.'

'Would you like another beer?'

'No... I would like you to get undressed and get into bed. I will join you,' she said smiling again.

I brushed my teeth first and then stripped off to my boxers under the watchful eye of Mariann and climbed underneath the duvet, then she rinsed her mouth with toothpaste and stripped off down to her thong, discarding her bra, exposing her breasts and fine body before she climbed in beside me, pulling me in closer to her as the bed being only single was tight but adequate.

'That's better, don't you think, Mac?'

Remembering temptation, I answered her, 'Yes, it is.'

She spoke softly, 'My boyfriend is in the army and has been away for six weeks now, so you understand how I miss him.'

'I know how you feel, yes,' I replied with the thought of Fox in my mind.

'We go to sleep now, and thanks for letting me stay here with you tonight.'

'Here, is that comfortable for you?' I asked, giving her most of the bed but moving half my body on top of hers.

'Better yes, but no hanky panky,' she replied, firmly placing my arm across her waist.

'I feel awkward like this,' I admitted to her.

'Me too, but understand my need.'

'Would it be okay if I got you off to sleep like my girl?' I asked her.

'Try it. As I said, I miss a man's company so it will be nice,' she whispered back.

So with Mariann giving me her permission, I moved into a more loving position against her body and slowly began to gently stroke her shoulders and upper arm, and felt her body relax more with every stroke. I laid my head next to hers, pulling her in a little closer. I felt the rise and fall of her chest gradually slowing and ten minutes later, it faded to nothing more than a faint pulse and her warm breath gently escaping from her lips. Then I too drifted off into the blackness of my platonic subconscious.

She woke me up when she got out of bed and started putting her clothes on. 'That has been the best night's sleep in weeks,' she commented smiling.

'You're welcome,' I replied smiling back at her.

She opened the door and turned saying, 'Thank you, Mac,' and quietly closed it behind her.

For the next few days, everything was very much the same, except I didn't keep Mariann company at night, though we did chat on several occasions in the presence of Jacques and Janika, but those two did keep each other company every night, in fact after we had parted for the rest of the evening. Then one week to the day I received a phone call from Bernie explaining he was in Bergen staying at the Hotel Admiral on the top floor with a bird's eye view of the Bryggen. He was furious that the hotel's underground parking was costing him £25 a night, yet the hotel room was only costing him £95 per night. I told him we would be there tomorrow evening after work as it being Saturday meant we did not have to be in work till the Monday, which in the meantime gave us ample time to do some reconnaissance around Bergen. I informed Jacques that the Bolt had landed and was indoors, to which he grinned and said in a relieved tone, 'Thank fuck for that!'

'He's expecting us there tomorrow after work.'

'Tell him to be in the centre somewhere where we can easily find him.'

The next morning, we went to work and at the end of the shift, we hurriedly made our way back to A22 and took a hasty shower and got into fresh clothes. We then called a taxi from reception as the camp bus to Bergen did not leave till 8 pm. The taxi arrived in no time and just over an hour and twenty minutes later, we were in the centre of Bergen right on the marina.

'Where do we meet Bernie?' Jacques asked enthusiastically.

'You won't believe this, but we have to find the church.'

'Couldn't he have found somewhere a little more or less convenient, Mac?'

'Well, you know Bernie, mate,' I said laughing.

'Yeah, you're right, I guess it's to be expected,' he replied laughing too.

We went into a bar and ordered a beer and when the barman put them on the bar, I asked him directions to the church which he gladly gave, looking at us stupidly. He told us that it was directly behind the bar, giving us the left, left, right treatment but smiling as he spoke. I thanked him as we swiftly finished off our beers and followed the route the barman had given us and five minutes later, we were stood opposite the church.

We crossed the road and entered into the eerie silence that all churches tend to exhibit. I turned to Jacques and said, 'It's a fucking damn shame double glazing windows don't have this effect.'

'How do you mean?' he replied with a puzzled look on his face.

'Every time I walk into a holy place, the outside world is silenced by its presence?'

'Really? I never noticed.'

'Look, there's Mick.'

'Where?'

'Over there, see him?' I said, pointing him out to the left of us.

'Yes, but where's Bernie?'

'Dunno, let's ask Mick,' I said, making our way over to him and sitting behind him.

'Psst,' Jacques whispered.

Mick jumped and upon turning around, he said, 'Hi. You frightened the crap out of me.'

'Hi, Mick. Where's Bernie, is he here?'

'Yes. He's in there.'

Looking in the direction he nodded to, but unable to see him, I said, 'Where to?'

'Sorry, my fault, he's in the confession room bit behind that curtain over there, see,' he replied, pointing to a crimson red drawn curtain.

'Confession?' Jacques exclaimed.

'Yeah, he's been in there for all of thirty minutes already,' Mick replied laughing.

'What has he got to confess?' I asked.

'I did ask him but he said that if he told me, it would not be a confession. As I am not a man of the cloth.'

Laughing, Jacques asked Mick, 'What's the hotel like?'

'Fucking expensive,' Mick replied glumly.

'Language, you're in a house of the Almighty,' I reminded him.

'Shit, sorry, I forgot,' Mick replied sheepishly.

Just then Bernie emerged from the confession booth displaying a huge grin on his face like he had just won a lottery roll over. 'Good to see you, my fine friends,' he announced in fine spirits!

'What was all that about in there then?' I asked him amusingly.

'Ah, it was nothing, just something I had to get off my chest.'

'It must have been real bad for you to stay in there for all of nearly forty minutes?' Jacques told him.

'That's because the guy behind the screen kept interrupting me,' Bernie replied.

'Do you feel better now it's all off your chest?' I asked him trying not to laugh.

'Yes, as a matter of fact, I do. It's like a huge weight has been lifted off my shoulders.'

'Can we get out of here now, I'm bored shitless,' Mick informed Bernie.

'Watch your language for fuck's sake, this place is sacred,' Bernie told him sitting down next to Mick.

'Is everything we need in the van?' I asked them both.

'Yes, of course it is,' Bernie replied.

'And where is the van now?'

'Parked underneath the hotel in its car park, out of sight.'

'What if somebody looks inside and spots the plasma?' Jacques asked him.

'Well, they will not see anything as I blacked the windows out, thinking ahead like,' he replied grinning from ear to ear.

'Good move, mate, and what of CCTV in the hotel and parking bays?'

'Ah well, we might have a problem.'

'In what way?'

'There isn't any anywhere as far as I can see,' he said laughing.

'You're joking?' I replied.

'Honestly, Mac, take a look around for yourself,' he said still laughing.

'Have you located the jeweller's whereabouts?' Jacques asked him.

'Yes, we have.'

'Well, come on then, spit it out.'

'Mick, you take Jacques back to the hotel with you and I'll bring Mac with me.'

'When?' he asked.

'Now is a good time as any, if that's okay with you two?'

'Are you sure this is a wise move? What if we're noticed?' I questioned.

'Trust me, Mac, we won't be.'

'What do you think, Jacques?'

'If Bernie says it's okay, Mac, then I guess we'll be fine.'

'Right then, you go with Mick and we'll be along shortly,' Bernie told them.

'Okay, let's go, Mick, lead the way,' Jacques said standing up, inviting Mick go ahead of him.

'Yeah, let's get out of here. I don't like this talking over the shoulder stuff, it creeps me out,' muttered Bernie.

We remained seated in the church for five minutes longer after Mick and Jacques had left, when Bernie rose to his feet with me trailing close behind him. We made our way out onto the street, leaving the eerie silence of the church behind us and headed to the hotel. Ten minutes later, we arrived at the Admiral

Hotel and made our entrance through the main doors with Bernie telling me to head straight for the lifts and not to stop, which I did without question. The receptionist looked up momentarily giving Bernie a quick smile and then attended to his business again behind his desk. We exited the lift on the top floor and entered his room, where Mick and Jacques were waiting for us patiently but smiling. The building had been an old six-story warehouse that had been impressively converted to a hotel back in the 1980s, situated directly on the Bryggen, overlooking the marina filled with sports cruisers and other pleasure boats.

Its tall structure captivated the skyline comparing it to its slightly smaller neighbouring buildings and hotels along the Sundt's Gateway, but with the added advantage of an open view across the marina to the Bryggen, with our target staring back at us full in the face, goading us for now. Bernie produced a pair of binoculars and handed them to me even though the light of day was fading fast and asked me to take a look across the marina towards the Radisson Hotel. I sighted the hotel in question opposite us and said to Bernie, 'Got it.'

'Now look to the right on the next block. The first shop on the corner is the jeweller's.'

'Got it,' I replied and adjusted the focus on the binoculars.

'Take your time, Mac, and have a good look at the surrounding buildings,' Bernie suggested.

There it was, situated on the corner, and the rest of the buildings adjacent to it were retail shops which appeared to have no living accommodation above them, but there was a big problem and that was it was situated directly opposite the Radisson Hotel, which would severely hamper our operation. I quickly gave the binoculars to Jacques who surveyed the jeweller's shop and surrounding buildings, and after a few minutes, Jacques let out a shallow grunt and then turned to us saying, 'There is one major problem factor here.'

'The Radisson?' I replied.

'Yes. With people coming and going, and not to mention, it's open twenty four hours.'

'But it doesn't mean to say that we can't do it,' Bernie added.

'That's right, but there may be an even bigger problem to overcome.'

'What's that, Mac?'

'The telephone wires if they are underground, if we cut them then we may well be cutting the Radisson Hotel's phone wires too, as all the fibre optics basically run through one cable.'

'Then let's get over there and see if there are any overhead or underground cables,' Bernie insisted.

'Me and Jacques will go first as we need to do a little recon of the area for ourselves,' I told them.

'What about me and Bernie?' Mick asked.

'Have the hotel issued you with a tourist map of the area?' I asked them.

'Yes, here,' Mick said taking a map from a draw and handing it to me.

I took the map and went to the window studying it for a short time, and said to them, 'We're here and I take it this is the bar we had a drink in, Jacques.'

Jacques peered at the map and said, 'Yes, and that's the church we met in.'

'Right,' said Bernie.

'This area here has bars in it, I noticed earlier, so after we have finished our recon, me and Jacques will head to one of them and we'll meet for a quiet drink.'

'Right you are, Mac.'

'Leave here in thirty minutes' time, and Mick, try to get a sneaky look at the door locks of the jeweller's, but no more than ten seconds and then survey the whole block with Bernie, okay?'

'Okay, got it, Mac,' he replied.

I turned to Jacques and said, 'Right, mate, let's do it, see you guys later and don't forget to stroll around slowly.'

'See you later, guys,' Bernie said smiling and opened the door to let us out.

We walked past the receptionist without a hitch and out into the now dark evening making our way through the Torget, where we were to meet up with Bernie and Mick later, and slowly made our way along the Byggen towards the jeweller's, stopping firstly at a street stall purchasing a tray of chips and a can of black currant drink. We got on the block housing the jeweller's at the end, all the time inconspicuously looking for CCTV cameras and telecommunication drain lids, spotting no cameras but locating two telecommunication lids either end of the block of shops with one directly on the pavement outside the jeweller's. We turned right immediately after the jeweller's, up the Bugarden passing the Radisson Hotel on our left, but continued onwards and then took another right turn along the street at the rear of the jeweller's, noticing another telecommunication lid on the floor but still no CCTV cameras in the vicinity.

Jacques and I continued along the rear of the block until we reached the end again, taking a sharp right until we were back on the Bryggen. Heading back to the meeting place as we crossed over the road to walk along the marina's edge, I noticed Bernie and Mick on the opposite side of the road making their way in the direction we had just came from but paid no attention to them nor they to us. The time was now fast approaching 10 pm and the streets and bars started to fill with people, and as we turned back into the Torget, the seating and smoking areas outside the bars were nigh on full. We entered one of the many surrounding bars and after getting our drinks, we went outside to the large terrace that faced directly onto the marina. We took a seat at one of the few empty tables and waited for Bernie and Mick to arrive.

We sat there taking in our surroundings and made casual conversation like real tourists, talking about how nice Bergen is as we sipped our beers slowly until we were joined by Bernie and Mick, who complained that Norway was the most expensive place on earth with the beers setting us all back a monstrous 7.50p a pint.

'I'll be bankrupt at this bleeding rate,' Mick commented.

'Just take your time drinking it,' I informed him.

'Seen anything of interest?' I asked Bernie and Mick in almost a whisper.

'Nothing you probably haven't already seen,' Bernie replied.

'And you, Mick?' I asked.

'Nothing I haven't seen before,' he replied smiling.

'Good,' I said lighting a cigarette.

'It's got mighty lively with people, don't you think?' Mick said noticeably.

'Yes, that's because they don't come out till late due to the prices on alcohol,' Jacques said informatively.

'I'll get us some beers, chaps,' Bernie announced and headed to the bar with Jacques in tow to give him a hand.

'Can you do the locks in time?'

'Sure, Mac. They're a piece of cake,' Mick replied reassuringly.

'What do you think of it here so far?'

'Expensive, friendly and very laid back.'

'I got to agree with you on that,' I replied, finishing off my drink.

Returning back from the bar, Jacques said, 'This bar closes at 2 am and the nightclubs close at 4 am.'

'I say we stay here for the next two hours and see how it calms down.'

'I'm with you on that, Mac,' Bernie agreed.

By now it had just turned midnight and the bar was full to capacity and noticeably, so were the surrounding bars and restaurants, but looking across the marina for any sign that there might be residential accommodation above the block in our interest, there was no sign of any lights coming on in the windows above the adjoining shops to the jeweller's; the windows above remained in total darkness. We remained in the bar until it closed at 2 am, but by 1 am, the place had practically emptied, only leaving us with a handful of other people. We finished our drinks and stepped out onto the street (Torget), and looking around there were groups of people scattered here and there away from the main bar areas. Bernie suggested that he go back to the Admiral Hotel and keep watch from there on the jeweller's and the immediate area surrounding it, to which we agreed, leaving us three to check out the nightclubs. Jacques asked some very tipsy Norwegians where the nightclubs were and them being more than helpful, they gave us basic directions and after a brief walk, we were back in the hustle and bustle of the revellers again, finding ourselves in a queue outside a club called Smiler, but with the queue not making any progress forward, I turned to Jacques and Mick, and said, 'Fuck this queuing up lark, let's get something to eat.'

'Good idea, Mac. What about an Italian?' Jacques suggested.

'Where to?' Mick asked.

Motioning with his head, Jacques replied, 'Little Italy, over there.'

'Good spotting, Jacques.'

'Let's go then,' I said urging them both.

We were shown to a table outside with the area covered by a large parasol with a patio heater built into it, which was welcoming as the cold air had started to make its presence felt. We ate and drank wine until the clubs kicked out at 4 am and we were more than politely asked to leave Little Italy several times as they wanted to close for the evening, and after paying for the meal and drinks (that cost an arm and a leg), we strolled merrily back down to the Brygen amid the many intoxicated Norwegians to see how they might inadvertently affect our plans. We hung around till 5 am in the early Sunday morning hours when the streets finally began to empty, so we made our way back to the Admiral Hotel, entering through the underground car park and taking the lift up to the top floor to Mick and Bernie's hotel room, where Bernie was still sat at the window with his binoculars.

'How was your evening?' he asked us laughing.

'Oh, fine, mate, we ended up having an Italian meal,' I answered him.

'Jammy bastards,' he replied scowling.

'How have things been across the way?'

'Okay, Mac, apart from a few people stopping to look in the window of the jeweller's.'

'Hmm. We'll have to come up with a contingency plan regarding that,' I stated.

'I've already thought of that and it's in the van,' Bernie emphasised.

'Any police patrolling around?'

'Only a handful of patrol cars that went up and down the Bryggen a few times,' Bernie replied.

'Lady Luck might be on our side,' Jacques said hopefully.

'Maybe, maybe not when it comes down to it,' I reminded them all sternly.

The night had taken its toll on all of us and sleep was the only thing on our minds, with me and Jacques sleeping on the floor using Bernie and Mick's extra blankets, but not before Bernie opened the hotel room door and quite thoughtfully put the do-not-disturb sign on the door handle, before he jumped into his bed and turned out the bedside lamp wishing us all goodnight in turn that funnily reminded me of the Waltons. I and Jacques had been thoughtful to bring a pair of ear plugs each with us from work and as I inserted mine into my ears, I started thinking of Fox and fell into a peaceful sleep. We all woke a little after midday and an hour later, we were exiting the hotel through the underground car park into the almost deserted streets, locating an empty diner and ordered breakfasts all round. Once eaten, we strolled down the Torget and I explained our next course of plans for Mick to keep the room on in the Admiral Hotel and the van in the car park, and for Bernie to try and book himself a room in the Radisson Hotel, preferably on the street side facing the jeweller's by the Thursday or Friday in advance of the job, to which he stated he would book the room tomorrow by phone, that's if they're not fully booked.

I explained to Mick that he would have to stay in his existing room as he would be our main eyes and ears on the outside and that he would communicate to us via a two-way radio, to which he agreed but somewhat reluctantly. I told them both to go about their days like a tourist for the rest of the week until Saturday night when I and Jacques would return. I lit a cigarette and told the three of them to remain in the Torget area as I had to check something out on the

Bryggen but would be back in ten minutes. I strolled past the retail shops on the block that was in our interest and was relieved to find all the stores closed, as this was crucial for what I had in mind, but if one was open then the strategy would have to be approached in a completely different conceptive way.

Later that day, a little after 6 pm, me and Jacques caught the refinery bus back to the camp, leaving Bernie and Mick to their own devices but not before we had a few drinks with them first. Bernie said if it wasn't for the fact that the van had a plasma cutter in the back, he and Mick would be travelling around but he didn't want to take a chance on being stopped and searched by the police after making it this far without a hitch, so he said they would resort to public transport instead; after all, they had been around all the museums and other points of interest as described in their hotel information pack that had been placed in their hotel room for the guests to ponder through at their own leisure. The bus arrived back at the camp just after 7.30 pm and we made our way straight to the canteen to get a bite to eat before heading back to A22 to have a sauna and an early night, but on the way to A22, we bumped into Mariann and Janika who were very delighted to see us. Jacques naturally invited them to our block for a bottle or two to which they accepted but only after they had eaten first.

They made their way to the canteen and we made our way back to A22, and once inside, I got into my shorts and went to the sauna, leaving Jacques waiting for the girls. After 30 minutes, I went back to my room, showered first and then went to Jacques' room and knocked on his door. Mariann opened the door for me and I was handed a beer by Jacques who was sat next to Janika. The girls had done their best to pick our brains about our little time in Bergen but failed miserably as we named all the places we had been to, but left out Bernie and Mick so on the whole we pulled it off with ease, though we were asked if we went to certain bars and nightclubs in the centre, but we just shrugged it off and said we never seen them places, which delighted Janika as she quickly lent forward and kissed Jacques on the lips, and turning to Mariann she said, 'See, I told you.'

'Told her what?' I asked puzzled.

'That you are not like the other men on the camp here,' Mariann answered for her.

'So you think we were playing with you?' I asked them.

'Sorry, Mac, and to you too, Jacques,' she replied sorrowfully.

'It's okay, you are two ladies amongst many men, so you have the right to be cautious.'

'Better to be safe than sorry,' Jacques reminded them both.

Mariann smiled and said, 'Yes, that is true.'

This reassured the girls we were genuine enough and after another beer, I left the three of them saying I was tired, which I was, and went back to my room to my bed, turned off the light and drifted off to sleep thinking about Fox. The rest of the week was all work and we found out from Mariann and Janika that they would be finishing their 2-week rotations this coming Friday and would be departing on the Saturday morning, so when Friday night came around, we went to the camp pub for a few beers with no problems and I gave Mariann and Janika a parting kiss on the cheeks while Jacques and Janika went back to her room. I got into my bed and thought to myself, *roll on tomorrow*, I turned off the light and closed my eyes. Saturday, we were fortunate to be told that we would only be working half day due to a dangerous lift with the cranes and the site was to be cleared of all workers except for the personnel were involved in the lift, which was a godsend, so Jacques and I decided to do as little as possible that day to reserve energy for the jeweller's in the evening. After work, we went straight back to A22, showered and went to sleep for a few hours, and woke up at 4 pm. We both packed a spare set of clothes into a small backpack each and called a taxi to take us to Bergen. The taxi came and sped off away from the camp and arrived in Bergen at five thirty and went to a nearby bar Bernie had picked to meet us, and as we entered the bar, our beers were already on the table.

'You got a crystal ball or something?' I said to Bernie laughing.

'I wish, mate, as I could tell you the outcome of what lays ahead,' he replied giggling.

'You okay, Mick?'

'Fine, Mac, thanks.'

'Everything is in order and the room I got in the Radisson is directly facing the job, so there's one less pair of eyes to notice our activities.'

'Good, Bernie, but on this one I don't think it's going to count, mate.'

'Still one less is better than one more,' he replied.

'I have to agree, Bernie,' Jacques said, backing him up.

'I guess you're right, sorry, mate.'

'No, it's fine, Mac.'

'Right! I regret to inform you that we won't be going ahead until Sunday night but we still have work to do tonight,' I informed them.

'How come?' Mick enquired.

'There are a few details that need to be taken care of first.'

'What details, Mac?' Jacques asked eyeing me.

'Firstly, the alarm in the front, and secondly, the telecommunication cables must be cut at the rear of the jeweller's. Then we will see how things go.'

'Do you want anyone to go with you, Mac?'

'No, Jacques. You and Mick go back to the Admiral. Bernie, you wait here for me till I get back then we'll go to the Radisson, okay?'

'Where do we meet later?' Mick asked.

'In the Admiral at 10.30, but feel free to go out and about until then,' I replied.

'That's fine with me.'

'Me too,' Jacques added.

Jacques and Mick left a few minutes later and I left Bernie in the bar. Once outside, I put on my backpack and a cap, and walked off in the direction of the Radisson and produced a local map which I had kept from Mick at the Admiral a week earlier and began wandering up around the back of the block, slowly making my way to the jeweller's like a lost tourist but notably taking in every detail along the way that may help or hinder us. Finally after stopping at the rear of the jeweller's, I crossed over past the Radisson. I scanned the jeweller's for a second alarm whilst pretending to consult my map and with a few pre-meditated hand gestures as if finding my bearings, I walked past the Radisson and back onto the Bryggen, satisfied that there was only one alarm on the front of the jeweller's underneath its rain canopy that extended out from the wall – happy fucking days, I thought – and made my way back to Bernie the Bolt back in the bar. I removed my cap and put it inside my small backpack and went inside and ordered two pints, and then asked Bernie to join me outside, and once seated, I lit up a cigarette.

'Any problems, Mac?' he asked softly.

'Apart from the beer being too expensive, mate, all seems to be fine,' I replied.

'What are your intentions for tonight, if you don't mind me asking?'

'Don't worry about that for now, as I'll explain when we are all together.'

'How are things on the refinery?' he asked, changing the subject.

'The job's okay, and the accommodation's fine, but it's like a prison camp.'

'Just grin and bear it, mate.'

'Jacques knocked three scaffolders out for hassling this Norwegian girl called Janika.'

Bernie laughed and then commented, 'Did he win the girl's heart?'

'Naturally, mate, and she's a cracker too.'

'It's about time he got settled, don't you think?'

'Maybe, but he's happy the way things are, and he likes his space as you know.'

We finished our drinks and took a slow walk back along the Bryggen, past the jeweller's, and crossed over to the Radisson and sailed through the lobby to the lift while Bernie picked up his key from reception, and once inside his room, I took in the view from his window. With the jeweller's being directly opposite from us, I had the opportunity to look at it from a higher level and again I could see no further obstacles that may cause us an inconvenience. I opened the window and lit a cigarette, and focused on tomorrow evening whilst Bernie watched TV. When the time came, we made our way over to the Admiral Hotel, entering through the underground car park again and took the lift to the top floor, and once inside Mick's room, I told them the plan, keeping it simple and blatantly basic, asking Bernie to go down to the van and get a can of filler foam, one pair of surgical gloves, one syringe of Devcon (a strong adhesive for metal or concrete) and the heavy-duty cable cutters.

I placed the can of filler foam in the sink which I had filled with hot water, whilst Bernie went to the van and let it soak for five minutes and then peeled the label from the can to remove the barcode on it, as they can be traced back to distributors and retailers very much the same way as batch numbers. I wiped the can clean of any fingerprints, and placed the filler foam inside a bag and put it in my inside jacket pocket along with a pair of surgical gloves. I told Bernie and Mick they were to remain at the Admiral Hotel keeping a sharp look out for me and Jacques whilst we went and disabled the alarm on the jeweller's. Jacques would have a radio com in his ear to keep us informed of any unwanted guests that strayed or passed in our direction, relayed to him from Bernie in the crow's nest at the Admiral Hotel.

'Are we all clear on what you have to do?' I asked them, to which they all replied they were.

Jacques and I made our way towards the jeweller's keeping to the marina, casually strolling along making idle banter as we went, keeping a vigilant eye out around us. It was after 11.30 pm and the taxis were flowing along the Bryggen with a considerable amount of human traffic too, but this would not deter us from our goal. I took out the straw-like nozzle and began biting the end to flatten it so it would fit through the vents in the alarm, and as we crossed over the road, I slowed our pace down as we approached the corner of the Radisson Hotel. I looked left to the entrance of the hotel where there was a taxi parked with two people emerging from it as Jacques started to sing an Elvis song – *It's Now or Never* – as we walked under the canopy of the jeweller's, I quickly stepped in front of Jacques, opening my legs wide as Jacques quickly bent down, putting his head between them and lifted me up so I was now sat on his shoulders. He took a few steps forward so he was stood right underneath the alarm. I fixed the long nozzle to the can and inserted it into the vent in the side of the alarm and pressed the top down on the filler foam; there was a low rush of air and then the foam started filling the alarm when suddenly Jacques said, 'We got guests, Mac.'

I continued filling the alarm but screamed out, 'Stop playing around and put me down I might fall.' Letting out a false laugh.

As the people approached, Jacques laughed hysterically at the people passing by as they took a quick glance at our antics, laughing innocently back at us as they went about their business, not even noticing I was filling the alarm. A minute later, I told Jacques to put me down which he did with the two of us now in fits of real laughter. I put the can of filler foam inside a plastic carrier bag along with the surgical gloves and put them back in my jacket's inside pocket again.

'Thank fuck for that,' I said giggling.

'That old routine never ceases to fail,' Jacques replied giggling.

We giggled all the way back to the Admiral Hotel and once we were inside the hotel room, we were greeted with a nice cold bottle of beer from Bernie and Mick, and we all burst out laughing together as Bernie and Mick had been watching us from the hotel window and had seen Jacques lift me up on his shoulders, but the canopy had obscured me filling the alarm from their view. They readily admitted they were stood there panicking when the guests had walked past but were jumping up and down when we emerged uninterrupted. I lit a cigarette and we all clanked our bottles in a minor celebration as I reminded them we still had the telephone wires to cut next and told them that all three of them were to accompany me on cutting the underground telephone cables, positioning themselves accordingly to the plan I had drawn up for us. Once the telephone cables were disabled, Bernie and Mick would go one way and me and Jacques would go the other and meet back up at the Admiral Hotel.

'Are you all clear on where you have to take your positions?' I asked them.

'Yes, Mac,' they all replied in succession.

'Are you okay with it, Mick?' I asked.

'As ready as I'll ever be,' he replied, letting out a low sigh.

'Right then, gentlemen, let's do it,' I said smiling.

Jacques and Mick took the lead ahead of me and Bernie as the Bryggen started to get busy with people coming from everywhere. I told them to keep a cool head and stay focused. We all took a right turn up a narrow street that was deserted and then took a left turn which led us behind the far end of the block at the rear of the jeweller's. Here the street had its dark spots in between the street lights and as fortune would have it, the first telecommunication drain was in one of these dark spots and as we neared it, I told them to remember their places. Bernie stopped to the right of the telecommunication lid on the ground as Jacques took another step forward and stopped in front of us. As I dropped to the floor on one knee, Mick came in close behind and stopped boxing me in. I turned on the torch with a red lens and took a pair of hooks out of my waist band and inserted them into the holes in the cover and lifted it up, placing it to one side.

I shone the torch light on the mass of cables running underground and was amazed to find the telephone cable instantly without having to sift through the other cables to unearth it. I pulled the cable upwards so it bowed and taking the cable cutters from Bernie, I severed the cable and handed him the cable cutters back, just as Mick handed me the Devcon which I spread around the lip of the lid and replaced it firmly back into its position.

'One down, one to go,' I told them as we walked off towards the jeweller's.

'That went smooth,' Jacques remarked.

'Let's hope the next one does too,' Bernie said.

We all knew that the telecommunication drain outside the jeweller's was nothing more than a suicide mission and knew that this one would be the one to raise the alarm, but we had to cut the cable for better or worse. Our adrenalin was pumping gallons and we needed it.

'Are you all okay with the next one?' I asked them.

'We might as well be wearing a Rising Sun bandana on our heads,' Bernie stated.

'*Kamikaze!!* Mick said sweating.

'Keep your heads and stay focused,' Jacques said as we rounded the corner facing the Radisson Hotel.

Passing the Radisson Hotel, the only person visible was the bellhop standing just outside the doors with no other person in the street. We walked past and rounded the corner of the jeweller's where the activity in the area was more alive with cars and taxis going up and down the Bryggen. We had to walk past the jeweller's and the telecommunication drain to let two couples pass us by then turned back around and followed them back towards the jeweller's, and once they had passed the Radisson Hotel, a stream of cars came our way.

'This is no good, Mac, it's too busy here,' Bernie stated.

'He's right, Mac, there's people on foot and cars everywhere. We'll be spotted in an instant, mate,' Jacques said.

'It's tonight or never,' I told them as we too passed the Radisson Hotel.

'This is madness,' Mick stated.

'And there is method to the madness. Are you with me?' I asked them.

'But Mac…' Bernie started to say when I cut him off.

'Are you all with me on this?' I asked them all again.

'Yes,' came their replies to which I said, 'Good. Now let's turn ourselves around and sort this fucking cable out.'

We turned back around and headed back towards the jeweller's in formation, telling them that there was going to be no fucking about as we were going to stop at the telecommunication drain and get the job done no matter who or what was around and cut that fucking cable. Passing the Radisson Hotel, we crossed over the road to the jeweller's and just outside the shop, Bernie stepped to the side as Jacques took his pace forward. I dropped on one knee again and put the hooks in the holes of the lid and pulled up, but the lid didn't budge; I tried again and it still wouldn't budge.

'Come on, hurry it up,' Bernie said.

'The drain lid is stuck,' I replied.

'Shit,' Mick said.

Jacques turned around and said, 'Give me one of the hooks, I'll pull and you pull.'

I gave him a hook and we both pulled, but it wouldn't budge.

'Pull gain,' I said.

'Hurry up, we got cars heading towards us,' Bernie announced.

'Shit, we got a taxi coming behind us,' Mick said.

'Fuck 'um,' I said and told Jacques to pull on the count of three, and as we did, the lid popped off. Four people exited the Radisson Hotel and two people popped up from out of nowhere.

'It's on top!!' Bernie said panicking.

'Give me the fucking cutters,' I grunted out at Bernie.

Bernie handed me the cable cutters as I shone the torch in the hole and searched frantically for the telecom cable.

'Fucking hurry up,' Jacques hooted.

I scrambled through the mass of cables and found the telecom cable and severed it instantly and said, 'Devcon!'

Mick handed me the Devcon and said, 'There's two people right behind us.'

I squeezed the Devcon out around the lip of the lid and replaced it and quickly stood on top of it for good measure as the two people walked past us giving us a warm smile; we all smiled back at them.

'That was fucking close,' Bernie said out of the corner of his mouth.

'Too fucking close,' Jacques added.

'You guys are nuts,' Mick stated.

'Let's get the fuck outta here!' I barked as I lit up a cigarette and walked off with the others in tow.

We got back to the Admiral Hotel and hit the mini bar in our hotel room for a nice chilled beer and reflected on our madness with cold sweat and laughter. Bernie rang the Radisson Hotel and as soon as they picked up the phone, he killed the call and then he called the jeweller's and got a dead tone to all our jubilation after which we all freshened up and hit the Bryggen for a hearty meal and a few well-deserved beers. After we had eaten, we went to a club called Smiler and after paying 100 Krone (£10) each to get in, we found out the club had three floors. The ground floor had a Norwegian rock band playing on stage; although we couldn't understand what they were singing, the crowd was going absolutely mental to it. We went up to the first floor that had a massive dance floor to the rear and a smaller one to the front, both were packed to suffocation with people dancing to trance music. Jacques and Mick got chatting to two girls and disappeared only half hour later; they came back to us without the girls.

'Where've the girls gone, I thought you was right in there, guys,' I asked them.

'Mate, you won't believe how much I just paid for this double vodka for her,' Jacques replied fretting.

I started laughing and asked him, 'How much?'

Jacques shook his head and said, 'Fucking sixteen quid!!'

Bernie pissed himself laughing and said, 'I'm glad Chantelle's not here.'

'What's your excuse, Mick?'

'The same as Jacques's, I just paid thirty-two quid for two doubles,' he gloated.

'You better make it last then,' Bernie told him, laughing his bollocks off.

I went to the bar and got two cocktail umbrellas and put one in each of their drinks. 'For you,' I said laughing.

'You taking the piss,' Jacques said laughing along with Mick.

'Now it looks more like thirty-two quid's worth, mate,' I told them, still laughing along with Bernie who was in hysterics at them.

We left early around 2 am and headed back to our hotels even though we all wanted to stay out partying, but more pressing affairs cancelled this notion though it had been a fun night in more ways than one. When me and Bernie returned to the Radisson, I asked him, 'Did you bring the two-way radios from the van?'

'Yes, Mac, they're in the closet in the bag.'

'Good. Let's get them out and put them on charge overnight for good measure.'

'I'll get them,' he replied eagerly.

He plugged the base in and said, 'I modified the floor in the van to transport the diamonds.'

'Good man, and did you remove the serial numbers from the plasma cutter?'

'Yes, the day we arrived here, Mac.'

'And everything else is in order?' I asked.

'Sure it is. Don't fret, mate, all is well.'

'Right, mate, we better get some shut-eye as tomorrow could be a long night.'

'Nah, we'll be away in no time,' he replied grinning from ear to ear.

I grinned back at him and put the do-not-disturb sign outside on the door handle and said, 'Lights out?'

'Why don't we have a nightcap from the mini bar for a good lay-in?' he suggested.

'Yes, mate, I'll go for that,' I replied lighting a cigarette and opened the window to blow the smoke out.

'What do you fancy, as we got beer, whiskey, rum, cognac, gin?'

'A bottle of lager will be fine, mate, thanks.'

'How do you think Mick will handle it all tomorrow?' He asked raising his eye brow whilst handing me the bottle.

I took a sip and ran it around my mouth then answered him, 'He'll be fine, mate.'

'I hope you're right, Mac.'

'If he loses his bottle opening the door, there might be a slight hitch, but he still has to watch our backs with the radio but I'm confident he'll play his part,' I assured Bernie puffing on my cigarette.

The next day after lunch, we met back at the Admiral Hotel in Mick's room and went over the plan again and again, and when it was clear to all, Bernie went down to the van and checked all the equipment was secured to the top of the plasma cutter, as it all had to be taken inside the jeweller's in an instant with no return trips back to the van for anything, as timing was of the essence here. On his return, Bernie showed Mick his radio and told him to keep the earpiece in at all times and through the window I showed Mick his boundaries to keep a watchful eye on when we were to put the equipment inside the jeweller's along with the distances to inform us if anyone on foot was to pass us while we were inside to tell us to stop and when they had passed to inform us to recommence our work. Then I broke the bad news to Mick, 'You'll have to take the deadlock and the Yale lock out just as daylight starts to fade.'

'But I thought it would be dark when I opened the door?' he asked nervously.

I reassured him and said, 'It will be fine, I'll be there with you with Bernie in my ear watching over us.'

'Don't worry, mate, I'll keep you safe,' Bernie told Mick giving him a pat on the back.

'Are you guys worried at all?' Mick asked us.

'We're not worried, Mick, it will all be fine,' Jacques told him scowling.

'Yeah, that's right, Mick, no worries,' Bernie added smiling at him.

Steering the conversation away from Mick, I said, 'Bernie, you're driving the van while me and Jacques offload the equipment.'

'Check,' they both replied.

'Have you got the lock puller and drill up here?' I asked Bernie.

'Yes, Mac, they're under the bed with the drill still on charge,' he replied.

'Right, what's the time now?' I asked no one in particular.

'Just gone 3 pm,' Mick answered.

'Okay, I'm going to get some rest and suggest you do the same, and I'll come round here tonight at 7 pm. Bernie, are you coming back to the Radisson?'

'I'm right behind you, Mac,' he replied.

At 7:10 pm we both exited the Radisson and joined Mick and Jacques back at the Admiral Hotel only to find Mick's nerves were getting the better of him. I made him a coffee and told him to relax, and told Mick all would be well as the street will be practically deserted.

'You must try not to panic as you'll only spook yourself and us for that matter. Try to look at it as normal work and if you can't go through with it then say now,' Jacques told him sternly.

Mick replied saying, 'I'll be fine…just give me a minute.'

'You've got half an hour, mate, okay?'

'Yeah, Mac, I'm good,' he replied half smiling.

'Jacques, how is it looking out there?'

Without turning around, he said 'All's quiet on the Bryggen.'

'Bernie?'

'Yes, Mac?'

'Have you got the earpieces for the two-ways?'

'They're right here, Mac, and the radios are fully charged.'

'Excellent,' I replied lighting a cigarette and then asked Mick to join Jacques at the window to see how quiet it was.

'Here, Mick, take a seat and have a watch while I make a coffee, mate,' Jacques told him, throwing me a scowl.

'Bernie, be a good sport and get Mick his equipment out, would you?'

'No probs, Mac,' he replied reaching for the drill and lock puller from underneath one of the beds then placed them both on top of it.

'How's it looking out there, Mick?'

'Like you said, quiet,' he replied looking more himself.

I smiled and said, 'Told you.'

The time came for me and Mick to go and sort the locks out on the jeweller's, with Mick being a lot more composed in himself. I put the two-way radio in my inside jacket pocket and inserted the earpiece into my ear whilst Mick donned a shoulder harness with his drill clipped to it and put his jacket on over the top to conceal it while I carried the lock puller for good measure concealed underneath my jacket. We performed a final radio check and made our way out of the Admiral Hotel via the underground car park, passing through the Torget which had a fair amount of people in that area, but that was because of the bars and restaurants there. Mick looked a little edgy, looking around too much as if everyone knew what he was about to do, and Bernie was in my ear telling me of the people up ahead and to slow our pace down which we did, giving me a chance to light a cigarette when Bernie told me to stand too, as there was a couple admiring the diamonds in the window and a few minutes later they moved off and so did we. I reminded Mick to pay no attention to anything else and just sort the locks out as our backs was covered and on Bernie's instructions, he said to get ready to cross over from the marina, adding all was quiet outside the Radisson. Mick and I crossed over the road and walked till we were outside the jeweller's when I heard 'good to go' in my ear from Bernie.

I turned to Mick and said, 'Now is you finest hour.'

Mick got the drill out and dropped down on one knee and started drilling away and in less than two minutes, Mick said, 'Done, Mac.' As he stood up and I gave him the lock puller, no more than twenty seconds had passed when there was a dull thud and again Mick said, 'Done,' handing me the lock puller back with the barrel of the lock still attached to the end of it. Bernie was in my ear, 'Three persons heading your way from the Radisson.'

I quickly unpeeled a strip of graph tape and put it over the hole where the lock had been and said to Mick, 'Let's go.'

'Thank fuck for that,' he stated.

'Thank fuck for you,' I said laughing and led Mick around the corner past the trio, telling Bernie, 'Job done.' We walked past the Radisson and turned right along the back of jeweller's and back on to the Bryggen again and walked along the marina and back to the Admiral Hotel where we were warmly welcomed.

Jacques and Bernie had a lot of admiration for Mick in the way that he had performed his skill, taking the locks out faster than he had first predicted but in all honesty, there was no time for jubilation or celebrations as we were far from done yet. We rested for an hour, making our final checks, and went over our plan one last time, and at 9 pm we left Mick in the crow's nest of the Admiral hotel as me Jacques and Bernie made our way down to the van in the underground car park of the hotel. With Bernie at the wheel and Jacques sat upfront with him, I climbed in the back of the van and released the ratchet straps that were securing the plasma cutter making double sure I didn't undo the ratchet straps that were securing the rest of the equipment strapped on top of the plasma cutter. As we turned away from the Admiral hotel, I gave Mick a radio check to make sure all was working fine and told him to stay vigilant as we made our way towards the jeweller's. Bernie drove the van steadily through the Torget area that was deserted apart from a few people here and there; they were not to worry us with their presence. Bernie rounded the bend onto the Bryggen as Mick kept us informed via the radio com that all was quiet within the boundaries I had marked out for him to watch between. Bernie drove the van about a hundred metres past the jeweller's and casually did a U-turn in the road and headed back down the Bryggen as I opened the side loading door of the van about an inch so I could peer through the gap and started singing, 'Get your rocks off, get your rocks off, honey.'

After a last-minute check with Mick via the two-way radio that all was good to go, Bernie casually came to a halt outside the jeweller's, and with the all clear from Mick, I pulled the side loading door fully open as Jacques jumped out the van. I pushed the equipment to the open door as Jacques took a hold of the front. I pushed the plasma cutter out of the van only for the underbelly to get caught on the side step and with a hard shove from me, a cuss from Bernie and a pull from Jacques, it landed on the pavement with a bit of a thud, all we could do now was get all the equipment inside. Mick was still repeating himself, 'Good to go.' As we got the equipment to the door, Jacques tore the tape off and pulled the Yale lock's lever back then quickly grabbed hold of the door handle and shoulder nudged the door open, dragging the plasma cutter inside with him as I pushed it from the rear until we reached the back end of the shop. With no time for looking at the gems in the display counters, we made our exit out at lightning speed and as Jacques made for the van, I closed the door shut, slid the Yale locking lever back in its closed position, replacing the tape over the hole and jumped in the back of the van, pulling the side door closed. Bernie casually pulled away, we all started laughing our bollocks off.

Safely back at the Admiral Hotel, we went up to the crow's nest and on entering, Mick was still at the window checking the Bryggen through the binoculars. I asked him, 'How's it looking out there?'

'Welcome back. It's all looking good,' he replied.

'Great, but we watch and wait for the next hour,' I told them, lighting up a cigarette.

Over the next hour, we took it in turns watching the jeweller's with very little movement along the Bryggen apart from a few cars passing and a few people going into the Radisson Hotel, otherwise the area was deserted. We now knew that the job was more than good to go but still kept a vigil on the jeweller's up until it was time for me, Jacques and Bernie to depart once again. At 11:45 pm, I gave Mick his final instructions and also told him he must not move from the window for any reason whatsoever over the next couple of hours, not even to go to bathroom but if he did want to use the bathroom, then he was to relieve himself in the plant pot next to him or in the waste paper bin. I reminded him of his duties as we left the crow's nest and tossed him a toilet roll as I closed the door behind us.

I popped the earpiece in my ear and got a check call back from Mick. We exited the Admiral hotel and casually made our way over to the jeweller's on foot passing two people when I got Mick in my ear from the crow's nest, 'Police patrol car cruising down the Bryggen.'

'Check,' I replied, repeating Mick's info to Jacques and Bernie.

'Fucking two weeks without almost a sighting and now they show up,' Bernie muttered.

'Where are they to now, Mick?'

'Just passing the job heading towards you,' he replied.

'Check,' I replied lighting up a cigarette.

'Here they come,' Jacques announced as they turned into the Torget.

They drove past us without batting an eyelid.

'Well, that changes things if they're in the area.'

'You got that right, Jacques,' Bernie told him.

I asked Mick in the crow's nest, 'How are we looking?'

'All's clear, Mac. It's good to go,'

'Check,' I replied.

I asked Jacques and Bernie if they were ready as we approached the jeweller's, to which they both said yes, and with a final check from Mick that the coast was clear, we put our gloves on and slipped inside the jeweller's, closing the front door behind us, jamming a little door stop under the base of the door which I had kindly loaned from the Admiral Hotel on the way out. We immediately undid the two straps holding the rest of our equipment to the plasma cutter as Bernie wasted no time in draping a black out screen over the pane of glass in the front door screening anyone's vision who may look into the jeweller's on passing by, but with the time now getting on just after midnight, it seemed highly unlikely this would happen but all the same, you never know when a straddler could appear. With the screen in place and the rest of the windows covered in velvet backed panels, obscuring the inside of the jeweller's, though the panels could be individually slid apart to access the diamonds in the windows, we switched our headlamps on with the lenses coated in a red film to prevent any bright light giving us away but emitting enough light so we could see what we were doing, the three of us put on our flame retardant overalls.

Bernie went to work connecting the plasma to the transformer and the mains whilst sorting out the rest of the equipment, me and Jacques looked for any smoke alarms finding one in the front of the shop and one more in a small kitchen at the rear of the shop. Both fire alarms were disabled simply by stretching a rubber surgical glove over them and then wrapping them heavily in duct tape so they resembled an over-bandaged finger. Next, we cleared everything from around the safe (its size being very impressive) and cut away a few square metres of the carpet revealing the stone flooring underneath, replacing the area with fire-retardant blankets.

'Bernie, are you set yet?'

'Almost there. I just need help to erect this screen in front of the counter and then we're all good, Mac,' he replied.

With the large screen erected, I said, 'Ready to rock, Jacques?'

'Get a final check from Mick and then I'll begin,' he replied.

With the okay from Mick, Jacques got down to business behind the screen whilst me and Bernie could only sit back and wait for our turn to use the plasma. Jacques was gouging the metal away from the side of the safe with good progress compared to mine and Bernie's efforts back in France when Mick informed me that he'd spotted a police car slowly driving up the Bryggen. I immediately stopped Jacques and after two minutes of nerve-racking silence, Mick gave me the all clear, informing me that the police had gone from his boundaries and looked to be leaving the area; we breathed a sigh of relief and got Jacques back to business. Me and Bernie started emptying the two long display cabinets of their diamonds either side of the shop, carefully putting the gems in our black hold-alls when Mick was in my ear again, warning me of two people coming out from the Radisson Hotel. I stopped Jacques again and after a few minutes, Mick informed us that they had smoked a cigarette each and went back inside the Radisson again. I told Jacques we were good to go and when I looked at Bernie, he was smiling at me with a big diamond smile as he had jokingly placed a load of diamonds between his teeth; naturally I laughed, briefly seeing the funny side of his antics and when the moment had passed, we carried on bagging the diamonds from both counters again.

After an hour, Jacques stopped gouging as he was drained, dripping with sweat and said the nozzle needed to be replaced. I handed Jacques the two-way, replaced the nozzle and then I set to work on the safe where Jacques had left off, but it wasn't long before I got a tap on the shoulder from Jacques telling me to stop. Mick informed him that the police car was back in the area again, cruising down the Bryggen which raised our nerves as we sat in silence until it had passed us by and when Mick could no longer see it on the Torget, he gave us the go ahead to start burning the safe once again. I went hard at it and after an hour, I too stopped, having fucked the nozzle up completely, replacing it with a new one. Bernie took over with only a little of the bottom outside plate to cut away and roughly after ten minutes, he stopped, allowing me and Jacques to remove the section of the plate and put it to one side so Bernie could now concentrate on the inner plates.

Jacques disappeared into the office only to emerge a while later with two cups of coffee smiling and said, 'Sorry, it's coffee, Mac, there's no tea.'

Smiling back, I replied, 'It'll do, thanks,' and lit up a cigarette to go with it.

'We are half way there, Mac.'

'Yes, I know, but the time is getting on and so must we,' I urged him.

'Then let's make the inner cut not as wide as the first?' Jacques suggested.

'I've been thinking that myself but we'll see how time fares,' I told him whilst taking a sip of coffee.

'Mac, it's just after 2 am and we have to make it back to the Mongstad.'

'Let Bernie finish his cut then we'll see what's what. Relax, mate, and drink your coffee before it gets cold,' I replied.

'How's your coffee, Mac?'

'Tastes like shit,' I replied laughing.

Bernie emerged from behind the screen, 'What the fuck's this?! Sat on your asses drinking coffee?'

'Why, could you smell it?' I asked giggling.

'No. I fucked the nozzle up, lads.'

'Bolt, drink my coffee whilst I change the nozzle,' Jacques told him.

'Cheers, mate, don't mind if I do,' Bernie replied, snatching the coffee from Jacques.

'How far you cut now?' I asked him.

'Just cutting up the side, Mac, why?'

'We're going to shorten the top and bottom cuts but keep the side's the same.'

'Best thing to do seeming time's getting on and I'm drenched, and this coffee is shit.'

'That and to get the fuck out of here,' I replied.

Jacques came back and said, 'Right, Bolt, you're set to go, mate.'

'Here, finish your coffee, it tastes like shit,' Bernie said handing Jacques back his cup.

'What do you mean my coffee's shit?'

'Told you, mate,' I said laughing.

Bernie continued gouging on the safe whilst Jacques stretched out on the floor with his hands behind his head while I kept in contact with Mick up in the crow's nest who informed us that outside was all quiet. With the time fast approaching 3 am, Bernie stopped and Jacques took over, and once he fitted a new nozzle for good measure, he was soon back at it gouging away. I went into the kitchen area out back and looked in the refrigerator and found a carton of juice and gave it to the Bolt who was more than happy to drink it dry, then he laid out on the floor to get a little rest.

'Soon be away, Mac?'

'Yes. not long now hopefully, mate.'

'You and Jacques need to get back to the camp and into work.'

'Yes, I know and we're going to be fucked too.'

'Try and pull a sicky in work,' he said thoughtfully.

'Exactly what I had in mind.'

'How're you going to get back, Mac?'

'We're going to have to catch a taxi, mate, don't worry, we'll be fine,' I replied.

'What about the rest of the stones in the windows, Mac?'

'Once we have emptied the safe, then we'll empty the windows.'

'Yeah, it's best to,' he replied yawning.

I lit a cigarette and asked Mick how we were looking outside; he replied saying everything was still good but he needed to take a poo. I told him not to leave the window and do it in the plant pot or something. I mouthed to the Bolt, "he can't hold it in," which flipped him into a fit of hysterical giggles along with me, now he was panicking about toilet paper so I told him to use the leaves from the plant or the toilet roll I tossed to him earlier. Bernie raised his head and said, 'Mick will be psychologically scarred for the rest of his life.'

I said, 'So will I too if I walk in that hotel room and see that plant stripped bare,' again we were in fits of hysteria with Mick cursing me in my ear calling me everything under the sun. Jacques appeared with a puzzled look on his face, seeing the state of me and Bernie, he asked, 'What's so funny?' When we told him, he was on his back laughing adding, 'Never mind Mick, he'll live. What about the poor plant?'

The fits subsided and Jacques told us only the top cut was left. Bernie sprang to his feet, took the gloves and shield from Jacques, and got stuck in gouging away in an instant. Jacques asked me for the two-way radio, he plugged the ear piece in his ear and said, 'Mick, how's the plant looking?'

There was a slight pause before he said quite aggressively, 'Fucking bare!!'

We both fell about laughing as Jacques handed me back the radio. I inserted the ear piece in my ear again and did my best to block out the mental picture of Mick dumping in a plant pot and wiping his ass with leaves out of my head so I could focus on more pressing affairs. I got another two hold-alls and passed one to Jacques and told him to unzip it as I unzipped mine and reaching inside, I motioned to Jacques to do the same and pulled out an inflatable rubber ring and began to blow it up with Jacques doing the same and once inflated, we inserted them into the bottom of the hold-alls. Bernie came from around the screen with a big smile on his face, holding a load of diamond necklaces; me and Jacques looked at him and the necklaces draping in his hands and jumped for joy along with Bernie then linking arms, we began dancing around in a circle swapping from one arm to the other and after a minute or two, we stopped and patted each other on the backs and began filling the hold-alls with necklaces, bracelets, rings, pendants and brooches along with a few odd watches and other items caked in diamonds from inside the safe.

Once it was emptied of all its contents, we took everything out of the windows while Mick kept watch on the Bryggen and the Radisson Hotel. When we had stripped the windows bare of its diamonds, we took off our overalls and placed them in the hold-alls along with the empty juice carton and cups we had the coffee in, along with the leather gauntlets and head screen as they were full of our D.N.A (even my cigarette butts were placed inside my overall pocket) we did a final check of the jeweller's to make sure that we hadn't left anything significant behind to put us in the frame apart from the plasma cutter, though the serial numbers had already been removed from it by Bernie. The time was now coming up to 4 am and I asked Mick if we were good to exit the jeweller's and after a slight pause from him, he replied, 'Come on home.'

I removed the little door stop from the bottom of the door and placed it in my pocket (as it had Admiral Hotel stamped on it) and with a last check from Mick in the crow's nest, we exited the jeweller's each clutching two hold-alls and made our way directly opposite the jeweller's to the marina. I put my hold-alls down and climbed over the railing and quietly dropped onto the decking below; once there, Jacques and Bernie dropped the six hold-alls down to me and walked away. I clipped them all together, kicked off my boots into the water and watched them slowly float off as I lowered myself into the cold water along with the bags and began swimming silently across the marina in the direction of the Admiral Hotel. Ten freezing minutes later, I was on the other side of the marina shivering and freezing my nuts off but because we put the inflatable rings in the bottom of the hold-alls for buoyancy, all I had to do was float along the wall and try find the rope that had been dropped previously that evening and attach the hold-alls to it and scale the wall and crossover into the shadows to await Jacques and Bernie's arrival. I didn't have to wait long either and though I was shivering, Jacques and Bernie pulled the hold-alls up out of the water and with the hold-alls in our possession, we went up the side of the Admiral Hotel and into the underground car park, offloading the bags into the back of the van first before taking the stairs up to the top floor, not the using lift so as not to alert the receptionist that there was somebody in the lift at that time of the morning.

Once inside the hotel room, I said jokingly, 'Pwoar! What's that smell?' and headed straight for the warmth of a hot shower, and after a good ten minutes, I emerged with a towel wrapped around my waist where I was warmly greeted with a cup of tea and a lit cigarette which was a welcome sight along with Mick handing me a blanket too to keep me warm. I said to them grinning, 'Well, chaps, we did it but we still have to get the diamonds back to France.'

'That'll be easy for us, Mac,' Bernie replied smugly.

I finished my tea and said to Mick, 'How about a celebratory drink?'

'Never thought you'd ask, Mac,' he replied and got the only four bottles from the mini bar.

As we toasted each other, I reminded them to keep the noise down as we did not want to wake any of the other guests in the hotel, reminding them the celebrations could begin once the diamonds were safely back in Agde, but for now let's keep it down a bit. I lit another cigarette and eyed the three of them grinning from ear to ear and nodded in approval of their courage and especially to Mick who used the plant pot to have a poo in, which he emptied down the toilet and washed out and re-potted the plant still breathing, minus a few leaves.

Me and Jacques finished our beer and left Mick and Bernie to carry on having a quiet drink, and after we had changed into our spare clothes, we said our goodbyes and to have a safe journey's back to France. We exited the hotel via the stairs and underground car park and found a phone box and called a taxi which came a few minutes later. The taxi driver asked us where we had been, so we filled him full of shit telling him we had met two women on Saturday night and had been staying with them all weekend partying, to which he laughed and commented that they must have made us very welcome to which I smiled and said, 'They were a pair of diamonds.'

We got back to the camp without any issues and the place was already alive with bodies, but me and Jacques went straight to sleep and didn't wake up till late in the afternoon when I went to our company's office and told the receptionist that we had been very ill since Saturday night but would return to work the following day. She said, 'Okay, get well, I'll pass the message on.'

I went back to my room, put in a pair of ear plugs and went straight back to sleep but not before I put a note under Jacques' door informing him that I had been to the office and explained our absence from work.

Later that evening, Jacques and I had a few celebratory bottles of beer in his room, toasting to us, Bernie and Mick, who by now should have departed from Bergen and were already making their way back to France via Denmark. We worked the rest of our rotation to the end of the week and on the Friday afternoon when the time came for us to leave (along with another two hundred workers), me and Jacques were more than jubilant especially when we was airborne with Norway below and behind us.

Chapter 9

Presents on Arrival

After a short stop over at Schiphol Airport in Amsterdam, we were Cardiff bound and once we had arrived and passed through customs, we were met by Fox in arrivals who had a leggy blonde woman in early thirties with her. Fox ran gracefully up to me with a huge smile on her face and threw her arms around me, kissing me passionately for a brief moment. 'It's great to see you. 'It's good to see you too. Who's your friend?' I asked her suspiciously...

'This is Isobelle Omerta, or Izzy for short, she's a present for Jacques, love,' Fox explained smiling and gave me a wink.

'A present? How come I don't get a prezzie?' I asked her glumly.

'Yours is waiting for you back at your apartment, babe,' she replied, slowly stepping backwards, eyeing me up and down with a naughty look on her face. She turned to Jacques and introduced Jacques to Izzy, who greeted him with an unexpected quick kiss on his lips before she followed Fox outside to the car park but not before glancing back over her shoulder smiling at Jacques.

'Hey, Mac.'

'Yes, mate?'

'What the fuck was all that about with that Izzy woman? he asked inquisitively.

'That, my good friend, is a present to you from Fox,' I explained.

'A present? Do I get to keep her then?'

'That's entirely up to you, mate,' I replied laughing.

'Shame it's not Christmas.'

'Why's that?'

'She'd look even better in a mother Christmas suit,' he replied squeezing his gaper through his jeans.

'It's the thought that counts, Jacques,' I reminded him.

'Sorry, Mac. Tell Fox I love my present.'

'I do too but keep that quiet!' I replied laughing.

We caught them both up in the car park and after putting our luggage in the boot of the car, Fox drove us home, dropping off Jacques and Izzy at his apartment first, telling Izzy to be gentle with him and vice versa. No sooner had the front door closed to my apartment, Fox tore my clothes off and dragged me into the shower with her, after which she very naughtily grabbed hold of my cock and led me naked and wet to the bedroom, where to my absolute shock and amazement, Sue (the girl next door) was waiting naked on the bed smiling at me. On each of the bedside tables was a bottle of champagne stood in ice buckets as they both shouted out together, 'Surprise!!'

Fox in her naked prowess slowly, deliberately crept up the bed to Sue and seductively kissed Sue on her lips before she turned to me smiling, licked her plump lips and said, 'Welcome home, honey, care to indulge yourself in some champagne?'

I was speechless momentarily. My cock pulsed as I collected my thoughts and grinning from ear to ear, I playfully replied, 'I'll have a flute or two,' and leapt onto the bed, laying between them both, first kissing Fox and then Sue who handed us both a glass of bubbly each to which I remarked, 'Bottoms up, ladies.'

They both took a sip of their champagne and then set their glasses aside and slowly started to seduce each other as I molested them both and poured little droplets of champagne over their naked bodies, which they started licking off each other. They both teased each other with ice cubes as they began to work their magic on me in unison, kissing, licking and sucking me devilishly from head to toe, working, sharing every part of my body between themselves, destroying my senses as I equally fought to obey their destructive methods as Fox generously fucked me while Sue sat on my face proudly displaying the bitch flaps of her now fully shaven pussy, which I graced with an eager tongue as she squeezed Fox's breasts vehemently then sucked her erect nipples with pouting red lips, lavishly flickering her devilish tongue over them.

They swapped over, so now Fox had my probing tongue inside her wet juicy cunt as Sue fucked my fat cock whilst Fox sucked her tits running her tongue around Sue's stiff nipples. My cock throbbed madly inside Sue's hot soaking cunt which she took advantage of and began fucking me harder, sending me into oblivion, to which Sue read instantly and slipped herself off her manic ride and grabbed my pulsating cock and began wanking it vigorously, to which Fox adhered, leaning forward whilst I continued to lick her hot soaked love hole just as I shot my hot cum out, which they both greeted wide-eyed and open-mouthed, sharing their spoil together, sucking my cock's last drops in turn. My hungry tongue pleasured Fox's delicious cunt all the more lavishly as Sue turned around on all fours in front of Fox, who neatly inserted two fingers inside Sue's soaking wet cunt and finger thrusted her G-spot, sending Sue into a groaning and panting bitch with expulsions of delirium erotica tremens.

Fox inserted a third finger and fucked Sue's cunt harder till Sue squirted her love juice over us screaming out, 'Oh god, fuck yeezzz,' through gritted teeth and collapsed in heaven on the bed breathless. My cock grew hard again and took Fox from behind on all fours and fucked her hard until she juddered with an orgasmic arc. I kept thrusting her wet cunt till my thick cock exploded inside her as I let out a loud gritty growl emptying my balls of fluid inside her battered soaked pussy while Sue grabbed my balls, pulling them downwards and squeezed them firmly, trying to squeeze every drop of fluid out of my battered love-soaked hairy balls whilst wanking her now bulbous clitoris with three frenzied fingers till she let out a stiffened battle cry and let go climatically drained!

The three of us collapsed onto the bed stroking and wildly kissing each other.

I thought to myself this is the best night of my life when Sue grabbed hold of my cock and began sucking it hard again when Fox gently pushed Sue away from my cock on to her back and began kissing and licking Sue's nipples, moving slowly down over Sue's torso as her flicking tongue raced down over her juiced cunt, tearing at it with decorum and precision. Both of them expelled hoarse pants of erotic self-indulgences capsulated with my own expulsions of pleasure as I wanked myself off watching them both in their isobaric chemistry with each other which they devilishly pursued in fucking me one on one, again fucking me into a sweat-soaked oblivion of dogmatic nymphomania.

I didn't hear from Jacques till the Monday morning when he told me Izzy had gone back to Kensington in London where she ran an escort agency. Fox explained that she met Isobelle while in prison (who was stitched up by a top Metropolitan Police Commander after he beat one of her girls in a drunken frenzy and refused to pay the escort fee of £1,800), Isobelle had taking Fox under her wing in prison that cemented a strong relationship between them both in more ways than one (no doubt?), but both had remained in contact with each other after both being released.

'What a weekend I had, Mac,' Jacques stated.

'Yeah, me too,' I exclaimed relishing the thoughts of the threesome.

'I called Robbie's wife to find out how he is.'

'How is he, any progress?'

'The doctors have reduced his medication and told Robbie's wife that he will remain in the same state.'

'Shit, mate. We need to get some money up to his family.'

'There's been a big whip round from work sites all over the country so there's money in the pot.'

'Yeah, but it won't be long before they all forget about him. You know the old saying: "Out of sight, out of mind."'

'I know, Mac. Have you heard from the Bolt and Mick?'

'Not yet, but it won't be long before we do, I can assure you.'

'As soon as he's back, let me know and we'll get the first flight out, okay?'

'Sure thing, I'll ring him in a bit.'

'Right you are, Mac. I'm off for a sauna.'

'Haven't you had enough steam over the weekend?' I asked him.

Laughing, he replied, 'Say hi to Fox and thank her again for Izzy.'

'Tell her yourself when you see her next.'

'For sure, Mac.'

'Will do, mate,' I replied assuring him.

I got a phone call from Bernie late that Monday evening stating that he got the groceries in if we fancy dinner. I told him to set the table and then rang Jacques to inform him that Bernie and Mick had invited us to dinner, which delighted him to say the least. I regretfully told Fox that I was to go to Agde which didn't go down too well, only for her to insist that she came with us so I rang the Bolt and told him to set another place at the table, only for him to question who the place was for and when I told him it was for Fox, he just giggled and said, 'Be a pleasure, Mac. Fox is welcome anytime.'

Fox was over the moon with joy when I said she was going to France and eighteen hours later, we were all in Agde sat in the garden drinking wine and beers and introducing Chantelle to Jacques and especially Fox who got on like a house on fire with each other as they could talk about their girlie stuff and before we knew it, they were making their way down to the town leaving us to the man stuff or so they thought. Bernie sat there grinning from ear to ear and asked us, 'Do you want to see it?'

'You're damn right we do,' I replied eagerly.

He sprang to his feet, whipped his shirt off and pointed to the top of his arm. 'What do you think of this then?' he asked us, proudly displaying a tattoo of Chantelle's name.

'That's... err... very nice, mate,' I replied stunned, thinking he was going to show us the diamonds.

Bernie thrust his shoulder in Jacques' face and asked, 'Jacques, what do you think?'

'I think it's bloody great, mate.'

'Dog's bollocks, I reckon,' Bernie said.

'What does Chantelle think of it?' Jacques asked him.

'Erm, I... er... haven't showed it to her yet,' he answered sheepishly.

'Why not?' I asked him.

'Well, Mac, the timing is not right just yet.'

'So when is a good time?' I asked inquisitively.

'When it's a good time of course,' he replied smiling.

'I agree, Bolt. Now where are the diamonds?' I asked him.

'There inside the safe. Why?' he replied coyly.

'Because we would like to see them,' Jacques told him.

'Oh right, follow me, gentlemen,' he replied in an official tone.

Rubbing our hands together and smiling, we followed Bernie into the house and through into the kitchen, where he slid back a large wooden panel in the wall revealing a digital lock. After entering the code, there was a click and then a door panel slowly opened outwards; Bernie grinned and opened the door to its full extent and turned on the light that revealed a wide stone staircase leading down to the old wine cellar.

'If you please, chaps, follow me.'

'Anymore places around the house like this, Bolt?' Jacques asked him.

'Thought you may like this feature,' he replied, pleased with himself.

We followed the staircase down where it opened out into a large cellar.

'How the hell did I not know about this?' I asked in astonishment.

Bernie giggled and then informed us that he had found it months ago whilst taking the old plaster of the walls ready for the fitted kitchen and after incorporating the panels, he decided to get a little creative and hide it out the way, even going so far as to line the rear of the door panel with one-inch steel plate so when tapped, it gave the sound of a solid wall behind it; ingenious to a degree, but nonetheless he wanted to keep it as a surprise for a rainy day like now.

There were at least two hundred bottles of vintage wine left in the racks covered in dust and cobwebs that would be worth a small fortune on their own and up against the rear wall was the safe that Mick had driven over with in the van.

'Fuck me, how did you two manage to get that down here?' I asked Bernie and Mick in amazement.

'It took an engine hoist, a few pieces of wood and a lot of determination, right, Mick?'

'Damn right, Bernie,' Mick replied smiling.

'Well, I never,' Jacques exclaimed.

'Me neither,' I added, scratching my head in amazement.

Bernie wasted no time opening the safe and handed us bag after bag of the gems, all carefully tagged, from necklaces, bracelets, ring's to earrings and so on, but even under the low lighting they shone magnificently as we laid them out on a cloth-covered table. Mick disappeared shortly before returning with four bottles of beer to toast our success but Jacques said, 'Fuck that. Let's do the vintage stuff,' and pulled a dusty bottle of wine from the rack, pulled out the cork with his teeth and took a slug, passing it to me and I in turn passed it to Bernie who passed it to Mick.

'Have you got any idea how much it's all worth yet?' Jacques asked them both.

'I'm afraid not, Jacques. This is only the second time we've taken them out so we can share the spoils of adding them all up together,' Bernie told him.

'Well, there's no time like the present, chaps,' I said lighting up a cigarette.

'Best I get some pens and paper then,' Bernie suggested.

'Try and find a calculator too.'

'I don't have one,' he replied and disappeared back upstairs.

When he returned a short while later, we each took a bag and carefully emptied them out and began writing down the prices ready to be added up later, when all of a sudden from behind us we heard Fox say, 'Well, well, boys, you have been busy bees, haven't you, eh?'

All four of us froze then relaxing I asked, 'Where's Chantelle to?'

'Relax, she's with her parents,' Fox replied, eyeing all the gems.

Bernie jumped to his feet and exclaimed, 'What! Her parents are here too? In the house!!'

Fox giggled and told Bernie, 'Relax, they're in the bar down in the town talking.'

'Thank God for that,' he replied, adding, 'You nearly gave me a heart attack.'

'Do you know something, babe?' I asked her. shaking my head slowly in disbelief.

'I know them diamonds are a girl's best friend and a pig's ass makes bacon,' she replied giggling.

'You, my love, have an unruly time of showing up,' I told her grinning.

'Like at the right time?' she asked.

'Always,' I replied smiling.

'Well, now that we've got that out of the way, do you boys want a hand here?' she asked.

'Only with the counting, love.'

'Then let's count, boys,' she replied, taking her place at the table; she looked like a kid in a candy shop.

Jacques said to Fox, 'Glad to have you on board and thanks for my present, she was fantastic.'

'Glad you enjoyed her,' Fox replied smiling.

'Several times over,' Jacques emphasised, smiling back at her.

Fox smiled back at Jacques as she thought to herself, *So did I.*

It took us the best part of several hours to sort through the diamonds, making various lists of all the gems on the table and let Fox add them all up, stating the grand figure came in at just over three point two million pounds sterling. Bernie asked Fox to double check the figures again as he danced about jubilantly taking small swigs out of a vintage bottle of wine.

Breathing a sigh of relief, Fox looked up at us dumbfounded but smiling she said, 'Jesus H Christ, you're fucking minted, boys.'

Bernie moonwalked over to Fox and asked excitedly, 'How much this time?'

Fox stood up and started moving her arms up and down, turning from side to side like a robot when she suddenly jolted to a stop in Bernie's face and said, 'Three point two million, two hundred and forty-five thousand pounds,' and burst out laughing.

We all jumped up and down hugging each other, laughing our heads off exuberantly for quite some time and when we gathered our thoughts, Bernie brought out a bottle of champagne, shaking it madly and when he popped the cork, the champagne erupted from the bottle as he sprayed it all over us and the diamonds then he made a toast to Robbie and our good fortune then took a swig from the bottle and passed it on to the rest of us.

'Fox?'

'Yes, Bernie?'

'You won't say anything to Chantelle, will you, Fox?'

'Only if you give me a necklace, bracelet and matching earrings,' she replied laughing.

'Done,' he replied sheepishly red-faced.

Giggling to herself, she told him, 'Lighten up, Bolt. I'm just joking with you.'

'Oh right, but I still would have given them to you for your silence,' he admitted.

'I know,' she replied, kissing him on the cheek.

'Let's shut this place up and go to town and celebrate?' I suggested to them.

'Sounds like a grand idea to me,' Jacques agreed along with everyone else.

Chapter 10

Alter – The Jew

We arrived back in the UK the next morning and the three of us drove straight up to London to Isobelle's apartment in Kensington where were warmly greeted by her but she had her eyes firmly fixed on Jacques. Izzy told us to make ourselves at home and allocated me and Fox a plush bedroom and said, 'Excuse us,' she turned around and cupped Jacques by the balls and said to him, 'Your bedroom is in here with me.'

Smiling at her, Jacques replied, 'Lead the way.'

'There's something about you, Mr Jacques Couture,' she stated, gazing into his eyes.

'You can put your hand on it later,' he replied.

'Oh, I think I already have, darling,' she said, squeezing his balls firmer.

Fox whispered in my ear, 'I knew they would suit each other.'

'How come?' I whispered back.

Fox looked at me sympathetically and whispered, 'A woman's instinct, love.'

'Is that so?'

Fox gently nudged me in my side with her elbow and whispered, 'You men know nothing of women?'

I whispered back, 'Is there any point in trying?'

Fox pouted her lips and after a silent pause, she casually replied, 'Nope!'

Izzy wasted no time in whisking us around the West End in her yellow Bentley, first taking us to DiMaggio's restaurant where Izzy was made a huge fuss of the moment. She walked through the door by a very camp waiter called Clarence, who kept ending every sentence with darling. Over dinner, we had the pleasure of meeting the owner Roberto briefly, who informed Clarence to see to Izzy's every need. Roberto kissed Izzy's hand and then excused himself. After a lavish fine dining, we left DiMaggio's, and Izzy took us to Bar 66 where again she was hugely fussed over and presented with a bottle of champagne and a non-alcoholic cocktail for her.

I turned to Izzy asking her if she had ever heard of Geldschranks.

'I presume you are referring to the diamond establishment in Bond St?' she replied.

'Yes, as a matter of fact, I am.'

Staring at me, she cautiously asked, 'Why?'

'My old friend Alter works there and it's been a while since I last saw him,' I informed her.

'My god! You know Alter and Jacob?' she exclaimed in disbelief.

'I know Alter, but who's Jacob?'

'His half-brother of course, darling,'

'I never knew he had a half-brother,' I told her frowning.

'And Alter don't just work there, darling, he owns the place, or half of it at least.'

'Really? Christ.'

'How do you know Alter?' she enquired wryly.

'People used to bully him in school over his foot, so a few of us kept him under our wing,' I replied, enlightening her.

'That's decent of you, love,' Fox said, kissing me on the cheek.

'What a small world we live in,' Izzy remarked.

'We need to see him urgently regarding a private matter,' Jacques informed her.

'Why don't you keep me company and let Mac and Fox go,' Izzy suggested to him.

'Sounds okay to me, Mac.'

'And it's okay by us too,' I told him.

Isobelle made a call on her mobile and said, 'Hi darling, no darling, but I'm graced with the company of an old friend of yours darling who would like to say hello. It's Alter,' she whispered and handed me the phone.

Alter was totally shocked that I was in Isobelle's company, but I explained briefly that she knew Fox more than me and I needed to see him regarding an urgent matter. He said he would be delighted and told me to come to his shop in Bond St in an hour, stating that he would be there to greet us personally to which I agreed and handed Izzy her phone back.

My observations got the better of me so I casually asked Izzy, 'How is it everything is on the house for you?'

After a brief silence, Izzy explained that she has arrangements with quite a lot of establishment owners, stating that she uses their premises for her girls to meet clients, who wine and dine them there, earning the owners a small fortune which in turn earns her a nice little fortune too, and as they all use her services, if a businessman or businesswoman is away from home who desires to be graced with a beautiful woman's company for the evening, then Izzy's perks were being free gourmet meals, champagne, top-notch hotels and the occasional exotic holiday here and there with her guarantee of assured discretion the clients keep coming back and with over twenty absolute stunning women on her books at £1800 basic per girl for a two hours chat, the figures add up enormously for all parties involved.

She even stated that she was once given a yacht as a present on Cowes Week, a sailing event on the Isle of Wight, for taking care of a Texan oil tycoon and eleven of his friends for forty-eight hours. Unfortunately, the oil tycoon died three weeks later of a heart attack in a massage parlour in Singapore. Remarkable, I thought to myself, hence her driving a Bentley and having a lavish apartment in Kensington.

We entered Geldshcranks and as promised, we were greeted by Alter stood leaning on a cane and on seeing me, a warm smile spread across his face and across mine too, as he greeted us with the Jewish formality 'Shalom' and a firm handshake. Alter took us his through to his office out back.

He spoke softly, 'Mac, my dear friend, it's been a very long time, I thought you had forgotten all about me, please, both of you, sit down.'

'I know, my friend, but you are sincerely thought of often,' I replied solemnly.

'And who is this angel that graces us with her presence?' he asked looking at Fox.

'This is Melody Fox-Wright, my future wife,' I replied triumphantly.

'Ah, your magnificent beauty is testament that you are indeed an angel.'

Fox smiled at him and said, 'Thank you, Alter, I'm flattered.'

'You are welcome, my dear,' he told her, then turning to me he asked, 'What is so urgent, my friend, that I may be of assistance to you?'

'Alter… I don't mean to put you on the spot, but I'd like you to look at something for me.'

He looked at me through wise eyes and said, 'What is it you would like me to look at?'

I nodded to Fox who took a small red box from her bag and handed it over to Alter, who eyed us both perceptually before he opened the box. Alter gently eased the lid off the little red box and his eyes lit up instantly and reached for his eye piece. After taking the ring out the box, he spent several moments looking at it before he spoke, 'This, my dear friend, is a very nice piece known as a True Blue, set in platinum, with a pear-shaped four-carat diamond.'

'And its value?' I asked inquisitively.

He stood up and limped over to an old picture on the wall of a group of Jewish men standing proudly and stared at it for a while in silence before he said without turning around, 'Are you in some kind of trouble, my old friend?'

'No and yes, but nothing life-threatening,' I replied assumingly.

'You should know the value of this piece then as it's never been worn,' he stated, limping slowly back over to his desk and upon him sitting down again, he looked at us both in silence before he spoke, 'I could retail this ring for forty k if you need my help.'

'We do, Alter, how much would you be prepared to pay for it?'

'Just as I thought,' he replied as a smile appeared on his face then he continued adding, 'For you, Mac… thirty, maybe thirty-five k as an old friend.'

'Thank you, that's very generous of you, Alter, but I have something else to ask of you and is of even greater importance,' I said.

He leaned back in his chair behind his desk and asked, 'How many more do you have, my friend?'

'A lot, and I mean a lot,' I stated.

He thought momentarily looking back at the old picture on the wall and in a calm but stern voice, he said, 'I can help you but you have to be more than honest with me when I ask you something.'

'I'm not in the habit of lying, Alter, especially to you. What do you want to ask?'

'Why come to me and not take them to some gangster out there somewhere?'

'Because I trust you and it's not that you owe me anything in anyway. It's just I…'

Alter cut in and protested, 'Oh, but I do, Mac, all the times you stopped people from tormenting me about my foot in school…'

176

Cutting him short, I told him, 'Alter, that's what friends do in school and in life is look out for each other.'

'Yes of course, forgive me. How many more do you have, my friend?' he asked gathering his thoughts.

Smiling I replied, 'Just over three million in sterling.'

Alter reeled in his chair coughing and then he laughed spurting out, 'You are going to need all the Jewish community to help you get rid of that amount,' and carried on laughing.

'What's so funny?' Fox asked him.

'Why the profits of course, my angel,' he replied and went into a fit of laughter again with me and Fox joining him.

Eventually, the laughter subsided, and we finalised a few details with Alter, who was more than happy to help us out, possibly in more ways than one if need be, though he offered us thirty-five k there and then for the ring. I told him to keep it and settle up later returning his trust. We explained our relationship with Isobelle and met Alter's half-brother Jacob, who after a lot of Yiddish with Alter, was by now my new Jewish best friend though he didn't quite know it yet. We left them both smiling on the shop floor as we strode off up Bond St casually hand in hand when Fox commented, 'I like them both, but Alter is the sweetest.'

'He thinks you're pretty sweet too,' I commented.

'Now, now, lover boy, don't go getting jealous,' she replied giggling.

The next day (Sunday) late in the afternoon, we said goodbye to Izzy and thanked her for a wonderful weekend. Though she begged us to stay, we assured her we would see her again, probably sooner rather than later.

We arrived back in Barry Island early that evening and after taking Jacques to his apartment, I immediately called Bernie informing him that all went well with the Jews and told him to get ready to roll shortly, when he announced that Mick was coming back to the UK in a day or two.

I told him it was okay and to let Mick come and for him to await further instructions possibly within the next few days too as I had half a plan in mind but needed to make certain adjustments. I had to find a way to import the diamonds from France into the UK as certain opportunities had now arisen within the last day or two to be taken full advantage of.

Mick returned from France two days later as predicted which was a good thing while Jacques had gone up to see Robbie Duggan in person and find out what the final diagnosis was from the doctors. I had a chat with Fox and told her that we would need to borrow Isobelle's yacht, to which she smiled and winked at me saying she would take care of it, making the phone call to Izzy there and then. After a short conversation with Izzy, Fox hung up and smiled saying it was sorted, but we would have to pick the keys up from Izzy in person which would mean a trip to London again, but Fox insisted on making the journey herself and after a hug and kiss, she grabbed the car keys and said, 'See you soon.'

'What, you're leaving now this minute?' I asked her stunned.

'Better to go now, babe,' she replied smiling.

I knew she was right, but I still wanted her to stay, so not letting my feelings for her stand in the way, I let her go after a long meaningful kiss, telling her I loved her.

I got a call from Jacques the next morning saying Robbie had taken a turn for the worse and that the doctors stated the next twenty-four hours would be critical for him. Before ending the call, Jacques informed me that he would make his way back to Barry Island and call me upon his arrival which he did the following day around lunchtime, and no sooner had that call ended, Mick was on the other end and when that call ended, Fox was on the phone stating she had just come over the Severn Bridge and did I want to take her for lunch to which I agreed after deciding we should meet at the White Horse for a simple pub lunch.

Jacques rang back with the same idea so I told him the White Horse and just for good measure, I rang Mick and asked him if he fancied a bite to eat at the White Horse, to which he agreed, but coincidently told me Jacques had just asked him the same thing no more than ten minutes ago on the phone.

Fuck it, I thought, ending the call. I was the first to arrive which made me feel better, then Jacques and Mick turned up and a short while later, Fox elegantly walked through the doors, kissed me on the cheek and sat down and said, 'Okay, boys, it's like a family reunion.'

'That's what I was thinking,' I replied.

'Well, it is, kind of … in a funny way,' Mick said hesitantly.

'Well, it would be if Bernie was here,' Jacques added.

Looking at Fox, I said, 'Did everything go okay?'

'Of course it did, babe,' she replied giving me a wink.

After we had finished our typical pub lunch in the form of lasagne and chips, Fox held up the keys to the yacht and jingled them for all to see and said, 'Here you go, boys,' and placed them on the table.

'What are the keys for? Mick asked her puzzled.

'The keys to the yacht,' she replied smiling.

'Boat, what boat?' Jacques asked her even more puzzled.

'It's a yacht, not a boat,' she told him rolling her eyes.

'And what is the yacht for?' he asked cynically.

Fox turned to me with a look of bewilderment on her face, so turning back to Jacques and Mick, I said, 'Forgive me but we're going on a little sea trip, guys.'

'You have a nasty habit of springing surprises on people when they least expect it,' Jacques said sighing.

'I'm not too clever on the open waves,' Mick declared sorrowfully.

'Oh yeah, and why is that, Mick?' Fox enquired.

'Because I got no sea legs and throw up a lot,' he confessed grimly.

Fox giggled and said wryly, 'Aw, Mick, you poor thing.'

'Sod sitting next to you then,' Jacques remarked, teasing Mick.

'I'll drink to that, Jacques,' I said.

'Take no notice of them, Mick,' Fox told him.

'I don't anymore, Fox. And just as a matter of curiosity, where are we going on it?'

'That's a good question, Mick, and I bet Mac is dying to tell us, aren't you, Mac?' Jacques said sternly looking me in the eye.

'We are going to the Channel Islands to meet the Bolt and collect some rocks, if you get my drift,' I informed them.

'I think we are overlooking something here?' Jacques announced.

'What are we overlooking, mate?' I asked him troubled.

'Like who's going to sail the damn thing?'

'It's not that type of yacht, it's more a sport cruiser, and I'm going to navigate it,' Fox told him full of herself, grinning from ear to ear.

'You're kidding us right, Mac?'

'Fortunately, Jacques, the lady is going to drive it,' I replied grinning too.

'But how?' Mick asked her.

'My dad taught me a thing or two on his sailing yacht when I was a kid growing up, including navigation and chart reading, along with other stuff,' she informed him and took a sip of her drink then smiled at them both, who in turn looked at each other and then back at Fox wide-eyed in disbelief.

'Trust me, she's good, very, very good,' I told them.

'Well, fuck me,' Jacques squawked.

'No thanks, you're not my type,' Fox replied, relishing the moment to comment.

'I never meant it that way,' Jacques explained apologetically.

'I know, Jacques, and neither did I, so lighten up and get off the defensive,' she told him.

'Okay you two, pack it in, it feels like Bernie's present,' I told them.

'That's what I was thinking, but why the Channel Islands?' Mick asked.

'It's easier for Bernie to meet us half way and the Channel Islands are lovely, you'll enjoy them, trust me,' I replied.

'But that's a bit more than half way,' Mick pointed out.

'Mick?'

'Yes, Mac?'

'Shh.'

'So when do we set sail?' Mick asked.

'Cruise,' Fox reminded him assertively.

'As soon as the Bolt is ready,' I told Mick.

'Erm, when will that be?' Mick shyly asked.

'When he's ready,' Jacques told him stiffly.

'Okay, no need to bite my head off, I was only asking,' Mick replied innocently.

'You boys need to chill out,' Fox told them.

'No offence, Mick, but I think you spent too much time around Bernie and it's rubbed off on you,' Jacques told him.

'How do you mean?' Mick asked frowning at him.

'Is he winding me up?' Jacques asked me and Fox, but we both burst out laughing whilst Mick sat there grinning.

Jacques got over it eventually and forgave Mick, but Mick did point out that it was as if Bernie was present, so in essence we were all together again in spirit and I suppose there was method to his madness but on the whole I don't think Mick should push things too far with Jacques in the little time they had known each other as Jacques can put a sudden halt to shit like that in an instant that Mick would regret for the rest of his life but they made up so that's that. Jacques got around to Robbie again and fearing the worst to come (as the doctors put it), Fox put her hand on top of his and gave it a sympathetic squeeze of reassuring comfort. Fox faked a good yawn and remarked how tired she was whilst rubbing my leg with her foot and with me being ever the gentleman, I made our excuses to Mick and Jacques and departed back to the apartment where we headed directly for the bedroom.

Life carried on as normal for all of us for a few days apart from Mick who happened upon chance to bump into Sara at McArthur Glen retail outlet in Bridgend, though he was unaware that Sara's husband was with her and had his back to Mick whilst looking at a rail of shorts when Mick casually asked Sara, "When can I see you again?" But as he said these fatal words, Sara's face turned pale and expressionless as her husband had overheard him say it to Sara. Sara denied all knowledge of Mick, telling her husband that Mick was talking to someone else and not her, but this made her husband even more enraged. Her husband told her to shut up and stop insulting his intelligence, and after a rowdy confrontation in the shop, he chased Mick through the centre of the retail park, screaming he was going to fucking kill him first then Sara, but Mick shitting himself, quickly hailed the security guards and said the guy chasing him was a lunatic who was trying to kill him. Four burly security guards set about Mick's assailant, rugby-tackling him around the waist, felling the poor guy to the floor, leaving Mick to make his escape only to pass Sara on his way back through the shopping area when she started hysterically screaming like a dement at Mick everything under the sun for bringing it on top for her, saying she was going to rip his eyes out and deep fry them as she ran towards him banshee style.

Mick unfroze and called for help again, and pointed her out to another approaching security guard and cried out, 'There's another one,' and made good his escape calling her a "fucking nutcase" over his shoulder and hot-footed it back to his car shaking, out of breath and dripping with sweat, thanking his lucky stars that he was not in a hospital again.

I received the news we had been waiting for from Bernie, stating he was ready to roll and that he would meet us at the Marmalade Café in St Helier in the Channel Islands, and rather than book ourselves into a hotel, we thought it better to stay onboard the yacht. Fox and Jacques were delighted by the news when I told them but Mick on the other hand was silent, and when I informed Alter by telephone, he was ecstatic with the thought of all the diamonds and said he would make plans himself. With a plan set in place, it was time for us to depart for St Helier and for good measure, we took an unhurried drive down to Southampton, staying there overnight in an area close to the city centre known as The Polygon, staying in different B&B's apart from me and Fox. Opposite our B&B was a pub called the May Flower, so we headed in through the doors early in the evening and had a few light drinks accompanied by a meal before heading back to our B&Bs at around 10 pm as we had to be at the ferry terminal to catch the morning ferry to the Isle of Wight before it set sail at 8 am.

We sat in the lounge on board the ferry as it slowly began to move away from its berth and once outside the harbour, it picked up speed and gently bobbed up and down across the Solent towards the Isle of Wight. After we had berthed on the Island, we departed from the ferry, taking a slow drive to the marina where our yacht was moored courtesy of Isobelle. Mick looked under the weather and fell silent whereas I, Fox and Jacques were in high spirits and the conversation was basically limited to our surroundings (like tourists on an excursion), but Mick was getting paler by the minute sitting there in silence trying hard to keep a smile on his face and just stared out the passenger window in the back of the car until I asked him what was the matter. Looking more off colour, he replied, 'I don't feel so well after the ferry crossing.'

'I thought you did very well, after all, you managed to keep your breakfast down and not throw it up,' I told him.

'And not show yourself up,' Jacques remarked.

'Fox?'

'Yes, Mick?'

'Stop the car!' Mick barked.

'What?'

'Just stop the car please,' he begged her.

'Can't it wait till we get to the marina?' she asked him.

Noticing Mick starting to heave, I said to Fox, 'Quick, love, pull over fast.'

'Why?' she asked.

'Because Mick's about to share his breakfast with us,' I exclaimed.

'Oh shit, no! Not in the car,' she cried out and abruptly pulled over, skidding to a halt.

Mick's cheeks were now bulging outwards with his face green as his stomach content was slowly seeping through the corners of his mouth and dribbling down over his chin onto his shirt. Jacques was pissing himself laughing but quickly reached over and opened Mick's door and pushed him out on to the side of the road just in time as his stomach content spewed violently from his face time and time again until eventually he was just heaving and gagging for air. Jacques was now totally hysterical with laughter at Mick who was still on his hands and knees gasping for air and purple in the face with long thick stringy bile dangling from his mouth.

'I can't wait for him to get on this boat,' Jacques stated trying to conceal his hysterics.

'Don't be so cruel, Jacques,' Fox told him.

'I wish Bernie was here to see this,' Jacques stated.

'You bastards,' Mick cried out getting back inside the car.

'What have we done?' I asked him earnestly.

'Laughing at me, and you can pack it in, Jacques.'

'You should look at it from where I'm sat,' Jacques replied through fits of giggles.

'Are you all finished throwing your guts up?'

'Yes, Mac,' he replied sighing.

'Good,' I replied.

'You can clean up once we are onboard, Mick,' Fox told him sympathetically.

'Thanks, Fox.'

'Open your window, you stink.'

'Fuck you, Jacques.'

'Not smelling like that you won't,' Jacques jested, still giggling away.

Fox let out a little laugh and then pulled back on to the main road. She drove down to the marina and parked the car and headed towards the harbourmaster's office where she enquired where our yacht was, returning she said follow me. We trailed behind her along the walkways until she stopped and said, 'Here we are, boys, this is ours.'

'Which one?' I asked her.

Beaming from ear to ear, she pointed to a row of yachts and said, 'That one.'

'Which one?' Jacques asked.

'The one that's got *Pussy Galore* written across the back of it.'

'You're fucking joking, ain't you?' Mick asked her shocked.

'Not at all,' she replied smiling.

'That is one mighty impressive yacht, it must have cost a fortune?' Jacques stated.

'What do think, Mick?' Fox asked him.

'I don't care about the damn thing! I'm dreading it and I don't want to go on it.'

'You'll be fine, Mick.'

'Yeah right!' he replied solemnly.

'Any pussy onboard?' Jacques asked.

'Only Fox,' I replied smiling at him.

'Still, it is a nice yacht.'

'I have to agree with you, Jacques,' I said.

'Then let's board her and grab ourselves a bunk.'

'Sorry, only beds, so you'll have to make do,' Fox informed Jacques giggling.

'Bunk, bed, what's the difference, they both sleep, don't they?' he replied.

'You're right, but we're travelling in comfort, Jacques, but of course there is always the deck floor if the bed isn't to your liking?'

'No, the bed will be fine, Fox, thanks,' he stated smiling at her.

'I thought it might be,' she replied sarcastically.

Chapter 11

Murder in St Helier

We boarded the yacht and took a quick look around, familiarising ourselves with the cabins, plush fittings and lavish décor, and its layout. Jacques had instantly disappeared below decks as soon as we boarded, he re-appeared wearing matching white shorts, shirt, deck shoes and a cap. Mick looked nervous but was sporting the same attire and noticing them, I turned to Fox and said, 'Check them two out.'

She looked at both of them and burst out laughing saying, 'What the hell are they like?'

'Like two kids with a new toy,' I mused.

'Then it's best you go and join in, love.'

'What do you mean?'

'Go the whole hog and try to find the same kit,' she told me.

'You got to be joking, love...aren't you?'

'Please, pretty please, for me,' she said fluttering her eyelids at me.

'Okay, but don't laugh.'

'Who, me? No,' she replied.

Below decks in the cabins, I found the same clothes hanging in a wardrobe that funnily enough had what looked to be like the captain's attire, so I grabbed the cap and shirt and found a smaller pair of shorts in another cabin which I thought I'd get Fox to wear and after I had dressed up in my clothes, I took the rest up to Fox who was now at the helm on the bridge. 'Here you are, love, try these for size,' I said handing them over to her.

'Oh goody, thanks, babe. You look great,' she replied but continued, 'Help me out of this dress,' she said turning her back to me to unzip her, then she let the dress fall to the floor. She put the shirt on first; though a little big, she just tied the shirt in a knot around her midriff, exposing her waistline and put on her shorts retaining her high heels. 'There, how do I look, babe?'

'Absolutely stunning,' I replied admiring her new look.

'Well, ain't you going to give your Captain good luck kiss for the voyage ahead?'

'That's not the only thing the first engineer wants to give her,' I replied suggestively.

'Well, that'll have to wait, now come here and kiss me,' she ordered.

I kissed her lightly and placed the captain's cap on her head and said to her, 'Now you're twice as stunning,'

She replied in a flustered state, 'Careful, Mac, we'll be role-playing at this rate.'

'Then let's play.'

'Later perhaps? Now go and untie us,' she ordered.

'Aye aye, Captain,' I replied saluting her.

She started the engines and did all that radio chat informing the harbourmaster that we were departing and then called down to us to cast us off from its moorings and slowly cruised out of the marina into the Solent where the sea was getting rougher by the minute. Fox increased the power of the yacht's engines as poor Mick tied himself to the rail on the side of the yacht and hung his head over the side, stating that he knew this was a bad idea but Jacques reminded him to think of the money, which at this point Mick started to take a turn for the worse as the colour started to drain from his face.

Fox was at the helm and loving it, sat in the big captain's swivel chair cross-legged with her heels off and her cap turned to the back, tuning in radio stations eventually settling for some R&B. I made my way to the cooler inside and opened the door and found amongst the drinks a bottle of champagne which I cracked open and filled a flute up, taking it up to Fox at the helm who was having a ball singing along to the radio. 'Here you go, Captain,' I said handing her the glass.

'Why thank you, able seaman Mac,' she replied playfully.

'My pleasure, Captain,' I replied, stood to attention.

'Would able seaman Mac grace me with his presence at the captain's table this evening?'

'Able seaman Mac would be honoured to dine in the presence of such beauty.'

She winked at me and then said, 'How are the other seamen doing?'

'I regret to inform the Captain that able seaman Jacques is having a ball watching not-so-able seaman Mick, who has tied a rope around his waist and to the rail, and is currently throwing up over the side feeding the ocean's inhabitants and the trailing seagulls, all to able seaman Jacques's amusement,' I replied laughing.

'Tell able seaman Jacques to leave not-so-able seaman Mick alone,' she said laughing.

'Aye aye, Captain. Anything else for the Captain?' I asked.

Fox laughed and said, 'Would able seaman Mac be so kind as to go and look after non-able seaman Mick and perhaps take him some water?'

'Aye Captain. Anything else for the Captain?'

'No. Able seaman Mac is dismissed until further required,' she replied pissing herself laughing.

'Aye aye, Captain,' I replied sharply and double footed it to not-so-able seaman Mick.

I went to see Mick and handed him a bottle of water which he placed between his legs without saying anything and put his head back over the side. I looked across to Jacques who was sat there watching Mick with interest. I motioned to Jacques to follow me with a nod of my head, but he shook his head from side to side and put two fingers to his eyes and pointed them back at Mick. I scowled at Jacques and waved him to come inside, reluctantly he came in and as I handed him a beer from the cooler, I said to him, 'How can you watch him like that?'

'Easy, Mac, it beats looking at the sea and it's more entertaining seeing the faces he pulls when he throws up.'

'He must hate you,' I told him through mild laughter.

'What for?'

'Cos you're sat there with a big grin on your face.'

He shrugged his shoulders and said, 'So what, it's funny.'

'I know, but let's give him some space by himself.'

'Thanks for the beer, Mac, I'm going to keep an eye on Mick,' he said and went back outside seating himself opposite Mick swigging his beer and grinning again.

And that's very much how the six-hour crossing continued with Jacques watching Mick and me sat alongside Fox at the helm until we hit the Channel Islands and moored in St Aubin's Bay in Jersey. The harbour with its vast sand lined shore with its bars and restaurants as well as its hotels is the jewel in the crown of Jersey with its fishing boats and pleasure yachts moored peacefully side by side all being overlooked by the magnificent splendour of St Aubin's Fort. The time was now approaching 2 pm in the afternoon when suddenly out of the blue we were boarded by two policemen and a WPC, one of them being a Sergeant who was alerted by a member of the public who reported that there was a dead man tied to the back of a yacht in the marina.

We all looked at poor Mick who was still tied to the rail by the waist as one of the policeman gestured to his fellow colleagues with his head in the direction of Mick who still had his head hung over the side in a lifeless state. A smile began to appear on all their faces when the Sergeant stepped forward and said, 'Would any of you mind explaining why that man is tied to the rail?'

'Sure,' Fox called out, stepping out onto the deck in all her glory.

The three police officers looked at each other and then back at Fox when one of them managed to say, 'Enlighten us, Miss...'

'Fox-Wright,' she stated firmly then turned to me and Jacques, and said, 'Will you two check the fuel and hydraulics?'

'Aye, Captain,' I replied, winking at her and quickly made my way inside closely followed by Jacques.

'Err... Miss Fox-Wright,' the Sergeant mumbled.

'Captain Fox-Wright,' she emphasised asking him, 'And you are?'

'Err... I'm Sergeant Lake, this is WPC La'Roux and this is PC Caprice,' he replied introducing himself and his two police colleagues with a broad smile.

'Well, this is a nice welcome party I must say,' Fox stated, unbuttoning the top of her shirt a little more, producing a little more cleavage adding, 'God, it's hot today,' and winked at the WPC who with embarrassment began to blush.

'And where have you just come from, Captain?' the Sergeant asked her suspiciously.

'Why, from the Isle of Wight of course, Sergeant.'

'And you have documentation for all on board I take it, err, Captain?'

'Why yes, I'll go and get them for you, Sergeant, if you like?' Fox offered.

'That would be of help to us,' he told her scrupulously as he glanced over at Mick.

Fox smiled and said, 'One moment please, Sergeant, while I go and get them for you.'

She came inside but I already had our passports in my hand for her. I kissed her on the lips and told her, 'You're doing brilliant, love.'

'So far, so good,' she sighed and took our passports out to the Sergeant.

'Here you are, Sergeant. I think you'll find everything is in order.'

He looked at all the passports and then throwing a cautious look at Fox, he asked, 'Just the four of you on board, Captain Wright?'

'That's Captain Fox-Wright, Sergeant, and yes, just the four of us. Feel free to take a look around,' she said moving to one side so they could pass by.

The WPC took a step forward but the Sergeant idly waved his hand at her and then turned to Fox saying, 'I don't think that will be necessary as everything looks to be in order,' and handed her the passports back.

'Thank you but like I said, feel free, Sergeant,' she told him smiling whilst pushing her breasts out at him.

Stumbling for words, the Sergeant cleared his throat, 'Err...herm... I... err...mean we have to follow up on reports. I hope you understand it's procedure, you see?'

'I think you have been misinformed about a dead body, as Mick there is very much alive, it's just he has no sea legs at present,' Fox informed them all.

'Would you mind if we asked him a few questions, Miss...err I mean Captain?' the Sergeant asked eyeing her eagerly.

'Not at all, Sergeant, I doubt if you can get a straight answer out of him in that state. We've been trying for the last six hours during the crossing,' she informed the trio.

'You must see it from our perspective,' he told her fumbling for his notebook.

'I do, Sergeant. Now if you will please excuse me, I have more important affairs to tend to,' she told him assertively.

'And what affairs would they be?' he asked, dabbing his brow with a hanky.

'Nothing that would be of interest to you, Sergeant, but if you must know, I need to take a long hot shower as the crossing has got me all clammy,' she replied pouting her lips.

'Oh... err... really?' the Sergeant stammered, licking his lips.

'Are you calling me a liar, Sergeant?' Fox asked him angrily.

'No, Captain,' he whimpered.

A wry smile broke out on Fox's face as she firmly said, 'Good.' Then turned her back on him and went inside with her hands covering her mouth to muffle her laughter.

Me and Jacques were in silent fits of silent laughter too, but we kept our eye on the police through the tinted glass windows as they untied the rope from around Mick's waist and sat him upright and gave him a few mouthfuls of his water just as a fishing boat passed, creating a rocking motion from its wake which was all Mick needed to make him throw up again, literally spraying the Sergeant and PC Caprice with vomit. Mick didn't even say sorry and just flopped his head back over the side and went limp again. This made our day, but Fox was at hand offering them each a bar towel to clean themselves up with which they eagerly accepted. They were happy that Mick was very much alive and said that they were sorry for any inconvenience that they had caused and for any intrusion. Fox waved them off and returned back inside where we all fell into fits of howling hysterical laughter that lasted what seemed like ages when Mick came through the door. 'I guess that took care of them,' he said grinning as he too burst into laughter with us.

Later, he told us that he had fallen asleep and was waking when the police had arrived but thought it better to remain dead (as the police put it) and when they offered him the water, he could not resist the offer as he felt it coming back up almost instantly and thought to himself, *let them have it*. But he did say that he was feeling rather hungry as we all was so we got freshened up and headed for shore with us three hoping Mick could keep his food down though by now he had regained some colour back to his face and even looked to be a little more on the brighter side.

Jacques told him not to go for any seafood but instead to have potatoes and other vegetables without any sauces as that would only make him heave again. Mick kindly thanked him for his advice but told him to stick it up his ass telling Jacques that he was not forgiven for sitting there laughing his head off for six hours watching him vomit over the side of the boat and called Jacques a sick bastard. Fox and I paid no attention to their bickering but laughed at them all the same, after all, they were pals.

We all praised Fox for her cool, calm collectiveness on how she had handled the police situation back on the yacht in her Captain's role.

That night to our delight, we got a text message from Bernie saying to rendezvous at the Marmalade Café in St Helier at around midday the following day. Fox bought a few provisions for onboard the yacht and we all peacefully spent the evening there talking about bygones and later after a few glasses of alcohol out on deck, we all retired to our separate quarters apart from me and Fox.

The next morning we sat out on the deck having a light breakfast while basking in the morning sun along with the fresh gentle breeze that blew across the harbour that was coming in from the west. We kept our vigilance about us, smiling and waving at the fisherman and pleasure yachtsmen coming and going on their boats. We discussed the matter of the diamonds quietly and all present were concerned for Bernie as how he was bringing them onto the island and after long deliberations, it was agreed that Mick would stay with the yacht just in case anyone took too much interest in it.

Jacques was to sit outside the Marmalade Café as a precaution while Fox and I would be seated inside awaiting Bernie's arrival. Jacques decided to make his way on foot to the meeting place, taking in the sights along the way whilst me and Fox took a taxi, arriving ahead of Jacques and seated ourselves away from the window and ordered scrambled eggs with toast, crepes with honey and a pot of tea (hence the light breakfast aboard the yacht earlier), and waited for the Bolt to arrive. It wasn't long before we noticed Jacques taking his position outside; he casually began reading a newspaper and gave his order to a waiter.

We took our time eating our food and ordered another pot of tea playing for time, when to my astonishment, in walked the Bolt dressed in a pink Hawaiian shirt, shorts, Jesus creepers, a baseball cap and wearing yellow-rimmed sunglasses. On noticing us, he smiled and walked proudly towards us. bumping into a table on the way over. I scowled at him and motioned for him to take his sunglasses off as Fox quietly pissed herself laughing at him in his ridiculous clothing.

'Is he for fucking real?' I whispered to her.

'I think it suits him, love,' Fox mused.

'He resembles a piñata,' I told her.

'What you trying to say, Mac, that he sticks out?' she asked.

'Sticks out?! I give up,' I replied shaking my head.

Bernie sat down and summoned a waitress over and ordered a latte with pie and chips, then asked why Jacques looked like he'd seen a ghost.

I said to him, 'Have you looked in the mirror at yourself?'

'Why, what's wrong with me?' Bernie replied feeling his face.

'Your clothes,' I whispered.

'How'd you mean? They're all brand new. I bought them especially for today. Are you jealous or something, Mac?'

'You stick out like a sore thumb, mate,' I told him.

'No, I don't.'

'Yes, you do.'

'No, I don't, it's the fashion,' he stated.

'You're supposed to be casual and not get noticed.'

'As far as I can see, you're the only one taking any notice,' he replied in a huff.

'They could spot you from Mars in that outfit.'

'Who? The little green men?' Bernie jested with two curled fingers.

'Well, they wouldn't abduct you wearing that clobber, you'd scare the little fucks off.'

'He's jealous, Fox.'

'Don't bring me into it,' she told him laughing.

'And for the record, Bolt, I'm not jealous.'

'Yes, you are, because my shirt is better than yours,' Bernie said smugly.

'No, it isn't.'

'I think it is.'

'You think what you like,' I told him.

'And I'll wear what I like too,' he replied smiling at me.

Fox interjected and said, 'Now, now, boys, quit squabbling and stay focused.'

There was a brief silence that ended with Bernie saying that it was nice to see us in such fine spirits and good health, likewise we told him the same then turning the conversation to the diamonds. Bernie sat upright and beamed a huge smile and told us that he had put them all in the false floor in the van which he had parked in the pay and display car park to the rear of the cafe and that he would bring them to the yacht under the cover of darkness to which we agreed was by far the safest way. Suddenly, Jacques came through the door at an alarming pace and as he hastily walked past us, he mouthed 'police' several times to us as he made his way to the gents. I looked towards the direction of the main door and in walked WPC La'Roux from the previous day. She noticed us immediately and made her way towards us, greeting us with a broad smile and in an over-friendly tone said, 'Good afternoon, I take it your friend is feeling better today?'

'Why yes he is, thank you, but he's resting on board,' Fox replied.

'It's a shame the poor man has to go through it all again on the return leg.'

'That has got him a little bothered,' I told the WPC.

'And when will you be returning, Miss Fox-Wright, or is it Captain?' the WPC asked, emphasising the latter.

Fox looked uneasy but calmly replied, 'In a day or two, after we have done a little maintenance onboard, why do you ask?'

'Oh, no particular reason, just making conversation that's all and it's nice to meet new people and have a drink or two in one's free time, if you catch my drift, Captain,' she replied, giving Fox a wink.

Fox produced a warm smile and said, 'If you like, you can leave me your phone number and I'll call you once the maintenance is complete.'

WPC La'Roux's face lit up; producing her notebook, she scribbled her phone number down, tore out the page and handed it to Fox saying, 'Anytime after 8 pm. Enjoy your stay and please call if you need anything as local knowledge is priceless.'

With a saucy expression, Fox took the piece of paper and glanced at it and said, 'After 8 pm it is…Nicola,' emphasizing her first name.

The WPC bade us all a good day then turned on her heel and made her way to the deli counter and bought a pack of sandwiches before she left but just as she was about to exit the café, she glanced over to us, or rather at Fox, and smiled.

'That was the most blatant cheekiest bitch I've ever met,' Fox said angrily.

'Well, you started it off on the yacht, love,' I told her.

'It was supposed to make her feel uncomfortable and put her off guard,' she stated.

'I don't like it, she's on the sniff, I reckon,' Bernie said whilst lowering his sunglasses back down over his eyes.

'Too bloody right she's on the sniff, Bolt, she's sniffing after me,' Fox said riled.

'That's fine, so long as she's not sniffing after the diamonds,' he replied.

'Oh, is it now?' Fox exclaimed.

'Cool it for now and we'll deal with the WPC later, okay love?' I said reassuring her.

'Fucking bitch,' Fox muttered.

'I'm going to the gents to tell Jacques that all is okay and Fox…'

'Yes, Mac?'

'Your face is cherry red,' I told her.

'Oh, that bitch Nicola is so fucking dead!' she whispered.

'Poor cop,' Bernie stated.

I went to the gents and informed Jacques what had just taken place and he too did not like the smell of it but found the scenario between Fox and the WPC highly amusing.

We all left the Marmalade Café making our way back to the yacht. Fox was still furious and took a cold shower whilst Jacques scanned the harbour and surrounding buildings through binoculars from behind the tinted windows of the bridge for any signs of people who may well be watching us whilst me and Mick kept ourselves busy out on deck pretending to do maintenance checks. The Bolt on the other hand had taken a sharp left turn as soon as he was outside the café telling us he's going sightseeing around the island and would not be back till after it was dark. Fox came up to the bridge in her captain's outfit more herself and told Jacques to put the binoculars away as he had the wrong end of the stick and not to be so paranoid as it was her the WPC was after and not anyone else.

Jacques paused for thought smiling momentarily picturing the two of them together then shook himself out of it as Fox glared at him in disgust saying, 'You're are so sick-minded.'

'Sorry,' he confessed and scampered before Fox scrammed his eyes out.

As the afternoon turned to dusk then to darkness, we all felt uncomfortable with the earlier meeting in the café. I had pointed out why had the WPC not asked about the Bolt. But Fox was quick to point out that the WPC was besotted with her, stating only women's intuitional knowledge would know this but she would take care of it when she had thought it through properly.

Jacques and Mick sat in silence looking through the onboard yachting magazines whilst I on the other hand was playing host to them all by serving up line-caught mackerel and salad along with a cold beer, which Fox downed one after another until she became unsteady on her feet, alarming us all but we said nothing of it to her or each other.

I followed her outside and put my arms around her and kissed her on the neck and told her not to let it get to her. She squeezed my arms and told me it was fine but was worried in case the WPC had checked her name out on the police computer and it came back that she had been to prison for fraud and deception. I assured her the WPC had not without her date of birth and address, but Fox said there was something in the WPC's eyes other than love at first sight. I gave her a reassuring hug but said nothing as she gave my arms a gentle squeeze.

Bernie arrived a little past midnight carrying the hold-alls and sweating profusely. He quickly made his way inside placing them on the floor. 'Thank fuck for that,' he said exhausted.

'You should have come and got us,' I told him.

'No point in us all getting collared with these, is there?' he sighed.

'You're a good man, Bolt,' Jacques told him.

'Thanks, mate, but I could do with a cold beer right now,' he said sitting down.

'And rightfully deserved too,' Mick said handing him a bottle from the cooler.

'Cheers, Mick, I didn't know you cared.'

'I don't,' Mick replied joking.

'Where's Fox to?' he asked.

'She was tired and had an early night,' I told him, knowing she was fast asleep from the beers earlier on in the evening.

'Bless her,' he said and necked back the bottle, finishing it with a long ahhhh.

'Did anyone see you along the moorings?' I asked him.

'Nah, they're all sleeping like babies,' Bernie replied.

'Good.'

'Shall I take the bags down and put them in their place?' Jacques suggested.

'Yes, good idea, and Mick, give him a hand, would you?'

'Sure, Mac.'

'Where are you hiding them to?' Bernie asked.

'Jacques unscrewed a panel below that should accommodate them nicely,' I replied.

'I'll crash here for the night if that's okay with you, after I've had another nightcap that is,' he stated.

'Help yourself to the beer, it's in the cooler there.' I told him.

Jacques and Mick returned and helped themselves to another beer to with me reminding everyone to keep the noise down as not to disturb our neighbouring yachtsman and Fox. After I had drank another bottle, I made my excuses and retired for the night, and it felt good to be next to the warmth of Fox's body, she stirred and folded her arms around me. The following morning, we were all sat out on the aft deck having a morning coffee when Mick pointed out WPC La'Roux was approaching us.

This of course infuriated Fox, made Jacques swear, and Bernie growled as he put his sunglasses on while I lit a cigarette and said to Fox, 'Here comes lover girl.'

'I'd love her with a bitch slap!' she replied.

Fox stood up and greeted her with a false smile and said, 'Good morning, WPC La'Roux, would you care to come onboard?'

'Good morning. I will,' she replied already having a foot on the gangplank.

'Can I offer you a drink, coffee perhaps?

'No thank you, I'm fine, I thought I may have missed you.'

'Really! In what way?' Fox asked her suggestively.

'Oh, I just thought you may have left during the night.'

'Well, as you can see, we are very much still here,' Fox replied beaming a smile at her.

'I don't mean to pry, but your name is Melody Fox-Wright, isn't it?'

Alarm bells started ringing all round but Fox as cool as ever said, 'That's right, why do you ask?'

'Oh, no reason, just something came up on my computer but it can't possibly be you, I'm sure,' she said.

Fox seemed to freeze momentarily then said, 'Can't possibly be me what?'

'Just someone with the same name as you has been to prison for fraud and deception, but like I say, it can't possibly be you.'

'I should think not as I am a law-abiding citizen,' Fox replied harshly.

'Would it be too much for me to ask you for your date of birth just as a matter of elimination?' WPC La'Roux asked Fox with a tone of irony in her voice.

'This is very interesting, though I'm horrified that you could possibly imagine I am this person, but yes, you can have my birth details by all means. Why don't I come around to your place tonight after you finish work and bring them with me then?' Fox suggested winking at the WPC and stuck her finger in her mouth playfully.

La'Roux gave Fox a naughty look before she said, 'Yes, I think that would be very kind of you. Shall we say 8 pm and not before?'

Fox nodded slowly at her and said, 'That would be perfect, Nicola; you don't mind me calling you Nicola, do you?'

Blushing a little, she replied, 'So long as none of my colleagues are around.'

'I take it they won't be around tonight?' Fox asked her, raising an eyebrow.

'It will only be me and you, and they don't know I've come down here but like I said, it's just something on my computer,' she informed Fox and blushed again.

'Right then, 8 pm on the nail it is, Nicola,' Fox told her whilst playing with her hair.

'Great, see you later then,' smiling the WPC turned and headed back to shore, stopping to look back over her shoulder at Fox before going on her way again.

As soon as she was out of earshot, Fox cringed and doubled at the middle saying, 'I knew it from that look in her eye, there was more to this.'

'We need to go now,' Mick suggested.

'Maybe they're watching all of us right now as we sit here?' Bernie said.

'I doubt it, otherwise she would not have come alone,' I pointed out.

'That's right, Mac,' Jacques said agreeing with me.

'That bitch has got a screw loose if you ask me,' Bernie said.

'I hope you're not referring to me, Bolt,' Fox snapped at him.

'Now, now, Fox I was on about the copper,' he told her.

'Sorry, Bolt.'

'Apology accepted, mate,' Bernie replied to her.

'Right, let us weigh up the pros and cons here, shall we. 1: The bitch is onto Fox. 2: She's either sure it's Fox and is playing a game, and 3: she's the only one who knows at present which is good for us.'

'I think the bitch is trying to blackmail me into bed using scare tactics,' Fox cried out stamping her foot.

'Well, we have got to come up with some way of stopping her from digging any deeper by 8 pm tonight,' I told them.

'Like what, love?' Fox asked.

'Bernie?'

'Yes, Mac?'

'You take the next ferry back to France.'

'But you need me here.'

'No buts, mate, please, and Mick...'

'Yes?'

'You're going with Bernie.'

'What?' Mick replied astonished.

'Don't question me on this, Mick,' I told him.

'What's the matter, Mick, I cramp your style now, do I?' Bernie said grinning.

'Speak for yourself dressed in that shirt,' Mick replied.

'For fuck's sake, you two, pack it in, this is a serious dilemma Fox is in,' I reminded them.

'And us,' Jacques said, adding another point.

They both fell silent along with the grin on Bernie's face, 'You two leave now. Mick, grab your passport and things, and follow the Bolt.'

'Be quick, Mick, we only got about a three-hour wait till the next ferry,' Bernie said sarcastically but I let it go over my head.

'I'll deal with this bitch tonight on my own,' Fox stated.

'No, Melody, you will not, I will,' Jacques told her in a cold, cold tone.

'When the bloody hell have you ever called me Melody?!' she asked Jacques.

'Now when you are in danger.'

'That's very sweet of you, Jacques, but she is expecting me not you.'

'She won't see or hear me,' he told her.

'Listen, we have a few hours to decide what is best, and love, I don't want you doing anything irrational that you may regret later,' I told her.

Fox snapped back at me, 'What, like £1.5 million of my customer's money?!'

I let Fox's last remark go over my head, saying nothing in my defence as she too had realised herself that she had said the wrong thing, disappearing off the deck and going inside leaving me, Bernie and Jacques alone.

'She'll be okay in a minute, Mac,' Bernie said solemnly.

'More like an hour,' Jacques added.

'I know ... Fuck!' I shouted.

'I want to take care of it, Mac. We've come too far now for a measly WPC to go and fuck it up for us,' Jacques stated.

'We'll work something out after Mick and Bernie have gone, but for now let's try to gather our wits.'

Mick came back with his bag, 'Well, that's me all packed.'

'Good, when we get back, I'll call you to let you know all is okay,' I told him.

'Then it's goodbye for now. Come on, Mick,' Bernie said standing up and after parting handshakes, the two of them strolled off down along the harbour keeping a vigilant eye out as they went.

'I'll go check on Fox.'

'I'll hold the fort here, Mac,' said Jacques.

'Thanks,' I replied.

Fox was laying on the bed staring at the ceiling in deep thought with her hands behind her head with her legs crossed, rocking her feet from side to side rapidly, not even giving me a glance as I entered. I stood there for several minutes in silence looking at her, trying to think what was going through her mind when I asked, 'Penny for your thoughts?'

She spoke quietly, 'Mac...'

'Yes, love?'

'I'm sorry for blurting out that remark.'

'It's fine, don't worry yourself about that, I understand.'

'No, Mac, you don't. It was out of order what I said and not meant.'

I laid next to her and kissed her on the head and said, 'Believe me, love, it's okay.'

She put her arms around me and said, 'What am I going to do about the copper?'

'Well, that's for you, me and Jacques to decide.'

'Bernie and Mick have left already?' she asked.

'Just now, love.'

'No time for goodbyes, eh?'

'You know this situation is going to be difficult for all of us and there are only two options and both have serious consequences, don't they, love?'

'That's what I'm afraid of,' she replied.

'Me too, but we all have to decide which is the best one.'

'If we up anchor and take off now, she'll have customs on our case and they'll rip this yacht apart, Mac.'

'We can't have you in her place as it only takes a hair off your head to fall on the floor for DNA,' I told her.

'This is difficult for us, babe,' she said lowly.

'It's delicate, love, very delicate.'

'She has to be taken care of, Mac, you know that, don't you?' she said remorsefully.

I gave her a gentle squeeze and a kiss but that was all and went back up to Jacques who was sat inside with his back to me with a large glass of scotch whiskey in his hand, staring out through the tinted windows and without turning around he said, 'How is she?'

'She's had better days,' I replied.

'Haven't we all, huh?'

'The only option is to…'

Jacques cut me short saying, 'I take care of the cop bitch as that is the only real option, my friend,' he stated taking a mouthful of his scotch.

'That or up anchor and hope for the best,' I told him.

Jacques took a large gulp of the scotch and said hoarsely, 'No good, Mac, you know that and so does Fox.'

'I know.'

'So tonight I will go ashore and kill her painlessly as I am more used to it than you two and I have demons to fight anyway, so one more will not make a difference to my sleep, I can assure you of that,' he stated.

'Nobody expects you to do anything, Jacques, though I'd rather you stay here taking care of Fox…'

'Mac, you or Fox cannot kill her, it's not in your nature.'

'It's not in yours either but…'

Again, he cut me off, 'I will do it, now tell Fox to stop worrying and you too for that matter.'

Fox came from behind us unexpectedly and walked over to Jacques, taking his glass from his hand, she took a mouthful and handed it back to him looking first at me then at Jacques, she said, 'She's my problem and I don't expect either of you to do my dirty work.'

Jacques spoke assertively, 'I am more efficient in my methods, you would only hesitate and freeze up.'

'Fuck, this is a mess,' I shouted.

'It's my mess,' Fox stated.

'No, it's our mess, and I am going to do it, not you two, but I will need your help to get there, and Fox, you will have to come with me.'

'And me, what do I do?' I asked.

'You make sure the coast is clear and when I'm done with her, we up anchor and get the hell out of here.'

'What have you got in mind?' I asked him eagerly.

We discussed our options when Jacques came up with a plan that would involve us all playing a part, though mine and Fox's would be minor compared to Jacques, but it was as good as murder nonetheless, so with the plan agreed, all we had to do now was sit back and wait till nightfall and then go pay WPC

La'Roux a visit. The time passed slowly as if time itself was killing us as the light of day faded. Jacques was the only person to eat anything and he ate well, like a man condemned and this being his last meal. I watched him as he chewed slowly on every mouthful, savouring the taste, and after he had finished his plate, he went and got a bowl of chocolate ice cream, finishing it all off with an Irish coffee.

Fox paced up and down as did I, smoking cigarette after cigarette, our minds racing until Jacques told us to pack it in and sit down as we were making him on edge and told us to eat something as it would calm us down. As planned, Fox went to a phone box and rang WPC La'Roux, making an excuse that she would be slightly late due to maintenance work which was accepted. Fox got her address, then returned back to the yacht taking a long shower and slipped into a dress tying a scarf loosely around her neck. Jacques took a long shower and shaved, and joined us both looking over the map of the Island on his phone, telling us both what route to take on foot as no taxi was to be used in case of repercussions at a later date as taxi drivers take in everything. I made my way first to check the house and surrounding area, then ten minutes later, Fox was to leave followed closely by Jacques. As I made my way through the streets to the WPC's house, I had this paranoid feeling that every person was looking at me and they knew what I was doing, which gave me an overwhelming feeling to run back and tell Fox and Jacques that everyone knew that we were about to commit a sinister crime but brushed it off and reluctantly continued on my way until I reached the WPC's street.

My mind was doing overtime as my heart pounded faster and faster. I walked up the dimly-lit street past her house and noticed her hall light on inside; I picked up my pace and rounded the corner. I walked back down the street again on the opposite side, doing my best to stay in the dark of the dimly-lit street; having not seen any other persons I turned into a lane just opposite her house and waited in the shadows out of sight. It felt like I was stood there forever as the paranoia graduated with every second that went by, as my heart banged against my chest along with the pounding wrenching of my stomach… I felt sick!

Fox came into view with Jacques trailing a few steps behind her wearing his baseball cap. I left the shadows crossing over the road and as we passed each other, I told them all was quiet. Without stopping, they both continued onwards as I returned back to the shadows of the lane. I glanced at my watch which read 20:17 pm. I watched them as they stopped outside the WPC's house as Jacques stepped to one side of the front door out of sight whilst Fox rang the bell, taking one step backwards away from the door. She waited a few seconds when the WPC's door opened with the inner hallway light radiating outwards, illuminating Fox in an aura of pale light like an angel.

I could make out the brilliant smile on WPC La'Roux's face, full of life and happiness, beckoning Fox to come inside with an outstretched hand, when in a flash Jacques sprang into the light and thrust out his arm with his powerful hand, clamping the WPC around the throat; he crushed the cartilage in her throat then a loud crack echoed in my ears as I watched Jacques push her fallen limp lifeless body back inside the house along with himself, closing the door behind them.

Fox stood there in the darkness motionless, unable to move for a few seconds at first then she took a few steps backwards and started walking away from the house, slowly at first, her pace increasing sometimes half running, sometimes walking. I emerged from the shadows, hastily crossing over the road to meet her. I linked my arm through hers and could feel her whole body shaking violently as her heart pounded through her rib cage. Her face was white with shock, contorted with horror if not traumatized, yet she managed to utter, 'Did you hear her neck break?'

I lied to her replying, 'No.'

'It… It was horrific,' she uttered and then doubled over at the waist and vomited violently.

I managed to get her back to the yacht with Fox heading straight for the bathroom. I fixed myself a large neat scotch with trembling hands and fumbled to light a cigarette, which I inhaled deeply and downed the scotch in one setting, my throat on fire but it brought me back to my senses. Still trembling, I poured another scotch but couldn't get the picture of Jacques so violently breaking the WPC's neck out of my head; it hung there like a dark cloud constantly bursting each time with a crack!! I ran out to the aft deck and vomited over the side when I felt a hand on my shoulder which startled me so much, I almost fell overboard but got yanked backwards. I turned around quickly as Jacques released his grip on me saying, 'Sorry, Mac, I didn't mean to startle you.'

'Fuck! You scared the crap out of me.'

'Sorry,' he replied.

'It's okay, what… what have you done with the body?' I asked.

'You really want the details?'

'No, it's just…'

'Then leave it there. How's Fox?' he asked concerned.

'She's fucked up badly, mate.'

'I'm sorry for her, but we have to leave, like now,' he said regretfully.

'She's in no fit state to go anywhere at the moment,' I told him.

'Mac, listen to me, we have to leave now!' he emphasized.

'Then I'll go start the engines,' Fox said through a shaky voice emerging with a glass of vodka in one hand and a cigarette in her other.

'Fox, I'm sorry, but there was no other way,' Jacques said remorsefully.

'I'm glad you made it back, Jacques,' she told him with tears rolling down her cheek. She took a drag on her cigarette, looked at us both, exhaled the smoke loudly and then went back inside.

'I need a drink, Mac, you want one too?'

'Sure.'

'I'll be inside.'

'I'll join you in a minute,' I told him, lighting up another cigarette thinking of what he had just done and what sort of hell had he been through in the past and how does he handle all this shit or even sleep.

Fox steered the yacht out of the harbour and once we were in more open water, she punched in the coordinates and set the yacht to auto pilot. The three of us sat there saying nothing to each other and when I tried to comfort Fox, she gave me the cold shoulder. Jacques gathered the clothes we had worn bundling them into a sack which he overweighted and tossed them over board and came back inside, continuing to drink the scotch until the bottle was almost empty, then he made his excuses and went to his cabin leaving me and Fox alone together. After an hour of silence had passed, Fox came over and sat next to me throwing her arms around me as she put her head against my shoulder and began sobbing before she broke down crying.

I put my hand on the back of her head and pulled her in tight to my shoulder saying nothing, only comforting her, understanding her horror and torment as I too felt pained, only Fox's far exceeded mine. After what seemed like forever, her crying turned to juddering sobbing and then to small shudders of exhausted weeps as her body eventually gave in until the weeps stopped as her breathing became shallow and rhythmic in the silence that followed, and it wasn't long before she was fast asleep.

I slowly peeled myself away from her, carefully laying her down on the sofa and gently stretched her legs out, placing a cushion underneath her head. I went and got a blanket and placed it over her, kissing her lightly on the cheek and thought how at peace she looked but knew on the inside it was very much a different story for her. I poured myself the last of the scotch and went out on the aft deck in the now chilly sea air to face my demons of the earlier events in the evening, chain smoking and occasionally checking on Fox from time to time who sometimes stirred in her sleep, mumbling muffled words I couldn't make out as her face produced frowns and scowls of anguish, being tormented by the horror of Jacques's murderous hand.

I noticed lights on the horizon in the distance every now and again as we rose up on the crest of a wave, only to be extinguished as the yacht fell back down in a gully of dark water before it rose up again on the crest of the next wave. It would not be long before we were back on the Isle of Wight, I thought to myself finishing my scotch off and throwing the tumbler overboard. I went inside and knelt down in front of Fox, putting my hand on her shoulder and gently shook her saying, 'Wake up, love.'

She opened her eyes, instantly letting out a scream first and then checking her neck. She threw her arms around me yelling, 'It was terrible, Mac! I thought my neck was broken! And that God awful crack!!'

'It's okay, love. It's okay, you're fine, I'm here,' I told her.

Jacques came rushing to us, 'What's happened?'

With a sullen look on my face and cradling Fox, I said, 'I woke her up, we're nearing the Isle of Wight.'

'I thought…'

'I know, best you get dressed,' I told him.

'Okay, will do,' he replied and disappeared.

'Fox love, you have to steer us in, we're close, I can see lights,' I told her.

'Give me a few minutes to sort my head out, will you?'

'Sure, take as long as you like. Would you like a coffee?' I asked her.

'Yes, thank you, that'll be good,' she replied rising to her feet.

She smoked a cigarette as swiftly as she drank the coffee and went up to the bridge, taking another coffee with her, and took over from auto, manually steering the yacht into the marina and its moorings. We stayed onboard for the rest of the night until morning when we went ashore, leaving the diamonds on board in case we got stopped with them. We let the marina get a little busier then at around noon, we went back and retrieved the hold-alls, staying vigilant as we made our way back to the car, placing the hold-alls in the boot and headed for the ferry port with me behind the wheel.

We disembarked back in Southampton, and Fox called Izzy Omerta to let her know that we were all safely back and to which she marvelled as she got to see Jacques again, but we were all in agreement to leave out the gruesome details of WPC La'Roux's death but asked Izzy to give Alter a call and ask him to come see us as soon as we were back in London.

Chapter 12

Two Deaths Don't Make a Right?

We arrived in Kensington early in the afternoon and were greeted by Izzy, who was more than pleased to see us, especially Jacques who she gave a long hug and kiss while Fox and I promptly took the hold-alls from the boot and took them inside promptly, closely followed Izzy and Jacques. Izzy informed us that Alter would be calling later this evening as he was temporarily indisposed with business but sent his regards and asked his forgiveness for not being able to meet us straight away.

I contacted Bernie and Mick, letting them know that the diamonds were safe along with us, to which Bernie let out a big sigh of relief but wanted know how things had gone back in St Helier. I told him now was not the right time and didn't think there ever would be. Bernie fell silent for a few seconds but then said it was best that we left it there, to which I told him that would be best for all and would keep him updated with things here as and when they happened. Alter called before he arrived, telling us that he would be no more than 30 minutes but arrived an hour later full of apologies and smiles but was frustrated that he had to amble up a long flight of stairs to Izzy's apartment with his foot.

I persuaded Alter to climb on my back and gave him a piggy back up the staircase which amused him immensely, stating the last time he had a piggy back was from his father many, many years ago when he was a child.

I put him down at the top and watched him hobble into the lounge where the others greeted him warmly, especially Fox who again he referred to as an angel sent by the heavens and for once Fox didn't say anything, only giving him a quick smile.

'Have you got the diamonds with you?' he asked whilst sitting himself down.

'Yes, we do,' I replied.

Alter's eyes widened. 'Would be so kind as to show your old friend what they look like?'

'Jacques, would you do the honours?' I asked him.

'Of course,' he answered.

'Izzy love, can we borrow that table over there,' I asked pointing to an oblong table against the wall.

'Why yes, but be careful, it's antique, 17th century,' she replied.

I took the two vases off the table and placed the table in front of Alter, who at first seemed a little bewildered until I told him, 'It's for the diamonds so you can look at them properly.'

'Oh, I see, good thinking,' he replied chuckling.

Jacques placed two of the bags on top of the table and said, 'You're going to like this lot, Alter.'

Alter looked up at Jacques beaming and said, 'I think you're right, Mr Jacques.'

'Jacques is my forename, Alter,' Jacques informed him.

Alter looked at Jacques with deep embarrassment and said, 'Forgive me please.'

'It's okay, Alter, it was a simple assumption,' Jacques told him.

'Ladies and gentlemen, let's see what wonders you have brought me,' he said unzipping the hold-all. Alter slowly peeked inside, licking his lips then he let out a long sigh of relief and lifted out a hand full of diamond necklaces, saying to himself, *Yes, yes, you're pretty, look how you sparkle in the light, just how I imagined you to be.* Fox started giggling first followed by us.

'Fuck me!' Izzy said in astonishment looking at all the diamonds.

A little concerned with his behaviour, I asked, 'Is everything okay with you, Alter?'

Looking at up at me with an expression of marvel on his face like a kid in a toy shop, he replied, 'Why everything is fine with me, these beauties are better than I had expected.'

'So you're happy then?' Jacques implored.

'Yes indeed, Jacques,' he chuckled.

I went over and got the other hold-alls and placed them on the table in front of him and said, 'Now you're six times as happy, Alter,' and sat back down again giggling.

Clasping his hands together with delight, he replied in a fit of giggles, 'You're too kind, my lovelies, just too kind,' he repeated.

'So you more than happy, I take it?

'My dear Mac, I'm over the moon,' he exclaimed, falling back in his chair, chuckling like mad, which sparked us all off laughing with him but more so at his odd behaviour.

Alter continued in his bizarre manner with his eyepiece lodged in his eye socket which kept us highly amused as he looked through all the hold-alls containing the diamonds, smiling, giggling and mumbling to himself in Yiddish, forgetting that we were even there in the room with him.

A full two hours passed by before the scenario ended when Alter said that he was exhausted and his eye ached from his eyepiece; he rubbed his right eye smiling at us all saying, 'Well, you have quite a fancy collection, my friends, to say the least, and I see no problem for me in helping you.'

'So you're definitely happy with what you have seen?' I asked him.

Alter let out a little giggle, 'My dear Mac, do I look disappointed?'

'No, not at all,' I replied smiling at him.

'Then stop worrying, my friend, all is good if not better for us all,' he replied chuckling again.

'So what's our next move?'

Alter sat upright and cleared his throat and spoke firmly, 'I will arrange for these bags to be picked up by my chauffer and when this loot has been turned into cash, we can all live happily ever after.'

'How long will it take?' Jacques asked anxiously.

Alter raised his eyebrows and paused before he replied saying, 'It should take no more than, ooh, let's say a few days, just so people can lay their hands on good cash unless you can have it transferred to an account which would be wiser for all concerned.'

'I can't argue with that, Alter,' Jacques told him.

'Do you have an offshore account where the money can be sent to?' Alter asked.

'Yes, I do,' I replied.

'Then it will be wise for me to have it wired to you,' he said smiling.

I looked at Jacques and Fox who nodded in unison. 'That'll be fine,' I replied.

'Good. I never liked carrying large sums of money around, it always made me feel vulnerable.'

'We understand, Alter,' I replied grinning.

'Thank you for being so understanding, now if you will excuse me, I have further business to take care of that will be of benefit to us all,' Alter stated rising to his feet.

We all stood up and shook hands except for Fox and Isobelle, who gave Alter a kiss on his cheeks. Alter climbed on my back again as to aid him down the stairs, letting out the odd chuckle on the way back down the staircase. His chauffer immediately got out of the car and opened the rear door ready for him but before he got inside, Alter told us he would be in touch in good time. He said Shalom which I repeated back and watched him slowly limp to the car.

The chauffer closed his door and the rear window came down and as the car pulled off, Alter gave us a smiling wave and was gone.

Back upstairs, the celebrations had already begun as Izzy had popped open a bottle of bubbly and quickly handed me a glass, which I readily accepted and downed in one. I sat next to Fox who only sipped her glass, setting it to one side whilst Jacques and Izzy were all over each other.

The celebrations soon died down when Izzy suggested we all go out, but Fox was quick to answer her, saying she had a pain in her stomach and didn't feel up to it but for us three to go ahead; even though Izzy tried her hardest to get her to come, Fox was adamant, insisting she would only dampen the evening.

Jacques shot me a look as we both knew what was really troubling her so I told her I would stay too, but again she insisted that I go with them which I did reluctantly and after spending forty odd minutes in their company, I made an excuse telling them I had business to take care of. Jacques gave me a wink whilst Izzy gave me a sorrowful pout of her lips but let me go anyway. Once outside, I hailed a taxi only to get out a few blocks away from the house in Kensington. Finding a bar, I downed a few shots from the top shelf, all the time my thoughts were with Fox when her reality became my reality as the alcohol made an impact on my thoughts, leading me to relive the events of what happened to the WPC. A cold shudder ran down my spine so I ordered another Bacardi with the bar tender telling me to slow down, but I couldn't.

I left the bar some two hours later, making my way back to Fox, smoking as I walked. I took out my phone and rang her; she sent me a busy tone which rocked me then a minute later, I got a text message saying: "I'm here, will see you when you get back". I picked up my pace and quickly made my way back to her and when she opened the door, I could tell she had been crying. She threw her arms around my neck and squeezed me tight then releasing her grip, she took hold of my hand and closed the door, shutting the whole world out except WPC La'Roux and the sound of her neck breaking!

The next morning, Jacques made a phone call to Robbie's wife and through a mass of tears, she told him Robbie had a massive brain haemorrhage at around 8:25 pm two nights ago and died. The news devastated us all but left Jacques inconsolable. Later when we were alone, he pointed out that Robbie had died around the same time as WPC La'Roux did, which sent a shiver down my spine again, just as the lights in the house rapidly flickered on and off, adding an eerie atmosphere to the already strange coincidence.

This initially freaked us out so we left the comforts of the house, finding solitude in a nearby bar away from Fox and Izzy, downing a lot of Bacardi in silence until Jacques broke it, 'This is too much.'

'What is?'

'That fucking WPC and Robbie and the lights,' he whispered.

'It's just coincidence and bad timing.'

'Maybe, maybe not?' he replied.

'It was uncanny, yes, but that's about it, Jacques.'

'Still, it'll bother me more than you,' he said.

'Then do your best not to associate them,' I told him.

'Yeah right!'

'Fancy another drink?'

'That's a silly question to ask a guy in mourning, mate,' he reminded me.

'Sorry, mate,' I replied remorsefully.

We were still sat in the bar when Fox phoned me saying that Alter's chauffer was at the house to collect the diamonds. I told her to let him take them and assured her Jacques was coping with the bad news as best he could and gave her our location if she and Izzy fancied joining us, but Jacques blurted out 'bad idea,' so with Fox overhearing this remark, understandably she told me to keep an eye on him and to call her later if I needed to.

I told him Fox had overheard him to which he apologised and suggested we find another bar, which we did and continued knocking back the Bacardi and cokes until Jacques said he'd had enough and wanted to sleep. I suggested we get a cab back to Izzy's place, only for him to say that he was going to book into a hotel somewhere but for me to go on back without him. I refused telling him I would take him to a hotel and then go back as he was unsteady on his feet and after much disagreement, he finally gave in and we found a place nearby where

I helped him up to his hotel room, opened the door for him and watched as he made for the bed and fell on top of it with him telling me to leave him… I closed the door behind me.

I called Fox and told her what Jacques had done though this panicked her. I assured her that he would be okay and said I was getting a taxi back to the house.

Izzy was in a state when I got there, wanting to know where he was but I suggested that she leave him for now and to expect a late knock on her door sometime in the early hours from him, which she did at around 2 am from him. Izzy answered and I could faintly hear Jacques apologising to her as they passed by our bedroom door, though Fox was very much fast asleep. I was being kept awake by all the recent events. I wondered how Alter was doing with the diamonds as it was a lot of loot to let out of one's sight but waved any immoral thoughts away eventually falling off to sleep.

Alter phoned in the early afternoon the next day asking me for the offshore account details which I readily gave him and two hours later, he phoned again telling me that a large deposit had just been made into it; when I asked how much, he paused and told me £1,200,000, and to check the account for myself, reminding me more would follow in due course. I couldn't thank him enough, but Alter just beat back the appraisal, telling me to go and have a good lunch with my friends.

When I told the others, they were over the moon with joy, even Jacques perked up suggesting we all go celebrate which we did of course. We dined in style, naturally regretting Bernie and Mick weren't there to enjoy the spoils with us. I phoned Bernie and told him we were on a roll and to inform Mick of the sum deposited. Bernie said they were going to celebrate too and the line went dead.

I told the others of their reaction with Bernie cutting the call short, which we all laughed at while Jacques on the other hand was anxious to get some money up to Robbie's family.

I told him that would be fine but not to race ahead and wait till we had the final sum in, then give it to Robbie's family rather than a bit here and there, as they would appreciate it a whole lot more. Understanding this made sense, he agreed and ordered another bottle of champagne and again we toasted to his buddy and our departed friend Robbie Duggan. 40 minutes later, we got a distressed call from Alter saying that he had some very upsetting news for us and that he was on his way to Isobelle's. I immediately hailed the waiter asking for the bill pronto, causing confusion amongst us but told them there was no time for explanations, that we had to leave this instant. I informed them that something had gone wrong but did not know what exactly.

Jacques sensing another loss rose so fast from the table, he almost turned it over, sending the plates and glasses upon it crashing to the floor, the whites of his eyes turning a cold red, the veins in his right temple popped to the surface of his head with a look of ultimate rage written all over his face.

With fists clenched, his knuckles white, Jacques stormed out of the restaurant not even apologising for the mess on the floor. To top it all off, he pulled the front door open with such force that it hit the internal wall, shattering the plate glass window in it, leaving everyone in the establishment totally stunned and quite panic-stricken! Izzy took care of everything, begging the owner not to call the police, excusing Jacques for his behaviour, telling the owner he just found out his wife had died.

Izzy immediately offered to pay for all the damage, handing him her credit card; she told him to charge £1,000 from it and if the damage should cost any more to repair, to call her. The owner, naturally irate and cussing unhappily, accepted Izzy's offer, leaving us to make a rapid exit and catch up with Jacques who was stood outside one hand on hip scratching his head then grasping the back of his neck when some idiot in a pin-striped suit holding a briefcase walking past noticing his irate state, sarcastically said to him, 'Have a nice day.' Jacques arm shot out like a bolt of lightning, his fist clenched, catching the man square on in the side of the face. The blow was well struck to say the least, it lifted the poor guy off his feet, sending him gliding through the air until he came crashing back down on the pavement all of seven feet away in a twisted pile of body mass knocked out cold with Jacques shouting at him, 'You too, fuckwit!'

'Come on, let's go,' I told him panicking.

'Like run?' he asked.

'If you like, yes, so long as it gets you out of here,' I urged him.

'Jacques,' Izzy called.

'What!'

'I love you,' Izzy said.

'Really?' he replied smiling.

'Yes, darling,' she replied, linking her arm through his proudly.

'Yo, taxi!' I yelled.

A taxi cab pulled up alongside the curb and we all climbed in rapidly. The cab driver asked who the guy in the pin-striped suit was on the floor to which Jacques replied, 'Who, the tramp?'

Alter arrived looking dishevelled and as pale as a ghost and highly distraught. He glanced around the room at each of us in turn sorrowfully, almost ashamed, before he spoke to us in a quiet, almost dehydrated voice, 'Please, my friends, be seated. I have some very unfortunate news to tell you that you will not like.'

Jacques said still standing and raging said, 'Regarding the diamonds?'

'Please, Jacques, for all of us, be seated.'

'Jacques, do as Alter here asks,' I told him.

We all sat down staring at Alter who sat in a winged chair opposite us. He remained silent for some time, his head bowed then he looked up at us, raised his hands and began telling us of the unfortunate events that had occurred a few hours earlier with a few of his friends and associates that had left two badly beaten and one killed by a gang of robbers whilst closing the deal on the remaining diamonds. Alter's eyes started to fill up and modestly continued taking out his handkerchief, saying the door burst open and five burley looking guys wearing ski masks yielding baseball bats and hand guns demanded the diamonds and the cash used to buy the gems.

The diamonds were in open view of the robbers, as for the money they were told it was to be wired to accounts and that it simply wasn't there, but the robbers were having none of it. They were convinced it was stashed in the room somewhere or that someone waiting outside had the cash. After gagging everyone, they took their bats to two of the Jews' kneecaps; with no result, the robbers took a cushion, placed it over a Jew's face and shot him, spraying his brains all over the wall behind.

The tears were rolling down Alter's face as he told his story to us. Eventually the robbers fled with the diamonds, realising that was all they were going to get, only after they had ransacked the premises first. It was only then that Alter told us that the man they shot in the face was his beloved cousin, married with four children with another unborn child on the way.

Fox went over to Alter, sat at his side putting her arms around him to comfort him for his loss, to which he put his head into her bosom and wept uncontrollably, crying out in Hebrew. Fox pulled Alter in closer to him, cradling his head as the tears flowed down her cheeks along with Izzy's tears, who cried uncontrollably. Jacques put a consoling arm around Izzy and looked at me with cold menace in his eyes. We eyed each other intently, not needing to say a word as we both knew exactly what the other was thinking. I nodded to his intended justice and Jacques gave me a nod back in my acceptance of justice. The bulb in the wall lamp flickered hastily, went out for a second then burst into light again.

Chapter 13

Bootsie Burns and Major Barron

We left our girls to take care of Alter after having a word with Izzy to make a precious phone call to her friends in the underworld in the East End of London, Izzy arrange a meeting for us both in boozer called The Leg & Gartering Whitechapel. The taxi stopped outside The Leg & Garter and the driver asked us, 'Are you two sure you want to go in there?'

'Yes, why do you ask?'

'Just this boozer isn't for tourists, mate, if you get my drift.'

'And what makes you think we're tourists?' Jacques asked the driver.

The taxi driver was silent as he eyed us both in his rear-view mirror before he spoke, 'My deepest apologies, gentlemen. That'll be twenty-eight quid of your finest.'

I handed the driver £30 and said, 'Keep the change.'

'That's very generous of you, sir,' He replied and sped off.

The boozer was an old corner establishment that had aged with time, its black paint flaking on its wooden window frames as well as the split wooden doors being just as untidy and in need of a lick of paint, yet the pub sign that hung off the wall above the doorway displaying a seated woman's bare leg with a black garter half way up her thigh was pristinely painted to a high gloss finish. The doors were closed with the curtains drawn across the windows – quite unexpected for that early in the evening. I knocked on the door anyway and heard the bolt being drawn back and the locks turning, then one of the split doors opened and a small round pale face appeared with short cropped black hair with little piercing eyes and a smudged nose. His head looked too small for the rest of his broad five-foot five frame, dressed in a pristine black suit, white shirt and blue tie with a look of trouble written all over his face yet diversely he looked harmless. He spoke in his mother tongue, the strong cockney accent in all its flair.

'Ya Izzy's mates, lads?'

'Yes, that's right,' I answered.

'Well... don't keep the Guvna' waiting then,' he said and stepped aside from the door.

'Cheers, Dave,' Jacques said on entering with me in toe.

Puzzled, the cockney put his arm out, blocking Jacques from going any further and said, 'Er...sunshine, hold up a minute.'

'What?' Jacques replied, looking down at him.

'Do I know ya, sunshine, 'coz as far as I can fackin' rememba', I ain't never seen ya before in my life and now I'm wondering how the fack do ya know my name's Dave?'

'Guesswork.'

'So now ya guessing like a fackin' coppa then, are ya, sunshine? Ya fucking old bill, sunshine? Ere, Guvna', this cunt's old fackin' bill in disguise,' he said through gritted teeth and whipped out a handgun from inside his suit jacket and pointed it at us.

Jacques moved instinctively, grabbing the gun and bending the guy's wrist back almost to his forearm, taking the gun from him. Jacques instantly snapped the guy's leg putting his foot through the side of the cockney's knee and yanked him upwards in the air, using him like a shield aiming the gun in front of him as the cockney screamed out in agony, 'He broke my fackin' leg! He broke my fackin' leg!!'

Jacques ordered me to get behind him which I did instantly saying, 'What the fuck are you doing?'

Jacques threw me a look of disbelief and said, 'Self-defence, mate.'

A voice from inside the dark called out, 'Enough of this! Put your weapons away, lads. You too, my friends, and let poor Dave go for fuck's sake.'

Jacques did as he was asked and let poor Dave drop to the floor causing him to scream out in even more pain. I asked Jacques, 'Was that necessary with Dave?'

'Yes,' he replied.

I asked, 'You're not over-reacting just a little?'

'No! Not on the grounds that little fucker Dave had a gun, so instinct took over me.'

'Are you okay now?'

'I'm cool, Mac, it's under control here, trust me.'

'I'm trying.'

'You said that like you were getting hitched.'

'What? All romantic like?'

'Save it for Fox.'

'Of course,' I replied, scratching my clueless head.

'Good then, relax!!'

The lights came on at the far end of the bar showing four big guys and another figure sat at a table, a little on the thinner side, very rugged looking with a scar down his left cheek smiling at us with a fat cigar wedged in the side of his mouth.

'Quite an entrance you just made, is that fucking normal?' he asked.

'Only when a fool tries to pull a gun on me,' Jacques replied.

'Dave 2?'

'Yes, Guv.'

'Fix Dave 1. His fucking whining is giving me a headache!' instructed the man with the scar down his face.

'Fix him fix him, Guv?' Dave 2 asked.

'Do I 'ave to fucking repeat myself!'

'No, Guv,' replied Dave 2, who walked over to Dave 1 on the floor, looked down at him and said, 'Sorry, Dave,' pulled out a pistol and shot him twice in the chest!

'Now that's better, I can 'ere myself fink,' Scarface said, blowing out a huge puff of smoke from his cigar.

The scar-faced man began speaking when Dave 1 on the floor in a pool of blood began to move and moan.

'Shall I fix him for you, gentlemen?' Jacques asked.

Scarface shrugged saying, 'He's all yours.'

Jacques walked over and without hesitation put a bullet between his eyes adding, 'Sweet dreams, Dave 1.'

'Fuck me, you get better by the minute, sunshine, come on over 'ere 'n take a lion's lair,' Scarface jested with a wave of his hand.

'What's a lion's lair?' I asked puzzled.

'Fuck me! A fucking chair!!' he gloated out along through a cloud of cigar smoke.

We sat down in the two chairs opposite Scarface at the large table and after introducing ourselves, the Guvna' introduced himself as Bootsie Burns, whose reputation was notorious for putting people's feet in oversized Wellington boots, filling them to the top with concrete, dowsing them in petrol and setting them on fire!! On the other hand, he knew a thing or two, and had the greatest respect for Izzy who gave him an alibi some years back that saved him from a lengthy 18 years stretch in Wormwood Scrubs, so it was not hard to understand why Bootsie would drop and do anything for Izzy in an instant.

The first thing Bootsie wanted was for Jacques to join his gang but diplomatically, Jacques declined. Bootsie looked at Jacques in disbelief for a few seconds, frowning deeply, too deep for my liking (as I pictured the two of us screaming in burning agony in concrete Wellingtons) then Bootsie's face relaxed saying to give it some thought.

I explained the situation regarding the diamonds along with poor Alter's cousin being shot so mercilessly, to which Bootsie agreed saying it was terrible to shoot a man like that (really heartfelt coming from a man who sets people on fire up to their shins in concrete!) and knowing it was one of Izzy's closest friends only angered Bootsie all the more!! He looked at us both in turn with a fixed smile upon his face while his henchmen remained standing close, keeping a vigilant eye upon us yet giving us enough space to breathe.

I looked at the scar embedded on the left side of Bootsie Burns' face that ran from just above his eyebrow down his left cheek, curving past his lips and finishing in the middle of his chin. The scar was old and it had aged well with him – ugly, I thought to myself. Oddly, in some vile way, it enhanced Bootsie's character and deprivation. Bootsie silently transfixed his gaze on Jacques, his smile disappearing momentarily before it returned. Bootsie leaned forward over the table and extended his arm with an open palm and said, 'The gun.'

'Sure,' Jacques replied, releasing the clip from the butt of the gun, putting it on the table then stripped the gun down into several parts and placed them all in Bootsie's palm.

This scenario amused Bootsie who let out a faint giggle as he placed the gun parts down on the table and relaxed back in his chair, puffing away on his fat cigar blowing the smoke directly at us as a mere taunt at us both that he was in control here. Jacques waved a hand through his smoke to rid it of its nuisance which I followed suit, waving it out of my face too.

Bootsie's grin broadened at our dislike for his rude taunt before he said in his cockney mother tongue, 'I've 'eard a whispa' in the grapevine that the bunch of cunts that shot the Jew are now in possession of a quantity of diamonds that has got a lot of people's attention!'

'News travels fast,' I stated.

'Every bent fucking in the East End is interested in your diamonds, including me, but my interests have been diverted due to Izzy's involvement. Now, these cunts you're dealing with are no fucking mugs. They are of Eastern European countries, dealing in arms, drugs and prostitution! They don't give a flying fuck who they kill so long as they get what they want. They have substantial fire power and the balls to use it to great effect, being more kamikaze than a fucking kamikaze don't-give-a-fuck cunt.'

'Do you know where they are?' I asked.

'It just so happens they are locked away in a warehouse in the Isle of Dogs partying like fuck on your misfortunes, probably off their fucking heads on crack, sweets and anything else they can get down their filthy fucking necks.'

'Can you take me to the warehouse now?' Jacques asked.

'Larry?'

'Yes, Guv?' one of the henchmen replied.

'Bring the motor to the front for us. And put poor Dave 1 there in the boot too and find something to weigh the fucker down.'

'Yes, Guv.'

'George?'

'Yes, Guv?'

'Give Larry a hand and then clean Dave 1's fucking sauce up on the floor.'

'Yes, Guv.'

Once Larry and George had finished mopping the sauce/blood up on the floor, they put Dave 1 in the boot of the car along with a few heavy objects. Bootsie stubbed his cigar out on the table and walked to the front door of the boozer, turning around he said to me and Jacques, 'What are you two waiting for, a fucking invite?!'

We followed Bootsie and the remainder of his henchmen outside to the waiting cars, two silver Mercedes Benz with Larry behind the wheel. George opened the rear door for Bootsie; George was about to get in the back when Bootsie in a tone of remorse said to him, 'No, no! Not you, you docile twat! Get in the other car and follow us or you'll be joining Dave 1 in the boot!'

'Err… Right, Guv.'

'Too fucking right I'm right, now fuck off!!'

George as big as he was fucked off hastily. Bootsie gave us the nod to get in the car so Jacques sat in the front seat leaving me to sit in the back with Bootsie, which I didn't feel too happy about but all the same I got in beside him. The journey to the Isle of Dogs was shorter than I expected. Bootsie told Larry to drive to where the old mills used to be and pull up close to the Thames. Larry did as he was told, eventually driving down a pot-ridden road close to the embankment when Bootsie told him to stop the car and get rid of Dave 1.

Larry was still sat in the driver's seat when Bootsie flicked his ear and said, 'What the fuck are you waiting for, get out and give that big fucking numpty George a hand with Dave 1.'

'Yes, Guv,' Larry replied bolting out the car.

'Fucking idiots sometimes them boys, but they'll do anything I ask,' he stated proudly.

'Is the warehouse near here?' Jacques asked.

'Fuck sake, let's get rid of Dave 1 first, shall we?'

'Naturally,' I said in agreement but noticed Jacques scowling in the car's rear-view mirror.

There came a knock on the car window; it was George looking rather sullen. Bootsie pressed the button for the electric window but nothing happened so he opened the door and said, 'Is he gone?'

'Um, not yet, Guv.'

'Why the fuck not!'

'The tide's low, Guv, and there's at least forty feet of mud before we can put him in the water.'

'Well improvise, you silly bastards, and drag the poor fucker in!'

'But we might get stuck, Guv.'

Bootsie pulled a knife out from inside his suit jacket and pointed it at George saying, 'You pair will be fucking stuck in a minute with this nine-inch blade up your asses if you don't fucking 'urry up and get rid of Dave 1!!!'

George and Larry dragged Dave 1 under his arms through the dirt to the edge of the embankment and paused for a few seconds, shrugging their shoulders at each other before they both picked Dave 1 up by his arms and legs and threw him over the side. George and Larry shrugged their shoulders a few times at each other again then jumped over the side, vanishing out of sight. Bootsie lit up a cigar. I asked Bootsie if it was okay for me to smoke, to which he said yes but warned me not to drop any cigarette ash on the carpet or interior. I put my cigarettes back in my pocket rapidly.

In the 15 minutes that elapsed with Bootsie cursing George and Larry for taking too long to get rid of Dave 1's body, they suddenly reappeared caked in mud from head to toe. Jacques pissed himself laughing like me but Bootsie who was preoccupied with his own thoughts, hadn't noticed what was walking towards him when Bootsie said to us, ''Ere, you two! What's so fucking funny?'

'Take a look at the state of those two salamanders,' Jacques said.

'Sala what?' Bootsie replied puzzled.

'George and Larry,' I informed him with a nod of my head in their direction.

Bootsie turned his head in the direction of George and Larry and shook his head. 'What a fucking pair of pricks, just like pigs in shit, in they?' he gasped and asked them both, 'What the fuck have you two been up to, to get it that fucking state?'

'Larry got stuck in the mud and I…'

Bootsie leapt out the car waving his knife in the air at the pair of them, who had stopped in their tracks with just the whites of their eyes the only visible human parts of their body, looked at each other then back at Bootsie, who screamed at them, 'My fucking Nana who's got Alzheimer's could have dumped Dave and found her way back here in less fucking time than you pricks! And if you think you're getting in any of these cars in that fucking mess…fucking think again! Now, lose the fucking rags and get in the fucking car or I'll cut the fucking balls off the pair of you!!'

'Yes, Guv,' came both their replies.

Bootsie settled himself back inside the car and straightened his already straight tie and puffed on his cigar, mumbling under his breath between each puff. I lit up a cigarette, only this time I didn't ask Bootsie who didn't seem to mind, but reminded me to watch the cigarette ash on the carpet and interior. Larry who had stripped himself of his shoes, trousers and jacket was about to get in the car when Bootsie told him to lose all his clothing including his underpants; Larry tried to protest but Bootsie was having none of it, shouting a torrent of abuse at him. Reluctantly, Larry stripped bollock-naked and got in behind the wheel with instructions from his Guvna' to take us to the warehouse where the Eastern Europeans were holed up.

Larry drove fifty meters along the embankment around the first corner and stopped the car.

'Do you see that old building in front with the big wooden doors?' Bootsie pointed out.

'The double doors with the partially blacked out windows above?'

'That's where they are on the whole top floor,' Bootsie added.

'How many of them inside, do you reckon?' I asked him.

'Fuck knows! Ten to fifteen, maybe more?'

'Can you get your hands on any C4 or anything that goes bang?'

'You'll have to see Major Barron for that stuff,' Bootsie replied grinning.

'Who's Major Barron?' I asked out of curiosity.

'Ex-army chap that does a bit on the side, likes his guns, explosives too. He'll have what you need or something better.'

'When can we see this Major Barron?'

'Larry.'

'Yes, Guv?'

'Take us to the Major's house.'

'Yes, Guv.'

It turned out Major Barron was a little cautious at first, wanting nothing to do with me or Jacques but was more than ready to see Bootsie on his own.

'Now, now, Major, there's no need to fret, these are good lads,' Bootsie told him via the intercom.

'So say you, Bootsie. Anyway, what do they want?'

'They need your help…'

'I'm not in the mood for helping.'

'These lads have troubles with crackheads,' Bootsie stated.

'Why didn't you say so in the first place, Bootsie?' the Major replied.

'He hates crackheads. They mugged his old drinking pal. Gave him a fucking heart attack, died on the spot, the poor bastard,' Bootsie regretfully informed us.

'So he don't like crackheads then?' Jacques asked.

'Fucking 'ates 'em with a vengeance.'

'I do too.'

'Don't we fucking all!'

There was a buzzing sound and Bootsie pushed the door open saying, 'Welcome to Pandora's Box. Close the door behind you,' and led the way in.

'Why is it so dark?' I asked.

''Cos the Major is checking you out, isn't he?!'

'Where…? I can't see a damn thing!'

'Trust me, he can see us!'

'What's he looking for?' Jacques whispered.

'Guns, knives and the like, also he's scanning our brain patterns just to be on the safe side to make sure we're not aggressive.'

'So if your brain patterns don't fit, then you're not coming in?' I joked.

'More like if they don't fit, he'll kill you on the spot,' Bootsie whispered back.

'Okay, gentlemen, take a few steps forward if you please,' came the Major's tinny voice through a speaker from somewhere in the hallway.

We shuffled a few paces forward in the darkness when the Major told us to stop.

'Lose the knife in your left inside jacket pocket, Boostie.'

'Sorry, Major, forgot I had it on me.'

There came a loud metallic slam from behind us and a second later, the hall was illuminated; a large steel door behind us had sealed us in the wide hallway. Another door was in front of us.

'Open the door and wait for me in the study. Do make yourselves comfortable, gentlemen,' said the Major's tinny voice.

'And Bootsie?'

Sarcastically, Bootsie asked, 'What now, Major?'

'Put the knife on the shelf to your left or you'll get a bullet in your thick skull.'

'Alright, alright, it's on the shelf.'

'You may now proceed.'

'Thank you, Major,' Bootsie replied sarcastically again.

Bootsie pulled the door open and led us into the study, and it was obvious that he'd been through this scenario before. Entering the study, the wooden panelled walls were lined with built-in shelves that were filled with volumes of books from floor to ceiling. Another wall was dedicated to pictures hanging here and there, dissipating heroic scenes of various battles throughout the centuries. Military memorabilia was scattered around the study, from swords, flintlock guns and little bronze figurines. The air that filled the room was old with a tinge of dampness, as if unaired for quite some time, and the fireplace looked like it hadn't given warmth to the room in ages with its ashes un-kindled.

The heavy red velvet curtains that hung to the floor were partially opened letting in enough light to be noticed. And the net curtains behind looked to have seen better days and were now an off-white shade with a moth hole appearing in the centre, allowing a welcomed dot of light on the wooden panelled wall. A church bell faintly chimed off in the distance. Sitting there I noticed a particular picture of a handsome young man standing proudly dressed in combat camouflage in a plush jungle, holding his Bren gun in one hand across to his chest with an Alsatian sat at his side.

A small silver plaque fixed to the bottom of the frame was engraved with the words: *Malaya May 1954 "Raja" SAS Detachment.*

'Sorry to have kept you waiting, gentlemen,' came an ardent voice from behind us.

'Ah, Major Barron, always a pleasure,' Bootsie replied with a broad grin.

'Hardly any pleasure when you are involved in something, Bootsie. Now get to the point, man, I haven't got all day!' said the Major striding over to the fireplace, taking an at-ease stance.

'My friends...' Bootsie started to say.

'Ah yes. I almost forgot,' interrupted the Major continuing, 'Who the devil are they?' the Major asked, raising himself up on his toes then settling back down again on his heels while looking at me and Jacques piercingly.

'I'm Jacques.'

'I'm Mac.'

The Major winced and asked, 'How may I be of service to you, hmm?!'

'Bootsie recommended your services, sir,' Jacques replied.

'Ah, a gentleman with manners, I note, unlike Bootsie here.'

'I got manners, Major, just me mum's not around anymore to remind me of them.'

'Maybe I should clip you round the ear for her as a reminder of all her efforts!' replied the Major sharply.

Surprisingly, Bootsie made no reply and shot the Major a cautious look but the Major took no notice; instead, he turned to look at himself in the mirror that hung above the fireplace and twirled the ends of his walrus moustache then quickly checked his teeth before turning around setting back his once broad shoulders of his five-foot eight frame. His face was long to the neat jaw, his blue eyes bore the trademark of life while his hair had thinned with time yet he dressed immaculately, from his well-ironed blue and white pin-striped shirt open at the neck displaying an immaculate white cravat with both cuffs fastened with a pair of silver crossed Gurkha knives, down to the starched creases in his brown trousers to his black polished Oxford brogues that looked as new as the day they were bought yet outdated by today's style. He stood proud.

After a lengthy explanation regarding the purpose of our visit, Major Barron produced a smile and asked us to follow him, stating he was more than willing to help us rid society of crackheads and those who dealt in the plague of drugs that ran amok on the streets of Britain, convinced that if there was no dealer, there would be no addicts and less crime.

We trailed behind him out of the study along the hall towards the back of the house and into a large open kitchen where he opened a door that revealed a large well-stocked larder consisting mainly of tinned items. The Major bent down and dug out a small metal ring that was neatly tucked into the tiled floor and pulled upwards, lifting a small hinged section of the floor revealing a hidden staircase.

'Now be good, fellows, and don't touch anything down here, do you understand?' he implored.

'Okay,' Bootsie replied uninterested.

'Sure.'

'As you request, Major,' Jacques replied earnestly.

'Watch your step on the way down, it's rather steep,' he warned.

The Major lit the stairway with a switch on the wall and then disappeared down the staircase. Bootsie went first, followed by me then Jacques. The steep decline was encased by narrow walls and I was already starting to feel claustrophobic as we descended to the bottom where there was a heavy metal door with a digital keypad to the right.

The Major entered the code and the door swung inwards, one by one the strip lights on the ceiling illuminated revealing a huge vault with an arsenal only a small army would describe as Aladdin's cave. On every wall either side from the floor upwards was racks of guns of every type imaginable, the vault was the size of the ground floor of the house with thick supporting pillars spaced here and there.

'Fuck a duck,' said Bootsie.

'What the…' I started to say and let out a long whistle.

'The man's a fucking genius,' Jacques said through a fit of laughter.

'Calm yourselves, calm yourselves, there's more over here,' the Major announced.

The Major had been a busy man over the years collecting his arsenal of weaponry. He even had a little workshop at the far end of the cellar where he fine-tuned his weapons. It was something to see all the guns and other paraphernalia but standing upright on its fins was a rocket.

'Is that what I think it is?' asked Jacques.

'What do you think it is?' the Major asked, looking rather pleased with himself.

'I think that's an Exocet missile?'

'You have a good eye, young man,' the Major said amused.

'Fuck me! What do you want with one of those?' Bootsie asked the Major, taking a few steps back.

'Research, my dear boy, research.'

'And to think my ass was sat right over the top of that,' I said.

'Don't worry, it's not armed…yet,' replied the Major whimsically.

'So who are you going to annihilate with that?' Jacques asked.

'You, if you don't put that back on the bench,' snapped the Major.

'Sorry,' Jacques replied, putting a hand grenade back on the bench.

'How the hell did you get that missile down here?' I asked.

'With bloody great difficulty, my boy,' the Major snapped back.

'Is it safe to smoke?' Bootsie asked taking a cigar out from his pocket.

'Damn you, Bootsie! Are you trying to get us all killed! Of course it's not safe! If this lot goes up, so will half of bloody London for Christ sake!'

'Alright Major, no need to get fresh, I was only asking.'

'Get fresh? You're insane, Bootsie!' the Major snapped back.

'Now hang on a minute, Major, that's a bit stiff, in it, all things considered,' Bootsie replied looking around at all the weapons.

'I'll give you stiff if you carry on with this banter!' yelled the Major.

'Alright, keep your pants on, Major,' Bootsie told him.

The Major picked up a Glock 45 and pointed it at Bootsie and shouted, 'Zip it or I'll weld your face up with lead!!'

Bootsie quickly drew his thumb and forefinger across his lips motioning that they were zipped.

The Major lowered the Glock 45 and muttered, 'Now, where was I? Oh yes, crackheads.'

'Something that will go boom?' I reminded him.

'Ah yes. Big booms or little booms?' the Major asked enthusiastically.

'Both, if you can spare them,' Jacques said still looking around the walls.

The Major sighed and said, 'You're quite the joker.'

Bootsie frowned then shook it off.

'Got anything in the silent department?'

'Ah yes, stealth always been a favourite of mine,' the Major replied beckoning Jacques to follow him.

The Major stopped at the far wall and pressed a red mushroom-shaped button that raised the roller shutter in the blink of an eye, displaying the illuminated silent department of sniper rifles. Jacques rubbed his eyes and stared in disbelief saying, 'I recognize a few rifles but some of these are like something out of *Star Wars.*'

'Indeed, most of them are, my boy. You see, some are my prototypes and others simply never made it onto the military circuit and some need some work done on them with the rest just being fine to squeeze the trigger and blow someone's head off.'

Jacques pointed at a rifle in the middle saying, 'What the heck is that thing?'

'What thing? This one here?' the Major asked pointing at a rifle.

'Not that one, the one above it.'

'You have a good eye for craftsmanship. This, my boy, is a decent little fellow recently new to the market.'

'It can't be a sniper rifle, it's too small.'

The Major laughed as he lifted the rifle off the wall and handed it to Jacques saying, 'Take a look at this little triumph of engineering. The Remington .338 SMR.'

Jacques was pleased with what he was holding in his hands with a broad grin steadfast on his face, he said, 'Remarkable, Major.'

'Yes, it is indeed. Accurate at 1500 metres, X mark drop in trigger, 22-inch barrel with a ratchet mounted quod fast suppressor, eliminating muzzle flash by 98% along with sound reduction placed at 28 decibels.' The Major paused eyeing for a reaction.

Jacques remained silent as the Major continued with its specifications, 'It has a titanium action feed mechanism with a 15-shot detachable Teflon magazine box firing .338 Laupa Magnum rounds. It is 32 inches in its current closed position with a length of pull or if you wish with the butt fully extended at a mere 42 inches. Are you following what I am saying, young man?'

'Of course, Major,' Jacques replied.

'Good. Then I haven't been wasting my breath, have I?'

'No, Major.'

'Any questions, young man?'

'Just the one question, Major.'

'Well, come on then, ask me,' the Major urged Jacques.

'What about the scopes on it?'

'Bloody damn good question, young man. The scopes are compact and light 4th generation Thor 3 thermals, with a plug-in USB for downloading pictures that can be transmitted via portable devices such as satellite phones, laptops or a mobile phone with all appropriate software built in.

'Its other features are start-up in 1 second with a 6-hour battery life, coupled with a microbolometering of 320 x 240, making a high resolute thermal image to all eyes who view through the scope. Weighing in at a mere 16 lbs, combat ready,' he finished, looking pleased with his spec speech.

'So what does all that mean?' I asked, not being sure if I should ask.

'It means, my boy…'

'It's Ginger Rogers and Fred Astaire,' Jacques said cutting the Major off.

'I couldn't have said it better myself, my dear boy.'

'So the gun dances nicely?' Bootsie asked puzzled.

'You'll be dancing nicely if I mind to lay a few rounds at your feet!' the Major snapped back at him.

'Hang on, did you say…'

Bootsie was cut short, the Major was red in the face but calmly he informed Bootsie, 'It simply means that they were made for each other in all ways.'

'Oh right, got ya.'

'So it's the dog's bollocks?' I said.

'It's a fucking godsend,' Jacques exclaimed.

'Calm yourself, my boy, it's like you've never seen a gun before.'

Jacques shot the Major a wry look.

The Major was more than happy to help out with a few off-the-shelf items of his stock but was very, very reluctant to let the .388 MSR out his sight though, but once Bootsie reminded him that it was for crackheads, the Major agreed only on the condition it would be returned, to which Jacques assured him it would be.

We left Major Barron's home in good spirits and promised to see him soon. Larry opened the boot of the car and a large black hold-all holding the .338 rifle, explosives, suppressed Uzis and ammo was deposited inside.

'Told you the Major was the man, didn't I?' Bootsie stated lighting up a cigar.

'You sure did.'

'Well, I think we should have a little drink and then get you two on your way.'

'Not for me,' Jacques replied.

'Me neither,' I added.

'Oh yeah, you two got shooting to do,' Bootsie reminded himself.

Fox was grateful to hear my voice when I phoned and was panicked by our lack of communication throughout the evening, but I reassured her that I and Jacques would be there in the next hour which perked her up. Me and Jacques along with Bootsie and his henchmen returned back to the warehouse near the Isle of Dogs and offloaded the bag of weapons from the Major. Larry drove us back to Izzy's place, dropping us off on the corner of her street and as we parted with solid handshakes after wishing us good luck, Bootsie said grinning, 'Don't forget you pair owe me one,' and sped off.

Back at the house, Fox threw her arms around me squeezing hard like I'd been away for decades while Izzy clamped Jacques by his crotch and led him straight to her bedroom.

Fox and I remained in the lounge talking and after a few minutes, we could hear Izzy's squeals and moanings coming from her bedroom which excited Fox that much, she tore herself out of her dress and then tore my clothes off dangerously excited. I gently pushed her back on the sofa which she took full advantage of by spreading her legs wide apart, giving me an open invite to her shaven haven. Goose bumps appeared all over her body, making her nipples hard as Izzy's squeals got louder. Fox grabbed at her breasts, pushing them together as she delicately licked the red plump of her top lip before draping the superfluity of her snaked tongue, letting it slowly cascade down to her stiffened nipple, seducing herself with precision whilst mischievously eyeing my cock.

Izzy's moans grew louder as Fox lent back on the sofa closing her eyes and smiled out of lust. I rubbed her clit hard as we both listened to Izzy's groans of pleasure growing in volume. I couldn't bear the strains of her lustful behaviour any longer and spread Fox's legs wider as I tasted her hot soft velvet pussy with the tip of my probing tongue as her body writhed in procession with Izzy's! My tongue lavished her wet cunt with precision. Fox gasped and violently imbedded her nails deep into my scalp and forcefully buried my wild tongue deeper inside her.

Her writhing twisting body and expulsions of pleasure echoed from her plump lips every time I sucked on her small ripe clitty. I couldn't bear it any longer and wrenched my head away from her imbedded talons and stood up, grabbing my stiffened bully and plunged its girth hard inside her cunt. I watched her face contort with lustful sin, her eyes wide and wild with the pain. I pulled it back out and sat on the sofa with my stiff cock resting on my stomach and grabbed Fox around her middle and pulled her on top of me as she reached around the back of my neck with one hand then raised herself up and grabbed my bully with her other hand and pushed my cock inside her juicy wet cunt as I pushed it deeper inside her till she had taken the cock's full length. Fox dominantly clamped both her legs around my back and pulled my face closer to her tits, which I sucked hard on as she rampantly fucked me, bouncing up and down fast and hard on my throbbing cock with her clutching cunt as she let out heavy gasps and superlative orgasmic squeals, united in baroque concertino with Izzy's orgasm as her legs tightened around my back, constricting me as her orgasmic body shuddered, grinding her soaking wet hoop down on my battered ejaculating cock, forcing it deeper inside her. She grabbed my face with both hands and kissed my lips hard and wild, and gasped out through deep shallow hot breaths.

'Thank... fuck... for you!

Chapter 14

Massacre on the Isle of Dogs

Later that evening, Izzy had driven Jacques to do a reconnaissance mission on the warehouse and returned two hours later. Jacques formulated a plan involving all of us apart from Izzy, whose only part was to drive us to the Isle of Dogs and pick us back up once we had finished our business there. Fox on the other hand was prepared to play a more vital role. Jacques had a way of putting his ideas across in a way that made you feel assured and confident with his past military experiences profiting in our favour.

Being focused, our mindsets had changed dramatically as we said goodbye to Izzy as she drove away from the Isle of Dogs to her safe haven. We retrieved the stashed hold-all of weapons and cautiously approached the warehouse on foot staying in the shadows of the night. Jacques positioned Fox on the 1st floor of a derelict building opposite the warehouse, giving her an easy line of fire with a close position for an impossible miss for accuracy. He handed Fox the MSR saying, 'Take a look through the scope into the other building and tell me what you can see.'

Fox took the sniper rifle and snuggly pressed it into her shoulder and looked through the scope and said in amazement, 'Wow, thermal people, these are good.'

'The best, how many people do you see?' he asked.

Fox said after a few seconds, 'I count thirteen.'

'Unlucky for some,' I remarked.

'Yeah, and it's about to get unluckier for them,' Jacques stated.

'I should say so,' I remarked.

'Are you clear on what you have to do, Fox?'

'Yes, Jacques. Squeeze the trigger and shoot the fuckers,' Fox replied unhindered.

'Remember, you only have 15 rounds in each magazine so take your time and try not to miss, and only fire on my command when I tell you to,' he reminded her.

Fox replied staunchly, 'Just because I fired my dad's shotgun several times don't mean I'm a trigger-happy serial killer you know.'

'Right. I get the picture, but just remember you're our eyes too, and if I or lover boy tell you to shoot, aim for their chests or their heads if you like.'

'Roger that,' she replied sternly.

'Are you ready, Mac?'

'About as ready as I'll ever be,' I replied exhaling a deep breath.

'Let's get on with it then,' Jacques ordered.

'Oh, and boys,' Fox said abruptly as we were just about to leave.

'What's up?' I asked.

Fox kept her eye in the thermal scope and without looking at us said, 'Do be careful.'

'That you can count on, Fox,' Jacques replied.

'I know,' she said assuring herself.

I followed Jacques staying in the dark shadows of the surrounding buildings as we crept up to the double wooden doors at the front of the warehouse where Jacques placed a device on the floor in the middle of the doors, covering it with a large empty plastic bucket he'd found and then quietly we both moved around to the side of the warehouse when Jacques stopped next to a big old extractor fan unit hanging on the wall that was long out of use. I took the weight of the fan's bulk as Jacques quietly dislodged it from the wall and together, we put it down on the floor, leaving a gaping hole in the wall large enough for us to slither through. Jacques carefully stood on top of the extractor fan unit itself and nimbly scrambled in through the hole in the wall. I passed Jacques our cache of weapons through the hole and then awkwardly slithered through the hole headfirst to Jacques who helped me in.

Jacques turned on his torch that was fitted with a red filtered lens and in its dull light, revealed we were now standing in a damp musty room that was partially filled with rotting cardboard boxes of old documents of some sort with a door to the right. Jacques tried the handle of the office door which opened, letting a beam of light shine in. Jacques instantly turned the torch off and ordered me to unzip the hold-all. I did as he ordered, quickly unzipping the bag that held our tiny but deadly arsenal of weapons.

'Pick a winner,' Jacques whispered.

'Like what?' I whispered to him.

Taking out two suppressed Uzis with the magazines taped together, Jacques handed them both to me as he whispered, 'Just point and squeeze the trigger,' then he put two grenades in each of my jacket pockets and said, 'Pull the pin and throw, simple.'

My heart rate increased its beats by a hundred and started sweating buckets whereas Jacques was as cool as a cucumber, focused, in his element and without a word, he armed himself with two suppressed Uzis and a handful of grenades plus a side arm.

Keeping in contact with Fox via radio com, she told us the targets were still on the first floor except for two others that were separately walking around the ground floor of the warehouse. Jacques slowly opened the door wider and stepped out but quickly stepped back inside closing the door almost closed.

'Guard,' he whispered and gestured for me to remain still.

I could now faintly hear the guard's footsteps on the concrete floor getting closer and closer. Jacques opened the door about an inch letting a beam of light shine into the room again and told me to get behind the door and remain still while he positioned himself the other side of the door just out of sight.

The footsteps came closer and closer until they abruptly stopped outside the office. I felt a bead of sweat run down the side of my face as the door slowly swung open and could see the guard stood there through the crack of the door with his gun in his hand. I held my breath trying not to breathe and lifted my gun up when suddenly he went reeling backwards with Jacques on top of him. I watched wide-eyed through the crack of the door as Jacques disarmed him in the blink of an eye, giving the guard no time to scream out though he tried, but all that came out of the guard's mouth was a low gargle as Jacques' hand was clamped firmly around the guard's throat and at the same time Jacques smashed the guard's gun into the side of his head, exploding the temple, killing the guard instantly. Jacques quietly dragged the dead bulk of the dead guard into the office and laid it on the floor. I stepped out from behind the door and looked at the guard's lifeless body then looked at Jacques who was completely unnerved, unmoved... just focused. The whites of his eyes shined brightly, too brightly.

'Are you alright, Mac?' he whispered.

'Yes! Yes, of course,' I answered back.

'Good man. Wait here, I'll be back shortly.'

'Where are you going?'

'To see where the other guard is.'

'But what if…'

'Just wait in here and if the other guard shows up, just shoot him and don't hesitate to pull the trigger,' he ordered and disappeared through the door.

I waited uncomfortably in the dark of the room for Jacques' return that seemed forever, when I heard his voice from behind the door call my name.

'What?' I replied.

'Open the door,' he whispered.

I immediately pulled the door open and was shocked to see he had a body slung over his shoulder. 'I caught the stupid bastard sleeping,' he said grinning.

'Is he dead?'

'What do you think? And it's a not a he, it's a she!' he replied.

'Probably,' I told him.

'Give me some credit, Mac, I knocked her out.' he replied laying the unconscious woman on the floor next to the dead guard.

After tying her up and gagging her, we got a radio check from Fox saying the others were still on the 1st floor. I could now hear music and their laughter from above us as we made our way across the ground floor of the warehouse which was littered with boxes and crates along with a hoard of fancy sports cars and 4 x 4 jeeps. We were both about to make our way up a wooden staircase to the first floor when a man's voice called down in a foreign dialect stopping us both dead in our tracks. We quickly retreated and hid underneath the open wooden staircase out of sight in the shadows when the man called out again.

Then the man slowly started to make his way down the staircase mumbling under his breath and as his foot came into view in front of me of the open staircase, Jacques motioned for me to yank it backwards. I did as Jacques wanted, sending the man flying down the last few steps with a crash as Jacques jumped out from underneath the staircase and fired off two shots into the man's body, killing him instantly.

'They're picking up weapons.' Fox alerted us.

'Then start shooting,' Jacques replied and ran up the staircase.

'Roger that,' Fox replied.

'Fuck it,' I said aloud and raced up the stairs behind Jacques who had just thrown two grenades into the room through the doorway.

'Get back!' he shouted at me.

I could hear a few windows pop followed by panic and automatic gun fire when there were two loud explosions that shook the building, collapsing part of the first floor onto the ground floor below, throwing up a large cloud of dust everywhere amid screams from those in the room above. A man staggered out from the dust cloud on the ground floor firing wildly, bullets tore into the hand rail and staircase, sending splints of wood flying in all directions hitting me in the leg and arm. I pointed the Uzis at him and squeezed their triggers, sending a double volley of bullets that tore into his chest, sending him reeling backwards into the silent dust cloud.

Jacques was busy firing both his Uzis in short bursts through the doorway and then retreating back behind the wall, repeating the process again and again and called down to me saying, 'Watch the ground floor!'

I ran back down the staircase to the ground floor and positioned myself behind a few wooden crates and looked up through the large hole in the wooden floor above and saw a man hiding, crouched next to a sofa firing at Jacques. I aimed my Uzis at him and fired, hitting him in the body and watched him as he fell down through the opening in the floor, landing on top of boxes, dead. Jacques tossed in another grenade that bounced off the sofa and fell through the hole above me. I dived over the top of some crates and laid flat on the floor behind them when it exploded, sending shards of wood and concrete in all directions. I lifted my head up over the crates and was instantly fired upon from somewhere above when there was another explosion overhead, which tore another hole in the floor above me and could see a woman reloading an assault rifle so I sprayed her in a volley of bullets, sending her through the hole in the floor, crashing onto the roof of a Ferrari, dead!

Fox was still shooting and said over the radio coms, 'It's like a fucking turkey shoot!'

Jacques was spraying bullets and I could see through the hole in the floor just the lower legs of a guy behind a desk firing back at Jacques. I took both the grenades out of my pockets, pulled the pins on them both and launched them both up through the hole in the floor and quickly ducked down behind the crates, again killing the guy instantly and bringing down half the floor above down on me, sending dust and debris flying everywhere.

The warehouse fell silent for a few brief seconds until Jacques shouted out to me, 'Are you okay?'

'Yes, I'm fine,' I yelled back.

'Stay where you are and cover those holes,' he shouted down.

'I'm on it,' I replied.

'Fox, you okay?' I asked her.

'I'm good guys. What's happening now?' she replied over the radio com.

'Do you see anything on the thermals?' Jacques asked her.

'I'll check,' she replied.

'Take your time, Fox,' Jacques told her.

'I am,' she snapped. Then went silent for a minute before she said excitedly, 'Oh! I got a live one hiding behind filing cabinets. Can I shoot him?'

'Can you get a clean shot at him?' Jacques asked her.

'Nah! He keeps moving in and out of the shot,'

'Shoot him straight through the cabinets, they're .338 Laupa rounds.'

Fox squeezed the trigger and said, 'Shit! I missed. He moved as I fired.'

'Can you spot anyone else alive?' I asked Fox.

'I'm looking now, honey.'

A few minutes later, Fox said, 'No one else breathing or moving except this sneaky shit.'

Jacques asked Fox, 'Can you see me waving my gun up and down in the doorway?'

'Yes, I can.'

'Okay. The middle of the wall facing you is your twelve o'clock. At what time do you see me in the doorway?'

'Err…three o'clock?'

'Good girl. Now, at what time is the guy hiding?'

'Nine o'clock.'

'Right. I want you to fire some shots at him while I try to move around the room, okay?'

'I got it, you just tell me when to fire,' Fox replied enthusiastically.

'Keep the holes covered down there.'

'I'm on them,' I called back.

'Ready, Fox?' Jacques asked her.

'Ready,' she answered.

'Fire!' Jacques ordered as he sprang across the room and hid behind what was left of a sofa.

No sooner had Fox started shooting at the cabinets, the guy threw his gun out and called out for us to stop shooting. Jacques told her to cease fire but keep him in her sights. Jacques checked the bodies scattered around the room for any signs of life before moving in on the helpless guy who was still in a crouching position with his hands held up above his head in surrender.

Jacques called out to the guy, 'Stand up slowly and come out,' and reminded the man that if he made any false moves, he'd be killed too.

'I come out, just don't shoot!!' he begged.

'Keep your hands up where I can see them.'

'Okay! Don't shoot! I'm coming out!!'

The man slowly stood up keeping his hands high above his head as Jacques cautiously made his way over to him and frisked him for any hidden weapons; he had none.

Jacques brought him downstairs with the muzzle of his Uzi firmly pressed into his back. The man was sweating profusely and shaking with fear. I went to get the bound woman from the room we had left tied up and just in the nick of time too, as she had already somehow managed to slip her hands free and was in the process of untying her feet; she looked up at me and cursed me, calling me a bastard!

We sat the two of them side by side on crates with their hands bound and with our guns pointed at them, fear stricken, they sat in silence looking at me and Jacques while we sat in silence looking back at them until the woman spat at us and screamed out, 'Fucking bastards!'

'That we are,' Jacques replied and spat back at her.

'Animal fuck,' she cried out at him.

'Shut the fuck up,' I told her.

'And you, you son of a pig, I kill you!' she screamed.

The man next to her said, 'Quiet, Anna!'

'Fuck you too,' she told him.

The man hit her in the face with his bound hands, sending her reeling backwards over the crate. 'Forgive her, she a little upset,' he told us.

Jacques calmly stood up, walked over to the man and punched him in the face, sending him flying off the crate, adding, 'I'm a little upset too.'

Fox joined us in questioning our two captives who said they were from Romania. The woman was a little on the thin side and had a pale complexion with dark hair and made a fatal comment on Fox's arrival, asking me and Jacques, 'Do you always work with whores?'

Fox gracefully walked over to her, studied the woman's face and then kicked her in the mouth adding, 'Shut it, bitch!'

'What do you want with us?' the man asked.

'We want our diamonds back that you stole from the Jews!' I told him.

The man nodded to himself before saying, 'If we give you the diamonds back, then you will kill us, yes?'

'So you still got them?' Fox asked.

'Of course we do,' said the woman wiping the blood from her mouth.

'I thought I told you to shut it!' Fox told her.

The woman flinched backwards as Jacques held out his arm, blocking Fox's advance on the woman. Jacques asked her, 'Where are the diamonds now?'

'For us to know, for you to find out,' said the man laughing.

'You think this is fucking funny?' I asked him.

'From where I'm sat, it's hilarious,' he replied, still laughing.

Jacques grabbed the man by the hair, pulling his head back so he was staring at the muzzle of the Uzi, and said, 'Where are they or I'll kill you.'

'You won't kill me if you want them back,' he said grinning.

Jacques took a step backwards, pointed the gun at the man who now had a smirk on his face and shot him in the leg. 'FUCK!!!!' he cried out in agony as he fell off the crate onto the floor.

Jacques turned the gun on the woman and said, 'You're next!'

'Fuck you bastards!!' she cried out.

Jacques shook his head very slowly saying, 'Wrong answer,' and then shot her in the leg.

The woman screamed out in terror as the bullet tore through her lower leg, sending her flying to the floor kicking her good leg wildly while her bound hands grabbed at her wounded leg. She cursed us in her own tongue as tears streamed down her checks. The man on the floor screamed out in defiance, 'You crazy bastards… You never find the diamonds.'

'Is that right?' Jacques asked.

'Yezzz, is right, you crazy fuckheads,' he replied through gritted teeth.

Jacques shot him in the knee cap in his other leg. The man let out a huge cry of pain and started rolling from side to side, shouting, 'Die, you fucks and your whore bitch!'

Fox pushed Jacques out of her way and pointed the MSR at the man wriggling around in agony and told us to, 'Pick that bitch up! I want her to watch this.'

'Fox, what are you doing?' I asked.

'Face that bitch this way!' Fox screamed at us both.

Jacques picked the woman up and dragged her over to where the man was and threw her down beside him. Fox kicked the man in the chest and said, 'What did you just call me, you fucking dog?!'

The man looked up at Fox smiling and said, 'You fucking whore bitch!'

Fox squeezed the trigger, sending a .338 Laupa Magnum round into the man's face, disintegrating his head and splattering the woman with skull fragments and brains, saturating her face with hot blood.

'I tell you!! I tell you!! I tell you!!' the woman screamed out hysterically and started crying uncontrollably.

Shocked and speechless at what Fox just did, I sat down and lit up a cigarette, puffing away frantically while Jacques on the other hand paid Fox a compliment saying, 'You should be a mercenary.'

'Nah, think I'll stick to being a lady of leisure,' she replied and then came over, taking the cigarette out of my hand and said calmly, 'You ok, babe?'

'Yes, are you?'

She took a deep drag of the cigarette and after exhaling a cloud of smoke, she said, 'Yes, babe.' Then handed my cigarette back to me adding, 'But these pissing boots are fucking killing me!

When the woman came to her senses, Jacques tied a tourniquet around her leg, stemming the flow of blood and handed her a cup of water which she reached out with shaking hands, spilling most of it over her blood-stained top and face in the process of drinking it. She was in shock, petrified and shaking, trying not to look at us. She told us the diamonds were in the safe upstairs which was locked but the key was hung around the neck of Dimi, who was now dead.

We took her upstairs so she could point Dimi out though he was hard to recognise due to the grenades tearing chunks out of him and minus a leg, but Jacques retrieved the key from him that hung around his neck and opened the safe and to our surprise, not only were the diamonds there but bundles of cash along with bags of drugs that contained ecstasy, crack, crystal meth, MDMA and two kilos of cocaine. We emptied the safe of our diamonds and the cash but left the drugs out of respect for Major Barron and his old drinking partner. Jacques told me and Fox to go wait outside in the shadows and to call Izzy and ask her to pick us back up where she had dropped us off, adding that he would join us shortly and for Fox to keep hold of the MSR and for me to throw my Uzis next to the sports cars downstairs and to watch out for the charge he had laid earlier under the tin in front the warehouse doors.

Fox walked over to the woman and placed two small bundles of cash in her lap; the shaking woman looked up at Fox confused and asked, 'What's this for?'

'To go back home to whatever country you came from,' Fox told her with a smile before following me out of the warehouse, leaving Jacques behind.

'Now what do I do?' she asked looking around the room and then back at Jacques.

Jacques looked at her for a moment and said, 'Nothing,' then shot her in the head!!

Jacques removed the charge from underneath the old tin and went back inside the warehouse, placing it underneath the fancy cars along with the C4 charges he had in the hold-all and all the guns, only Jacques kept a remote detonator and put it in his pocket and then exited via the little door in the big wooden double doors of the warehouse and hastily jogged to catch Fox and I up. Izzy arrived twenty five minutes after Jacques arrived and looked relieved to see us all in one piece but evidently nervous too. And as we drove away from the warehouse, none of us happened to notice Jacques slip his hand into his pocket and press the button that detonated the explosive charges which demolished the warehouse in a ball of flames, reducing it to nothing more than a pile of burning rubble. Izzy rapidly increased her speed instantly the moment the thunderous BOOM of an explosion rang out.

Chapter 15

R.I.P the Glasgow Ranger

The next few days were quiet to say the least. Alter was informed that his cousin's murderers had paid for their crime horrifically with their lives and the rest of the diamonds had been retrieved to add to his jubilance which he took care of personally though his chauffer had collected the diamonds from us, but as he promised, the money was in the bank by the end of business that day. Bootsie received a sum of money for his troubles though he tried to decline our gratitude, but we left it on the table along with Major Barron's MSR as promised along with a helpful token of our extreme for the Major's contributions in the form of a large sum of money to aid him in his gun hobbies.

We spent another two days with Izzy out on the town in the West End, partying a little before returning back to Barry Island (minus Jacques who remained in London) and its laid-back townie life. The past week had somewhat taken its toll on all of us and all I wanted to do was take a long hot shower and relax for a few days and try to forget everything that had happened, unlikely I thought, as I started stripping my clothes off to join Fox who begged me to join her in the shower when the phone rang. I tried to ignore it but I couldn't. I picked up the receiver and said, 'Hello.'

'Hiya, Mac, where you been?' said the voice on the other end.

'Bernie! I'll call you back,' I told him and disconnected the phone and joined Fox in the shower.

The national newspapers and national news stations on the television described the events on the Isle of Dogs as a gangland slaying where thirteen criminals had been slaughtered by a rival Eastern European underworld gang over drugs as they had found a large quantity of cocaine in a safe. The Chief Superintendent of the Metropolitan Police had merely commented on the situation as if unfazed by the event stating that, 'The streets of London would be a safer place to live without the drugs being sold on the street but investigations are continuing at present.'

The Chief Superintendent's comment laid emphasis on my vermicular paranoia, permitting it to ebb into the back of my mind as I had been expecting the door to the apartment to be kicked in at some inconvenient unearthly hour by a troop of screaming trigger-happy armed police, waving their MP5s in mine and Fox's face, shouting their famous battle cry, 'Police! Police! Nobody move! Stay where you are! You're under arrest!'... the thought lapped away in the back of my mind.

Mick and Bernie flew over from France to attend the funeral of Robert Duggan aka "The Jock".

Even though Mick had never met Robbie in person, he felt that he too should pay respects to the man who had improved his lifestyle in a very considerable way. The four of us, me, Jacques, Bernie and Mick made the long drive up to Glasgow in Scotland, arriving under the blanket of a star-filled clear night sky and settled into our hotel rooms which had been booked three days in advance.

The next morning at 10:00 am, we joined over two hundred mourners for Robbie's service that was held in a local church before he was buried in the church grounds with many tears being shed for the man his family and friends knew as Robbie and known to his work colleagues as Jock. We joined the majority of mourners at his favourite pub, The Castle, and toasted his life and death with a few large drams of fine Scotch. Over the next few hours as each hour passed, the pub became less occupied by mourners until eventually there was only a handful of Robbie's friends and immediate family left along with us.

I suggested to Jacques that this might be a good time to hand Jock's wife Robbie's share of money, to which he nodded and reached inside his jacket pulling out a small brown envelope. He interrupted the widow who was sat with her family, she smiled up at Jacques as he stood by her side and kindly asked her aside only after she had excused herself from her family and friends' presence, the widow took a few steps away from earshot with Jacques.

Jacques half smiled and handed Robbie's wife the small brown envelope which contained a 1st class return ticket to London dated two weeks from today together with a key numbered 203 with instructions to the safety deposit box that contained a generous £500,000 in cash at a London bank with a receipt for three nights at the Chester Hotel, Jacques asked her not to open it until she had got home. She refused the envelope at first but with Jacques's insistence placing it in her hand and gently folded the widow's fingers over it, Jacques smiled. The widow broke her curious bewilderment with a smile and kissed Jacques lightly on the cheek, then the widow glanced in our direction and acknowledged our presence with an inclined nod of her head as she walked back to join her family and placed the envelope in her hand bag and slowly zipped it to a close.

We remained in the pub until Robbie's widow and family left who once again thanked all those who remained for attending the funeral. A toast was performed by the Jock's uncle which we all drank to, then all the rest of the family left to mourn Robbie's passing in private.

'Now what?' I asked.

Jacques's eyebrows narrowed. Then he said, 'I guess we get blinding drunk, Mac?'

'Bloody good idea,' said Bernie.

'I'll third that,' said Mick.

'To Robbie "The Jock" Duggan,' I said standing up.

The three of them stood up and we all bellowed out with pride, 'TO ROBBIE!!'

Autumn was now in full swing with the leaves turning from their plush greens to reddish browns, falling from the trees scattering over the ground in the light but ever-increasing winds and with the drizzling rain that came with the wind, it pasted the leaves to the floor like a collage of summer memories just passed.

The early darkening evenings had crept in almost without warning, making the daytime hours vulnerable to mother nature's own humble way and with it came the chills a pre-warning of the winter months' blight ahead. Only a week, I thought to myself about Fox's probation ending, how it would be over forever, leaving her free to roam again with nothing holding her back, except my thoughts turned back to previous times when Fox had the freedom of sojourn, upturning my world as she quietly disappeared from my life again – a hazard of her unconditional love.

An unexpected part of my sub-conscious surfaced momentarily taunting me with its reflection over life's recent events, taking into account all that had happened. Like a marriage, for better or for worse, both had played their parts in the changing of my human abilities as a person. I never in a million years would have thought that these past few months would demoralise if not diminish my ethical upbringing that my parents had taught me, and taught me well, the differences of just and unjust livelihoods. My parents had construed in their sibling the adorning love of any parent installed in any good child only now these series of events had dismembered their every inhibition and expectation of me. My scorning conscience released its grip, interrupted by the telephone ringing; by the time I lifted the receiver, the line was dead.

Mick had bought himself a nice little house in France with his share of money half a mile away from our renovation project in Agde and found himself a petite French local woman called Marie Claire, who was well-suited for him plus she had helped him seal the purchase of his house using her Parisian influence, getting the house at a much lower price. Mick invited us over to view his new property and to meet his newfound love. So on Fox's last attendance at the probation office, when she emerged a free woman, I whisked her off to Agde to be reunited with Mick, Bernie and the girls with Jacques and Isobelle flying in from London.

Chapter 16

The Russian in Milan

I, Fox, Jacques and Izzy spent a spectacular week in Agde with Bernie, Chantelle, Mick and his new French girlfriend Marie Claire, who it turns out was a long-time friend of Chantelle. Marie Claire had an oval-shaped face with deep brown eyes, natural long lashes and pristine arched eye brows that centred her thin straight nose and a small mouth with cupid bow lips. She was petite framed at 5'6" with raven black tousled hair falling below her shoulders with a thin waistline and wore very little makeup apart from her cherry lipstick and a little mascara. She was a delightful woman who made Mick feel loved and cared for with both not being able to take their eyes of each other which was instantly observed by the rest of us.

Though Izzy playfully whispered to Fox, 'Honeymoon phase.'

At the end of the week, we left our friends in Agde as they had made plans of their own while I, Fox, Jacques and Izzy flew to Milan for a few days to spend time sightseeing, taking in all that Milan has to offer.

Every morning me and Fox woke up, we either made passionate love or just fucked each other senseless with our balcony doors wide open, giving any prying eyes from the opposite buildings an occasional glimpse of our naked bodies fucking each other as an occasional breeze made its unannounced entrance blowing the thin cotton draped net curtains covering the balcony doors upwards in the air, making them dance wildly and as the wind left our room, it let out a low whistle, drawing the draped net curtains to a close behind it, hiding our naked fucking bodies from view again.

The four of us spent every evening strolling hand in hand through the Milanese streets until we reached the Naviglio Grande Canal, dining in the many restaurants that lined either side of the canal, eating the most delicious cuisines and tasting many of Italy's fine wines after which we would hit a few rock or jazz bars and nightclubs via taxi rides and dance the night away until the early morning hours and then take a taxi back to our hotel.

Being in Milan, Fox had always wanted to visit the Pinacoteca di Brera and the Milan Cathedral, otherwise known as the Duomo, for all their grand splendours and historic significances as well as their magnificent architecture that graced the skyline, to which we all agreed that we would go visit them making a full day out for ourselves. The next morning, we all got up early and after having breakfast, the four of us set off from our hotel in a taxi and a short time later arrived at our first attraction, the Duomo in the Piazza del Duomo in the centre of Milan. The Duomo is the world's largest Gothic Cathedral, Fox informed us reading from a tourist guide booklet the receptionist had given her back at our hotel.

As we stood outside the Duomo and looked at the cathedral, all of us were struck by the sheer magnitude of it and its façade built of marble along with all 135 pinnacles reaching out from the roof to the heavens that were encumbered with an amazing 3,500 statues that encrusted the cathedral and on the highest pinnacle on the roof stood a 13.5-foot gilded statue of the Madonna, like she was watching over everybody some 376 feet above ground level. We followed Fox inside through one of its five huge heavy bronze doors where the cathedral's vastness is appreciated by all who grace its inner sanctuary, including its 40,000 worshipers that can fill the cathedral in all its majestic splendour and magnificence.

We all spent about an hour trailing behind Fox as she continued reading from her guide book, enlightening us with all the history of the cathedral which became rather interesting as we listened to her, only occasionally interrupting Fox to ask her questions to which she told us to be quiet and listen to her before she finally finished pointing out that once a year on the second Sunday in September, they publicly displayed a nail that is said to be from the cross Christ was crucified upon. From ground level, we chose to take the lift to the cathedral roof, each paying the few Euros as each of us opted out from walking up the staircase that leads up to the cathedral roof, which has tremendous views over Milan as far as the eye could see. And it's said that on a clear day, even the Alps are visible in the distance.

I lit a cigarette while taking in the views around me and got told off by an Italian official to the cathedral who was going ape shit with me whilst Fox, Jacques and Izzy had done a disappearing act pretending not to know me. After the embarrassment of the situation, we made our way back down via the lift again though we all wanted to take the stairs back down for the hell of it, but we changed our minds when we saw how out of breath the people were who were exiting the doorway that had the bright idea of walking up to the roof with most of whose faces resembled that of a sweating tomato.

After leaving the Piazza del Duomo some two and half hours later, we settled for a much-deserved relaxing cappuccino with a light lunch in one of the many surrounding restaurants before we headed off to our final destination for that day. We arrived at the Pinacoteca di Brera and after paying the entrance fee, we began our tour of Milan's most prestigious art gallery founded by Napoleon on the spoils of his many wars. While the Nazis looting that had taken place during World War II, and after the war had ended a select group of soldiers had recovered, most artifacts by Britain and America were returned and were now safely housed here for all visitors to appreciate. The art gallery is set in the heart of the Brera district with its main emphasis on Italian Renaissance such as Bellini, Carpaccio, Caravaggio and Giovanni to name but a few, with masterpieces from the 13th to 19th century hanging on every wall. Again, Fox graced us with her guided tour, informing us of the artists and their subjects as we moved from painting to painting until we came to Andrea Mantegna's *Dead Christ*, viewed from the sole of Jesus Christ's feet.

We were standing behind a large group of Chinese tourists silently admiring the painting when suddenly a man and a woman at the very front started arguing in what sounded like Russian. The Chinese tourist moved off in an instant, giving us a full view of both the man and woman arguing. The man had his two hands outstretched pointing at the painting of the *Dead Christ* and then he pointed his hands down at his own feet.

The woman was scowling and shaking her head violently in disagreement and walked away laughing and as the man turned around, Jacques's jaw dropped wide open with a look of disbelief on his face. The man who seemed to be arguing started to shout after the woman as she frantically walked off at a fast pace, babbling away in Russian to herself and showed the man her middle finger over her shoulder without even turning around.

'Oralik, is that you?' Jacques asked shocked.

The man turned directly to look at Jacques with a surprised look that instantly turned into a big silly grin and shouted out, 'Brother Couture! What the fuck!

Long time, no see,' he exclaimed triumphantly leaping forwards, almost knocking us out the way like skittles and embraced Jacques.

'Of all the people…what the hell are you doing here?' Jacques asked him still shocked.

'Enjoying my honeymoon, brother!' the man replied smugly.

The surprise on each of their faces was full of great joy to say the least while I, Fox and Izzy were totally bewildered by their jubilations. We looked at each other quite puzzled and shrugged our shoulders.

'Who is he?' Izzy asked.

'I haven't the foggiest,' Fox replied.

'Well… One thing's for sure.'

'What's that?' Izzy asked me.

'They certainly know each other,' I replied laughing.

Jacques looked at us with a huge smile on his face and said, 'Please meet my brilliant friend Oralik.'

Fox nudged Izzy letting out a tiny giggle, raised an eyebrow and whispered to her, 'I wonder if he's got a long tongue?'

'Should we buy him a Cornetto and find out?' she whispered back giggling.

'Pack it in, you two,' I whispered.

The thick-set Russian held out his hand proudly and said, 'Oralik Kalashnikov, descendant of the great Ivan Kalashnikov who invented the world's finest assault rifle.'

Izzy shook his hand and said amusingly, 'Isobelle Omerta… in the escort business.'

'Pleased to meet you, madam,' Oralik replied kissing her outstretched hand.

'Melody Fox-Wright, soon to be married,' she informed Oralik.

'Pleased to meet the bride,' he replied kissing Fox's hand.

'Mac, long-time friend of Jacques,' I told him extending my hand.

He shook it firmly adding, 'So you like a brother too, yes?'

Jacques interrupted, 'Yes, and a very dear brother.'

'Good, I like… I still not believe it's you Brother Couture, after all these years I thought you were fucking dead for sure,' Oralik said scratching his head but smiled fanatically at Jacques.

Jacques shook his head and laughed saying, 'Funnily enough, Oralik, I was just thinking the same thing about you too.'

The two of them pissed themselves laughing when Oralik said, 'Ironic we met here after all the shit we went through together, brother.'

'Yes, they were tough times, brother.'

Oralik let out a low laugh and said, 'Tough indeed, but we make it out okay, yes?'

'Yes, we made it out okay...and now isn't the time to remind ourselves of our misfortunes.'

Oralik turned to us, grinning wildly and said, ' We were soldiers of fortune. Has my brother told you?'

'Yes, on more than one occasion, brother,' I replied.

Oralik's expression changed to a somewhat exasperated look as if he wanted to tell many a story of their daysin the French Foreign Legion, then his face reverted back to a joyful smile. 'Good, so you know we are heroes among the elite of this world?'

'They do for sure, but for now we must leave that subject in the past, my brother,' Jacques told him.

'Of course, forgive me. How long you staying in Italy?' Oralik asked him.

'A few more days, then we fly back to the UK.'

'Good. Then you will have time to join me in few drinks to... how you say, remember?'

'Reminisce,' said Fox correcting him.

'Reminisce, yes. That's what I was looking to say, thank you,' Oralik told Fox.

'But we only just got here,' Fox reminded Jacques, glaring at him wildly.

'Is okay, you leave your wives to be, like my wife leave me, no problem,' Oralik replied, beaming from ear to ear.

Both Fox and Izzy threw Jacques a thunderous scowl and crossed their arms defensively. I joined them in my expression of disapproval by coughing uncontrollably.

'Eh... I er...maybe we can meet up later as this is part of our short schedule whilst we are here,' Jacques explained, trying his best as not to offend Oralik.

Oralik thought for a moment looking down at his bare feet then said smiling at us, 'I see, okay not difficult, but it be better without the wife, she has the hump with me so if I go back to the hotel, she want to come. Maybe upset the night?'

'They do it all the time, just something you have to put up with when you marry one,' Fox enlightened Oralik with a prude pout of her lips.

'Okay, Brother Couture, I see her point. I'm staying at the Grand Dunlin Plaza Hotel, so call me there or leave a message at the front desk,' he stated.

'I will for sure, you can count on it,' Jacques replied.

'Good, I leave you now as not to intrude on you and I have to find that damn mad wife of mine. I wish you all a happy day and see you soon.'

We said our goodbyes with promises of a reunion, to which Oralik smiled and was gone in a flash barefoot, leaving his shoes behind as he chased after his wife.

'Who the fucking hell was that?' Izzy demanded of Jacques.

'We were buddies a long time ago in the…'

Fox cut him short, 'The cheeky bastard! LEAVE your wives!! Is he bloody sane in the head?'

'Well yes, just a bit scatty sometimes, but a damn fine friend. Why?'

'Scatty!' Izzy yelled.

'Oralik's no less scattier than Bernie and you got on with him okay,' Jacques told her.

'Bernie does not need the men in white coats whereas I think brother Oralik does!' Fox commented.

'Can I make a suggestion here?' I asked.

They all looked at me in silence apart from Jacques who was trying his best to look occupied, fiddling for something in his pocket and no doubt wondering what was coming next.

'Why not forget about Oralik for the time being and carry on with our tour of this magnificent building with all its glorious masterpieces, eh?'

Fox produced a warm smile and linked her arm through mine and said, 'Christ, Mac, you sound like husband material. But hey, you've sold it to me.'

'I'll go with that,' Jacques added offering his arm to Izzy which she openly accepted.

Taking in the delights of our surroundings, the experience with Oralik soon passed as did the rest of the tour of the Pinacoteca di Brera some two hours later as did the rest of the day, stopping along the way back to the hotel at a small but illustrious little restaurant for a well-deserved large portion of Italian cuisine aided by a few small glasses of wine. Oralik's name didn't even get another mention as Fox and Izzy were too busy leading most of our conversations as we strolled romantically through the streets, taking in other sights and delights of the day, promiscuously omitting the Russian from conversation. We arrived back to the hotel just as night started to creep in with both Fox and Izzy looking relieved to say the least as the walk had turned into a scenic tour of side streets and alleyways, making the journey that little bit longer plus taking more toil on their feet in their high heels. The doorman greeted us all with a courtesy smile and politely opened the door for the girls, taking in the view of their asses as they strode in through the open door and upon noticing I was aware of his preying eyes, he quickly turned his attention to the taxi that had just parked curb-side, saving his bacon. He rushed down the steps to greet the occupants inside, luckily for him as Jacques had noticed too.

That evening whilst we were all together in the hotel bar having a few drinks, I asked the girls if they would like to do a lot of retail therapy the following day by themselves to which they both said yes, to mine and Jacques' delight as Milan is big on fashion and we like our girls to look good, plus it also gives us a break away from them. On the quiet, Jacques asked me why I had asked them and I told him we would go to the Dunlin Plaza and meet his old friend Oralik, which brought a huge smile to his face and nodded in agreement saying, 'Mum's the word.'

'For now at any rate,' I stated.

'How so?' he asked.

'We'll have to tell Fox and Izzy when we get back. But for now, just tell them we're going shopping too.'

'I'll drink to that, mate.'

The following morning, the girls were out of our sight as soon as breakfast was over, with them only having a quick coffee each, leaving me and Jacques on our own to finish our breakfasts. They gave us a quick kiss on the cheeks and like a pair of excited kids going off on a trip somewhere, they were gone frantically waving at us as they left.

'Give it ten minutes then we'll be off too.'

'Can't wait. Mac,' Jacques replied and sipped his coffee.

We took a taxi to Oralik's hotel to save us wandering around like headless chickens and admired the scenery as it went by more often than not at a slow pace due to the morning's hectic traffic that seemed to be on a constant loop, streaming from everywhere that bottled-necked us several times along the way, which only enraged the driver all the more as he blurted out obscenities, cursing at other drivers stuck in the traffic, occasionally sticking his middle finger up to them only to receive a torrent of abuse back which brought a wry smile to his face. He apologised to both of us on more than one occasion, stating that some people have no idea how to drive, calling them lunatics to be locked up, never to be free to drive on a road again.

All me and Jacques could do was nod our heads in agreement whilst trying to conceal our laughter as we were thoroughly enjoying watching the driver flailing his arms about and screaming out of his window at people with Jacques joining in with him on more than one occasion as to add fuel to the driver's angry outbursts. It took the driver what seemed like a day to reach Oralik's hotel and as ever, the driver was very apologetic for the delay getting us there once we had arrived.

Both of us did our best to calm him down and paid him with a tip thrown in for the entertainment along the way, which brought out a rapid Italian forte of dialect through gritted teeth before the driver spat on the floor, got in his taxi and gave us the middle finger as he sped off!

'What the fuck was all that about?' I asked Jacques.

'I tipped him about five pence in our money, mate,' he replied laughing.

'What the hell did you do that for after all he's done?'

'For the hell of it, mate. Hate to be the next guy to jump in his taxi and give a shit tip.'

I laughed and said, 'He'll crucify them.'

'With his middle finger I bet,' Jacques added laughing hysterically.

Once inside the Plaza Dunlin Hotel, we made our way to the receptionist and asked him to call Oralik in his suite, to which the receptionist informed us that Mr Kalashnikov did not want to be disturbed. Jacques reassured the receptionist that Mr Kalashnikov was expecting us and if he didn't inform Mr Kalashnikov of our arrival, he would be out of a job. A cold sweat broke out on the receptionist's brow when Jacques lifted up the telephone off the desk and handed it to him, to which the sweating receptionist feebly took from Jacques, agreeing to call Oralik informing him of our presence and would we kindly mind waiting in the lounge to the right.

We turned and were about to head for the lounge when the receptionist called out, 'Excuse me, gentlemen.'

We both turned back to look at him and said, 'Yes?'

'Who shall I say is waiting for him?'

'Tell him Couture,' Jacques replied.

'Err... Who?'

'Couture,' Jacques repeated himself, scowling at the receptionist.

'Don't worry, Mr Kalashnikov will understand,' I told the receptionist smiling.

The receptionist hesitatingly lifted the receiver from the phone and gestured with a sweep of his hand for us to go into the lounge whilst doing his best to produce a smile.

We did not have to wait long for Oralik to arrive. We could hear him ranting out in the foyer. We both slowly leaned forward from our seats and peered through the lounge's open archway to get a better view of the situation. Jacques burst out laughing instantly when he saw the receptionist kneeling on the floor with his hands clasped together as if praying before the Madonna, sobbing and whining repeatedly saying that he was sorry, when the receptionist suddenly lunged forward throwing his arms around Oralik's legs. Oralik's reaction could have not been better for Jacques's amusement.

'You crazy fuck, you! What you think I am, Jesus? I told you no disturb us when we happy making the passion for the babies. The phone rings and it put me off the lucky stroke!' he told the receptionist.

'Sorry, sorry, it won't happen again, I beg of you, Mr Kalashnikov,' bellowed the shaking receptionist.

'Mother of angels, you whine like a dog!' Oralik said cursing the receptionist.

Jacques was on his back laughing when he called out, 'Oralik, over here,'

Oralik turned in our direction and on seeing us, he kicked the receptionist away from his feet, 'Ah, brothers, this is nice of you to drop by.'

'I thought Couture would have got your attention?' Jacques said through a fit of laughter.

'I thought this silly bastard fuck here was playing me for the fool,' Oralik replied, picking the receptionist up by the scruff of the neck and proceeded to dust him down, telling him he was sorry but hoped he understood.

'Come on, he'll be okay,' Jacques told Oralik.

Oralik strode into the lounge barefoot with a huge grin on his face. 'Bad timing for the baby making and Mrs Kalashnikov, I think,' he stated.

'Forgive us for taking you away from your pleasures,' I said.

'Not at all, we've been at it many long days now to make sure of the conception. She should have stuck with gymnastics, at least I get a rest that way,' Oralik stated whilst seating himself opposite us.

There was more to Oralik than met the eye. On first diagnosis, it was clear to all that he was indeed of a scatty if not bizarre nature from the outset, but he also had hidden qualities and abilities that would only unfold the longer any person could manage to stay around him. At six foot with rugged looks, harsh jaw line, thick set with an athletic structure to his frame, short blonde hair that was almost shaven on the back and sides, it wasn't hard to figure out he was of ex-military origin which he was, having served alongside Jacques in the French Foreign Legion, spent a few undisclosed years in the Russian special forces along with being a helicopter pilot. His fortunes changed when he inherited from his great grandfather a huge sum of money that opened many doors all over Russia that linked Oralik to high-ranking politicians along with connections to the vast underworld of the Russian mafia. Oralik was not to be taken lightly as he had read all the books before he burnt the library.

The upside of it all was he was stinking rich as well as being a playboy back in his mother land and had enough money to command his own army as well as having some heavy military vehicles that he liked to play around in when he was not busy with life, a case of more money with sense… fortunately for the rest of the world.

His shirt was unfastened to his chest and displayed around his neck was a gold chain and hanging from it was a little glass phial that contained water housed in an ornate decorative silver over gold lattice shell. The water being from the Bolva river basin in Russia, where it is said in Russian folklore that if a droplet is drank, it cleanses and purifies the soul of sins and if added to any other water, it turns it to holy water.

'So…tell me Brother Couture and Brother Mac, how has life been treating you over the years?'

'Oh, so so. Nothing to write home about, but I can't complain.'

'Me neither,' I added.

'Same here, I suppose, but I have had misfortunes in it also. But now I am happily married to a crazy bitch.'

'We've had the odd misfortunes, haven't we, Mac?'

'We've had our fair share, I suppose.'

'How come? Please tell me more,' Oralik enquired.

'It would only bore you, brother.'

'Not at all, I would like to hear, it's been a long time so now we play catch-up, yes?'

'Well, where do I start…' Jacques said thinking aloud.

'Why, at the beginning as in all stories,' Oralik beamed.

Jacques told him of his exploits after leaving the French Foreign Legion. Oralik sat quietly listening and complimented Jacques on the good parts but showed deep regret on the not-so-good parts. I had to tell Oralik about my life from childhood to the present day and again he paid compliments to the good parts and regrets to the bad parts of my life. Oralik then told us of his exploits and then quite out of nowhere, his newlywed wife Anna came strutting into the lounge in a long black coat that almost touched the black high heels she was wearing. She looked at me and Jacques and apologised for her intrusion then turned to Oralik and fully opened her long black coat to reveal her semi-naked body wearing only black stockings, knickers and bra, and said through her glossed red lips, 'The passion can't wait, I need it now. Hurry up, damn you,' Anna begged him and hurriedly walked out of the lounge, only turning back to blow Oralik a kiss.

'See, brothers. She is fucking crazy in love with me. Sexy bitch always give me the boner,' Oralik stated grasping his manhood through his trousers.

'We better be going and let you get back with your wife,' Jacques said.

'Forgive me, but I think that is a good idea for now. But you come back before you go as I have a great business proposition for you both that will make you very rich men indeed, if I read between the lines correctly?'

'I think you've read correctly, wouldn't you agree, Mac?'

'Yes, I'm sure he has, and we are always open to a good proposition.'

'Good. Now if you excuse me, I have to go finish the passion.'

'A man's got to do what a man's got to do,' I said.

'More like a man's got to do what the woman needs, yes?' Oralik replied laughing.

We parted short of midday with firm handshakes and a promise of a get-together with the ladies in tow.

'So what do you think of him, Mac?'

'I wasn't sure at first but he's quite the character with his head screwed on.'

'That he is, I can assure you.'

'I wonder what the proposition will en-tail?'

'I have no idea but it will entail a lot of money. That I can promise us.'

'I can't wait to find out,' I replied grinning.

'Me too. Taxi!' Jacques shouted hailing a taxi.

I phoned Fox and Izzy to see if they wanted to meet up for lunch but as predicted, there was no reply from both of them with their phones going straight through to voicemail, so we decided to do a little shopping ourselves after which we had a bite to eat outside a restaurant under the canopy, taking in the hustle and bustle of the early afternoon, watching people flit past here and there. Much to our surprise, we spotted Fox and Izzy walking a distance away, loaded up with shopping bags of all colours, chatting away to each other as they walked until they sat down outside a restaurant just to the left of us across the way. We both quickly put our sunglasses on and ducked down slightly, trying not to be seen by them.

We eyed the pair of them as we ate our cannelloni when we noticed two guys sitting at the table opposite them, eyeing them both too when one called over to them. Not being able to hear what the man had said, we both sat bolt upright, pushed our plates away from us and leant forward straining our ears, though it was impossible to hear what they were saying anyway. Jacques folded his arms on the table whilst I lit a cigarette and inhaled deeply.

'This will be interesting,' I said exhaling.

'You're fucking right it will,' Jacques replied who was now rocking his fork back and forth between the fingers of his right hand.

Our girls took no notice of whatever the man had said and continued drinking their cappuccinos when the other man urged his friend on again. The man stood up and walked over to their table and ran his hands through his hair and began making hand gestures to his friend and himself.

'What do you make of it, Jacques?'

'Probably wants to get into their knickers, I reckon,' he replied angrily.

'That's understandable.'

'Yeah.'

'Do you think they'd…'

'Nah… Not their type, Mac.'

'Shit! They're sitting down at their table,' I whispered.

'Why are you whispering?' Jacques asked.

'Dunno,' I replied scratching my head.

Jacques sat back and crossed one leg over the other, raised his arm and rested his chin in his hand and said, 'Cheeky bastards.'

'Who, Fox and Izzy?'

'No! The two goons, mate.'

'Oh.'

'Fuck me, he's got hold of Izzy's hand!' Jacques shouted.

'The other fucker's got hold of Fox's!'

'The cheeky bastards,' he stated.

'Let's get over there, Jacques.'

'No! Wait a minute, let's see if they go off with them?'

'Are you kidding me!?'

'Wait a minute, Mac! We have to be sure.'

'Sure of what?'

'That they'll go off with them.'

'Those guys are holding their hands.'

'I can see that but wait.'

'Now they're stroking their palms!'

'That does it, let's get over there!' Jacques said suddenly changing his mind.

We ran across the square and were on top of the guys with fists clenched when Fox looked up and with a big smile and said, 'Hi guys, we're having our palms read.'

'I got a long lifeline,' said Izzy.

'Oh er... We were just passing and happened to notice you both...'

'Don't be such a fibber, we spotted you both having lunch over there and have been watching you ever since we sat down,' Fox giggled.

'Yeah, we thought you'd get the wrong impression and come running,' Izzy said through a fit of giggles.

'You should see your faces, boys, they're a picture,' Fox said giggling away.

'Why you pair of...'

'Wind ups?' Izzy concluded.

'Fucker's,' I replied laughing.

'I'm going to get you back for this, Isobelle Omerta, and you, Fox,' Jacques told them, both seeing the funny side of their antics.

'Well, don't just stand there, boys! Join us and have your fortunes read,' Fox said.

'I'm not having my hands felt by another man!' I declared.

'Me neither,' Jacques added.

'Don't be silly now, boys, they're both gay,' Izzy enlightened us.

The two gay guys looked at us and smiled when one added, 'The pleasure's all mine I can assure you.'

'Mine too,' the other gay guy added, pouting his lips and winking.

'Do you mind if we hot tail it out of here, girls?' Jacques asked them.

'No, we don't,' they both replied through a seizure of giggles.

'Men. They're all the same duck!' the gay guy said to Fox whilst whimsically shooing us away with his hand.

'Right... Well... Err... see you girls later then... I suppose,' Jacques said.

'Back at the hotel,' I added.

'Count on it, duck,' Izzy replied giggling.

'Oh, and boys,' Fox called out as we were leaving.

'What?' I asked.

'Now would be a good time to go back and pay your bill and explain to the police why you done a runner,' Fox reminded us with a nod of her head in the direction of the restaurant we had just ran from.

We both turned around and looked back towards the restaurant and could see the waiter pointing at us whilst talking to two policemen. 'Shit,' we both said aloud and quickly ran back to sort the mistake out with the waiter and policemen.

It was on our last evening in Milan at our hotel, just after we had finished eating in the hotel's restaurant and were crossing over the foyer into the lounge, when Anna, Oralik's wife, came storming through the front entrance looking vexed when the doorman came crashing through the doors after her with Oralik holding him by the scruff of the neck, dragging him up to the reception desk.

'Nasty bastard you! That's my wife!' Oralik yelled down at him.

'What the hell...' I started to say.

Fox interjected, 'Oh god no! It's that mad man and his wife.'

'Oh fuck,' Izzy sighed.

'Why is he manhandling the doorman?' I asked.

'I think we're about to find out,' Jacques replied smiling.

The receptionist shrunk and took a step back from his desk and asked Oralik quite bravely, 'Problem, sir?'

'Problem, yes! This dirty pervert looks at my Anna's ass as she walks in through the door,' Oralik told him angrily.

'Sorry, I no look,' the doorman pleaded to the receptionist.

'Don't lie, you filth!' Oralik barked, shaking him by the scruff of his coat.

The receptionist composed himself and asked Oralik in his most formal of mannerisms, 'Can you let him go, sir, please?'

'No! Not till I see the manager. I want to report the pervert for being a pervert,' Oralik told the receptionist adamantly.

'I not the pervert,' the doorman squeaked.

Oralik shook him a little more and said, 'Shut up, you filthy pervert dog.'

Anna blurted out a rapid volley of Russian, then said in crumpled English, 'He, the sexist man who, the ass that make him drool like a pervert dog he is.'

'Can you let him go sir, please?' the receptionist asked again.

Oralik threw the doorman to the floor adding, 'Sit, you filthy pervert dog. Now the manager, if you please,' Oralik asked the receptionist smiling.

'One moment, sir, while I get him,' the receptionist replied, trying his best to remain diplomatic and disappeared quickly.

We remained riveted to the floor where we stood, mouths agape apart from Jacques, who had a big cheesy smile and shouted out to Oralik, 'Brother, what's this?'

Oralik turned his attention to us and replied, 'Good evening, my friends. The bastard pervert looks to see my Anna's ass as she walk in through the door!'

'He done the same to our ladies. He's a snake,' Jacques told him.

'Why you slithering fuck of a pervert on your stomach!' Oralik yelled, pushing the poor doorman flat to the floor with his foot on his stomach adding, 'Now wriggle like the snake you are.'

The poor doorman went into snake mode, wriggling from side to side just as the manager came running up shouting, 'No! No! No! What is this?'

'The filthy snake, dog pervert, who eyes my wife's ass,' Oralik stated.

'Please, allow me, sir!' the manager said, who raised the doorman off the floor to his feet, proceeded to speak to him in a torrent of Italian dialect whilst gesturing with his hands at the doorman and to Oralik and then to Anna, pointing at her bum.

The doorman shrugged his shoulders, so Oralik clipped him across the head with the palm of his hand, followed by a volley of clips across the head through a volley of irate Italian again from the manager, who when finished speaking, held out his hand to the doorman. The sullen doorman regretfully took off his tunic and handed it to the manager, who then pointed to the door; even we were now laughing with Jacques at the odd scene in front of us. The doorman slowly turned around with his head hung low, not daring to look up and slowly started walking to the door. As he passed Anna, she too clipped him across the head whilst calling him god-knows-what in her mother tongue, finishing off in

English, Anna shouted at him as he was half way out the door calling him a 'Dirty dog snake pervert!'

The hotel manager deeply apologised to Oralik and Anna for the now sacked-like-a-dog doorman's rude behaviour and as a token of goodwill from the hotel, he invited them both along with us to accompany him to the lounge where he instructed the barman to give us a free bar and appointed a waiter to take care of our needs personally for the remainder of the evening. Oralik suddenly threw his arms around the hotel manager who let out a high-pitched yelp as Oralik hugged him as a show of his acceptance, but the manager turned pale, his small frame went limp and fainted in Oralik's arms. Anna, Fox and Izzy rushed to the manager's aid and sat him on a chair, and began frantically fanning him with cocktail menus off the bar, telling the waiter to fetch some water whilst Oralik looked down at him puzzled and said, 'What I do?'

'He'll live, brother,' Jacques reassured him.

'I only give him the friendly hug, he almost give me a heart attack. I thought he was dead!' Oralik confessed.

The manager gradually opened his eyes and through a dry gasp of breath, he said, 'You...you almost gave... me a heart attack,' then he casually fainted again.

Fox removed his tie and undid a few top buttons of his shirt saying, 'There, this will help.'

'That's the best bird that ever undressed him,' Jacques chuckled.

'You got that right, mate,' I replied grinning.

Fox was still leaning over in front of the manager when he started to come round again, moaning and as he slowly opened his eyes, his pupils dilated homing in on Fox's cleavage bursting out of her low-cut dress and like a startled horse, his feet began to jive as his eyes rolled in his head when his neck went limp and fell to the side fainting again. Me, Jacques and Oralik cracked up laughing while the girls giggled too at the manager's reaction.

'Don't laugh, it's rude, boys,' Fox stated while trying to conceal her giggles.

'It's fucking hysterical,' I replied, still laughing.

'He's made a right tit of himself,' Jacques said, laughing his bollocks off.

'Tits made my night,' Oralik joked, pissing himself laughing.

Fox shot us three a look that would kill and said, 'Go sit down!'

'But... I...'

'Now!' she said sternly.

Reluctantly, we left the girls to fuss the manager and took a table at the farthest end of the lounge, well away from the scenario at the bar which allowed us to overcome our laughter and ask Oralik about his proposition which turned out to be the Musee du Louvre in Paris. Oralik explained that a Russian Mafia boss was more than willing to pay extremely vast sums of money for a few masterpieces housed in the museum's art galleries, which would net us all literally millions of pounds.

Me and Jacques both sat back dumbfounded as Oralik eyed our reaction and drank champagne, swishing the remainder in the bottom of the glass around and around throughout our silence, whilst he trailed our thoughts with his own imaginative answers…none followed in that instance of his solitude. As for me and Jacques, we were drowning in millions of pound signs as we both looked at each other, smiled, then turned back to Oralik and both said together, 'You're on.'

The hotel manager eventually came around and thanked our women for their support and kindness, then embarrassingly disappeared from sight. The women re-joined us and we all laughed our heads off at the evening's events, from the doorman to the manager, as we drank the hotel's champagne bottle after bottle until we were all happily drunk at the hotel's expense. Oralik and Anna made their excuses to leave as it was close to midnight, so we all walked unsteadily from the lounge and across the foyer together and said our goodbyes through drunken slurs then waved them both off in their taxi. The four of us made our way to the lifts and up to our hotel rooms, where me and Fox slowly struggled to undress ourselves and fell into bed, giving each other the sloppiest of sloppy kisses after which we wrapped our arms around each other, mumbling sweet nothings as we moulded our bodies together in comfort. A smile spread across my face as we both fell happily asleep.

The next morning Jacques and Izzy decided to fly back to London while I and Fox flew back to Agde in France for a few days before returning back to the UK. Bernie picked us up at the airport and once we were back in Agde at our house, I explained to Bernie and Fox, Oralik's proposition of the Musee du Louvre, to which they both fell suddenly silent in their thoughts.

Fox laughed breaking the silence saying, 'You got to be bloody kidding me?'

'Not at all, love,' I said in response.

'That's madness if you ask me,' Bernie chuckled.

'And why is that, Bolt?' I asked.

'Have you got any idea how much security there is in that Louvre?'

'Not yet, no, but that's what we're going to find out when the time comes,' I told him.

'And when is that?' Fox asked amused.

'I was thinking of getting past Christmas and taking a peek in the New Year right after all the festivities,' I replied.

'And how do you plan on getting inside unnoticed and walking off with the paintings?' Bernie asked in bewilderment.

'That's what we've got to work out, I'm afraid.'

'Hang on a minute here, don't you think that if the Louvre could be robbed, it already would have been?' Fox stated.

'That's true,' Bernie said in agreement.

'Maybe it's been overlooked,' I replied eyeing their reactions.

'Maybe you're overlooking something, babe.'

'What's that, love?' I replied.

'Oralik is crazy, like the whole fucking idea.'

'Maybe you two are overlooking something too?' I told them both.

'And what would that be?' Bernie asked puzzled.

'How much we stand to earn if we can find a way to pull it off?'

'And how much we stand to lose if we get caught,' Fox added.

'Okay, points taken. But give it some thought from time to time. We get past the New Year's celebrations then we'll go take a peek. After all, there's no harm in looking, is there?' I said smiling.

Bernie grinned and said, 'Agreed.'

We both looked at Fox who was silent. She looked at each of us in turn, raised her eyebrows, pulled a long funny face for a few seconds and said, 'Okay, agreed.'

We drove over to Mick's house unannounced with Mick and Marie Claire welcoming us all with open arms. Fox side-tracked Marie Claire away from us, pointing at a little statue in the garden and remarked how lovely it was as they both walked over to it, giving Bernie and I the space we needed to ask Mick in on the job, but as we had guessed, he point blank refused to have anything to do with it though he thanked us for the invite and said he was happier than he had ever been with his life with Marie Claire and wished us all the luck in the world. Respecting his wishes, I changed the subject and suggested we go find the girls out in the garden to which Mick smiled and led the way. Me and Bernie looked at each other, shrugged our shoulders and followed Mick out to the garden.

The new year came and went in spectacular style with fireworks lighting the skies up with celebrations going on everywhere. Though Bernie and Mick were in France, me and Fox drove up to London to see New Year's Eve in with Jacques and Izzy, who laid on a lavish party at her house in Kensington, attended by her close circle of friends, with a lot of her escort girls playing waitresses, some of whom were saucily dressed in only their underwear, stockings, basques and suspenders. After a few drinks, Fox decided to join in with the waitresses and slipped out of her dress and heels, and gracefully walked around barefooted, semi-naked in her black and red sorbet laced knickers and bra, flirting like hell with the escort girls who responded to Fox seductively as she encouraged them to participate in her game of seduction. Fox came over to me and whispered in my ear, 'Now you've got something better to look at, darling.'

Sneakily, I squeezed her buttock and whispered back, 'Find us a present.'

'I'm working on it, darling,' she replied winking at me and strode off to mingle again.

Jacques came over and asked me nervously, 'What the hell is Fox doing?'

Grinning, I told him, 'Being herself, mate.'

New Year's Day I awoke to the sounds of last night's lust of tiny pants and gasps again. I sat up in bed and watched a naked blonde woman in her late twenties who was stood up with one foot resting on a stool with her leg spread wide apart with Fox kneeling between her legs delivering her tongue around the blonde's pussy. I could see Fox's hand between her own legs playing with her own pussy as she used two fingers expertly to spread the blonde's fissure wider apart and graciously licked her way into the blonde's wet cunt. The blonde opened her eyes and smiled momentarily at me before she licked her lips, inserting a finger and sucked hard on it whilst pinching her hard nipple with her other hand.

I threw back the bed covers and began slowly wanking myself off as the blonde's piercing blue eyes stared wildly at my stiffening cock. She looked down at Fox as her facial expression changed to a tight grimace blowing deeply out of her mouth as she grabbed a handful of Fox's hair and started panting wildly as she thrust her wet pussy hard into Fox's face. In their engagement of uniqueness, Fox worked her own pussy with two fingers, thrusting two frantic fingers in and out of the blonde's juiced cunt. The blonde's panting turned into a rapid barrage of low lustful cries, telling Fox, 'Don't stop, don't stop, don't stop, keep fucking me!'

My cock was full in its magnitude in my grasp as I slowly stroked away to both their exhibition. I continued watching them both with Fox oblivious to my raw epiphanies as the blonde's body stiffened with climax, carving her muscles statuesque as her face contorted to a deep red before her hand unleashed its grip on Fox's hair, rejecting her tongue, pushing Fox away from her soaking cunt as her love juice gushed from her!

Fox sucked on her two spoiled fingers and smiled up at the blonde woman satisfactorily as I made my way over to them both with my throbbing cock in my hand. Fox turned sharply looking up at me wild-eyed and devilishly panting and said, 'Happy New Year.'

I pulled Fox up off her knees and walked her across the bedroom and bent her over in front of the dressing table triple mirrors, spreading her legs wide apart with my foot and thrust my fat cock inside her hot soaked cunt and fucked her wildly, destroying her senses as her hands searched frantically for something to hold onto. Fox's breath partially steamed the mirrors on the dresser which she tried so desperately to wipe off so she could watch me fuck her from behind, slamming herself hard on my throbbing cock. She cried out as she started to cum, 'Don't fucking stop! Don't you dare stop fucking me, you bastard!'

The blonde woman lay sprawled on her back with her legs bent at the knees spread wide apart on the bedroom floor, molesting her own left breast's stiff nipple while finger fucking herself rampantly as she watched Fox getting fucked. Fox's body trembled and moments later, Fox cried out in her orgasmic pinnacle as my body tensioned, pumping my cum violently inside her love-soaked fuck hole and through a deep breath and gritted teeth, I managed to shout out at her 'HAPPY NEW YEAR TO YOU TOO!!'

Chapter 17

Masquerades in Paris

We arrived at Charles de Gaulle Airport and from there caught the metro to the centre of Paris, and once above ground, we caught a taxi to the Delphi Hotel on the Île Saint-Louis opposite Notre Dame Cathedral, and once we were booked in and shown to our rooms, I called Bernie at the Hotel La Cite and informed him of mine, Jacques and Fox's arrival. The following morning, we split up as pre-arranged to case the Musee du Louvre with both myself and Jacques entering separately while Fox and Bernie entered together, making out Bernie was blind. Bernie refused to enter the museum unless he was disguised, so firstly we had to find and buy him a blind man's white cane and dark glasses, which didn't take too long at all as it just so happened that as we were passing a café, we noticed a blind man with his guide dog sitting outside at a table with his stick lent up against the empty chair next to him, but he was still wearing his big dark glasses on his face. We all looked at each other shrugging our shoulders and nodding in approval so Jacques walked over to the blind man and was delicately removing the cane when the blind man's hand shot out at lightning speed, grabbing Jacques by the wrist.

We pissed ourselves laughing as Jacques froze on the spot when the blind man said to Jacques, 'Don't touch my coffee, waiter, I haven't finished drinking it yet.'

'Of course, sir,' Jacques replied sweating as the blind man let go of his wrist. Jacques picked the cane up and hurriedly walked off breathing a sigh of relief.

When he returned back to us with the cane, I asked laughing, 'What happened?'

Jacques let out another sigh of relief and said, 'Phew! I thought I was caught! He thought I was a waiter taking away his bloody coffee.'

'We still need his glasses,' Bernie said grumpily.

'If you want them, Bolt, you can go and fucking get them yourself,' Jacques told him.

'Right, I will,' he replied and walked into a bric-a-brac shop just behind us. Two minutes later, he emerged smiling and held up a pair of old chemistry glasses saying, 'These should do the job,'

'But they're clear glasses,' Jacques pointed out.

Bernie stopped in his tracks and said, 'How the hell will he know the difference. He's blind.'

'Oh yeah,' Jacques replied sulkily.

Bernie, whose French had improved over the past few months, approached the blind man and told him he was a policeman looking for a con artist who portrays himself as a blind man, and asked the blind man if he had any identification on him. The blind man started to protest when Bernie interrupted him, saying he was sorry for the inconvenience but he had to make sure he wasn't the man the police was looking for as a process of elimination. The blind man handed Bernie his wallet and said, 'Take a look for yourself!

To which Bernie replied, 'Please, could you remove your glasses, sir?'

Again, the blind man started to protest when Bernie reminded him that if he did not co-operate, he would have to arrest him. Reluctantly, the blind man removed his glasses and put them on the table saying, 'Does this resolve the matter?'

Bernie quickly switched the glasses and said, 'I think it does, sir, sorry for troubling you. And enjoy your coffee.'

The guide dog barked twice.

Bernie walked off as the blind man picked up the old chemistry glasses and put them on his face without noticing the difference and took a sip of his coffee, muttering away to himself in French.

To our astonishment, Bernie had pulled it off and when he came back to us, he said, 'I can't wait to see the masterpieces in the Louvre,'

'I beg to differ, Bolt, I can't see a damn thing through these glasses,' Jacques told him.

Bernie pulled a face and called Jacques a smartass.

Once we were all inside the Musee du Louvre, we all split up, taking different routes except for Bernie and Fox of course, who ambled along together though the ticket salesman shot them both a peculiar glance and then went back to selling tickets to the queue of tourists behind us. Fox stopped at a large white marble statue of a naked man with his arm held out and pretended to explain to Bernie what she was seeing to him when Bernie reached out to touch it, only to fondle the naked statue's genitalia, to which Fox started pissing herself laughing. Bernie asked her, 'Is it a bird of some sort with eggs?'

'Yes, it is,' she replied taking the piss out of Bernie adding, 'You learn quickly, Bolt.'

'That's what my tutor told me when I was studying mechanics,' he stated.

'That's why you're so good with nuts and bolts then?'

'Naturally,' he replied smiling.

'Oh, I can see you're a natural, mate.'

'Really?' Bernie mused.

'By how you're grabbing this Greek guy's cock and balls,' she told him and bent over at the waist laughing her head off.

Bernie lifted the glasses momentarily and let out a shriek and began walking off tapping his cane on the floor and bumped into a statue, only for Fox to go racing to his aid. After spending a few hours wandering around the Louvre, we all headed back to the hotel and came to the conclusion that the security was overwhelmingly tight but all agreed it was worth giving the Louvre another once over just to see if we had missed anything from our visit today. On our second visit, we went disguised as Scotsmen in full attire which we managed to hire from a fancy dress shop that I found online not too far away from our hotel. I Jacques and Bernie changed into our outfits which consisted of a tartan tamo' shanter cap with bright orange hair attached to it, a tartan kilt with white knee-high socks and a sporran.

All I could manage for Fox was a Sassie Lassie outfit consisting of a small tartan hat, a green tartan corset style dress with red diagonal opaque tights which did not amuse Fox very much, even though us lads found it to be quite exhilarating. Fox was in fits of laughter when she saw us in our disguises, to which Bernie grumbled that he wasn't wearing his outfit, but once Fox had composed herself and told Bernie he looked magnificent in his outfit, his spirit lifted and started Highland dancing around the hotel room, skipping here and there, much to all our amusement and fits of laughter.

When we arrived at the Musee du Louvre, and got a good few strange looks from people as we entered the building and got even more strange looks once we were inside, but crossing over the foyer to the ticket desk, the ticket salesman looked up shocked but retained his courtesy smile and said, 'Bonjour.'

Bernie brushed past us all and stepped up to the ticket counter, and looking the ticket seller in the eye, blurted out in his best Scottish accent, 'Alrite, pal, fur tikets!!'

'Pardon, sir,' came the ticket seller's reply.

Bernie barked back, 'Wat de fek? Youz bladdy def, pal?'

Very politely, the ticket seller asked with a raised eyebrow, 'Pardon me, sir. But are you wishing to buy tickets?'

'Fek I, pal, fur de new.'

'I'm sorry, sir, I don't follow,' the ticket seller replied baffled.

'Dini understan' English!'

'What?' the ticket seller asked, cocking his head to one side and straining his ear.

'Sees youz Jimmy! I fekin heed butt yas if you nos gives ma fur tikets fir me and my pals 'ere!'

'I still don't follow, sir,' the ticket seller replied confused.

I stepped forward and in a milder Scottish accent said, 'Four tickets, please.'

'You want four tickets?'

'I pal, please.'

'Where are you from?' the ticket seller asked whilst sorting out the tickets.

Bernie scowled at the man and said, 'Glasgow ya ninny!!'

The ticket seller raised his eyebrows at Bernie and handed me the four tickets smiling. We swiftly moved on in fits of laughter, more so at Bernie's antics other than anything else, and spent the next few hours again scanning every corner of the building interior for alarms and security camera's (which were everywhere) and counting the guards on duty, and still it looked impossible to penetrate until a plan started to form in my mind.

We all left the Musee du Louvre none the wiser (except for me) to our first visit, except for picking up on a few more laser alarms that we had failed to notice on our first visit but on the whole, they would be the least of our problems.

Back at the hotel, I telephoned Oralik who fell silent and listened intently to what I was telling him and once I had finished speaking, telling him about Bernie, he was in fits of laughter. His fits subsided and when he finally spoke, he was full of enthusiasm and agreed to the plan that I suggested, saying it was better that we hit the Louvre at night with less people being around with less traffic on the roads and that he would start preparing things at his end while we prepared things at our end.

I informed the others of what I had in mind and although they were all taken aback at first, they soon warmed to the plan to which they all agreed was probably the only way to rob the Musee du Louvre and stand a good chance of getting away with it. Bernie voiced a plan of his own too, to which we all listened intently and once he had spelled it out, we all agreed in favour of it. Now all we had to do was get the okay from Oralik that he too was ready and then finalise a night when the Louvre closed early to the public and surprise the hell out of the security guards who hopefully with a lot of luck on our side we would catch them all off guard. We prepared ourselves over the next few weeks and purchased the goods for the job ahead of us and working to a tight deadline, it didn't take very long for the eventful night of the Musee du Louvre to come around.

Chapter 18

Musee du Louvre – The Heist

Oralik flew the Bell UH-1 Iroquois helicopter high above the streets of Paris when suddenly the helicopter's nose dipped and we started descending downwards. Oralik yelled at me and Jacques over his shoulder, 'Hang on very tight, my brothers.'

The helicopter continued in its descent downwards at an even more alarming rate, throwing us further back into our seats. My eyes widened with panic thinking that the helicopter was malfunctioning. A cold sweat broke across my forehead when Oralik suddenly levelled the helicopter out of its descent just above the Eiffel Tower, barely missing the white beacon on top of it by a mere 20 feet!

'I always dreamed of doing that since I was a little boy, now it's off my bucket list,' Oralik yelled out over his shoulder, flying onwards towards the Musee du Louvre.

'That was a close one,' Jacques yelled back at him.

'Anything else you plan on doing in your bucket list while we're up here?' I yelled at him.

'Sorry if I shit you up, brothers,' Oralik yelled back at us.

'You did, you nut,' I screamed back.

'I know, brother, but you like, yes?'

'For fuck's sake,' I cussed out.

'Okay, my brothers, it's time to climb on the moto-cross bikes and perform safety checks, we're almost on top of the Louvre,' Oralik ordered.

We undid our harnesses and climbed on to our motocross bikes, checking that they were still securely strapped to the skid plate and donned our ski masks and helmets. We put our rucksacks on, making sure they were fastened tight to our chests and then gave each other a nod that we were ready.

'We're good to go,' Jacques yelled at Oralik.

'Get ready, I can see the Grand Gallery roof,' Oralik yelled at us.

'What happens if we fall off the bikes, brother?' I yelled at Oralik.

'You die and cause me great sadness, but you'll be okay, I think,' Oralik replied.

'Is he for fucking real?!' I said to Jacques.

'Oralik, pack the cappers in,' Jacques told him sternly.

'What I do? I have little fun with sense of humour. If you no like, no problem! But I like,' he replied laughing.

I sat on the motocross bike dumbfounded by Oralik's antics, taking in a deep breath before letting it out slowly when the helicopter came to a smooth stop and began hovering above the Musee du Louvre's Grand Gallery's roof. Oralik yelled out, 'Now go do your work, brothers, and make us rich men.'

'But you're already rich,' I yelled back at him.

'Yes, I know! Do you think I'm stupid?' he shouted back.

'I got my doubts sometimes,' I told him.

'See you in Agde,' Jacques shouted to Oralik pushing the winch button.

Oralik turned to face us smiling and said, 'Good luck to you, my brothers.'

I hung onto tightly to the handle bars of the bike as we began descending downwards and watched as the illuminated glass roof of the Grand Gallery sped to meet us. A few meters from impact, Jacques released the primary heavy metal skid plate, sending it into a twirling descent that smashed straight through the glass apex of the Grand Gallery roof, closely followed by us on the secondary skid plate with the motocross bikes strapped to it, hitting the floor of the gallery with only a light impact. Oralik had calculated the drop very well as it could have been harder or even fatal. We instantly released the straps holding the motor bikes to the secondary skid plate and Jacques told Oralik via radio com to winch the cable back up with the skid plate that formed part of the helicopter's floor.

We each threw a smoke grenade over our shoulders and sped off on the bikes through the museum along the ground floor of the Denon Wing to the staircase that led up to the 1st floor and stopped at the adjoining Sully Wing, we hurled another two smoke grenades down the hallways before moving on. As we came to the staircase, two frightened security guards stood in our path.

'Tasers! Take the one on the right,' Jacques said on his radio com.

'Check,' I replied pulling the taser from its holster, aiming it at the security guard and squeezed the trigger, and before I knew it, the guard was on the floor shaking violently alongside the other guard.

'Move up,' Jacques ordered.

I pulled back the throttle and followed him up the staircase to the 1st floor and again we deployed another two smoke grenades back down to the ground floor and hurled two more down the hallway of the Sully Wing on the 1st floor as we made our way around to our main goal and our ultimate prize: the Mona Lisa. Firstly, while Jacques was setting the breaching charges to the wall, I went to the Mona Lisa, it being the Russian Mafia's Grand Prix, and sprayed the glass case with a special formulated acid foam that would eat its way into the bullet-proof glass housing the Mona Lisa, rendering it useless to a minor blow. While the acid was taking its effect, I moved onto the other three paintings I had been assigned to steal. One by one, I cut them out of their frames and rolled them all up, putting them inside the alloy canister fastened to the side of my motor-cross bike.

Jacques on the other hand had finished setting the breaching charges to the museum wall and was busy removing his four paintings from their frames. Hot and sweating, I turned my attention back to the Mona Lisa and as assured, with only a light blow the glass shattered and I reached in for her. The gallery was now starting to fill very heavily with green smoke from the smoke grenades. A guard appeared out of the smoke coughing with a hanky over his mouth, only for Jacques to rush at him and knock him out with a heavy punch, sending the guard reeling back in to the sea of green smoke. I removed the Mona Lisa triumphantly and put her in the alloy cylinder along with the other three paintings and informed Jacques, 'I'm all done here.'

Oralik came over the radio com and said, 'Hey brothers! You have some serious company at the main entrance but I taking care of them for you, dropping the smoke grenades and stun grenades.'

'Almost done here, brother,' Jacques told Oralik.

'Brothers! I have to go now as I have competition up here with enemy choppers, so I leave to shake them off as they waving guns at me,' he said laughing.

'Is he for fucking real?' I said.

'Hey brother, I heard that and after all I do for you…'

'He was on about a guard,' Jacques told him.

'Okay, I go now, brothers,'

'Check,' I replied.

'Take your bike to that far wall,' Jacques ordered.

'Check,' I replied doing as he ordered.

A few seconds later, Jacques was next to my side on his moto-crosser holding a detonator in his hand and with a big grin said, 'Are you ready for this, brother?'

'As ready as I'll ever be. Let's get the fuck out of here,' I told him.

'Your wish is my command,' he said and detonated the breaching charges.

The explosion from the breaching charges tore a gaping hole in the gallery wall bigger than I had expected and as the air got sucked out with the smoke, I could see the night lights of Paris and the lovely lit Seine.

'See you on the other side, mate. I'll be two seconds behind you. Now make the jump!' Jacques ordered.

'See you at the boat,' I replied pulling the throttle back and sped towards the gaping hole in the museum wall.

The next moment I was gliding through the air with the ground beneath my feet and as if time had slowed to almost a standstill, I glanced to my right and noticed all the patriotic flashing lights of the police vehicles being smothered by green smoke. The bike landed hard and I accelerated to the Seine. 'I'm down!' I said in my radio com.

'Me too,' Jacques replied.

As I neared the Seine Wall, I slammed on the brakes too hard and felt the bike sliding away from underneath me, sending me tumbling along the floor to the river's edge, coming to an abrupt halt after a few hard rolls. I was trying to gather my thoughts when I felt myself being yanked up to my feet by Jacques who said, 'Jog on, mate, we got a boat to catch, and don't forget the paintings.'

A little dazed, I reached over the bike and unclipped the alloy cylinder with the paintings inside and climbed into the waiting boat where Bernie was waiting behind the helm. Smiling, he called out, 'Welcome aboard ship, mate,' and powered up the engines and sped off down the Seine.

'Are you okay, Mac?' Jacques asked.

'No broken bones if that's what you mean,' I replied.

'Then sit back and enjoy the ride,' Bernie shouted out.

Oralik came over the radio com, 'Fuck me! What an exit. I thought you kill yourselves for sure, brothers. You are truly mad men,' he exclaimed.

'Is that a fact?' I said.

''Course it's fact. Wait till you see this on the news tomorrow, brother!'

'Where are the police helicopters to?' Jacques asked.

'They far away looking for me. I am, how you say, the sneaky fuck. Yes?' he replied smugly.

'Lucky fuck more like it,' Bernie said.

'O shit, brothers!'

'What now,' I asked.

'You have two pirates coming up the river,' Oralik stated.

'What do you mean by pirates?' I asked him sarcastically.

'Police in boat,' he replied.

'Two police in a boat?' I asked.

'No. brother. Lots of police in two boats,' he replied.

'Shit! Did you get that Bernie?' I asked.

'Loud and clear. The smoke buoys are under that canvas,' Bernie replied pointing to them.

'What side of the Isles are they approaching, brother?' I asked Oralik.

'Looks like they going to split either side,' he informed us.

On hearing Oralik's message, Bernie swiftly took evasive action, steering the speedboat to the wall of Île de la Cité and stopped at a blind spot where we were hidden out of sight from the approaching patrol boats and waited. The patrol boats sped past us at full speed without noticing us and as they passed us, both me and Jacques threw two smoke buoys overboard as Bernie took off again at full throttle down the Seine away from the passing patrol boats, taking the right-hand side of the Île de la Cité and raced towards Fox, who was waiting for us at a rendezvous point along the embankment of the Pont de l'Archevêché in line with the channel that separated Île de la Cité and the Île Saint-Louis, which she had marked with a small blue fluorescent glow-stick attached to a length of fishing line hung over the side of the Seine that she immediately lowered down after the breaching charges had exploded the wall of the Louvre. Looking behind us, we could see the smoke buoys were screening us as planned but for good measure, we tossed another two overboard as Bernie continued racing forwards then called out, 'I see Fox's marker, get ready to dump the loot!

As the boat began to slow, I too could see the blue marker a few feet above the water line of the Seine and could make out Fox's silhouette above on the embankment. Bernie quickly manoeuvred the speedboat alongside the wall, stopping at the marker as Fox threw us down a large rucksack tied to a length of cord. I hastily put the two alloy cylinders inside the rucksack and pulled the drawstring to a close and locked its flap then called up to Fox to haul the rucksack back up.

Bernie fully opened the throttle of the speedboat as soon as the rucksack left my hand, sending me flying backwards, almost falling out of the boat, but Jacques was quick to catch hold of me and stopped me from falling overboard as we sped off down the Seine again to our final destination, where we were to ditch the speedboat and make for our getaway car. Ahead of us we could see the lights of another police patrol boat fast approaching us when Bernie yelled at us to hang on tight and spun the boat around in a tight circle before speeding back up the Seine towards the direction of the museum.

'What the fuck are you doing?' I shouted at him.

'Trust me, Mac! Throw two more smoke buoys overboard quickly,' he ordered.

We immediately tossed the smoke buoys overboard as Bernie changed his course, cutting back across to the right side of the Seine when after about 50 metres, he urged us to toss another two smoke buoys overboard and again repeating the process another 50 metres on. The river was now thick with green and red smoke. Bernie manoeuvred the boat in an arc so we were engulfed inside the thick curtain of smoke. At full throttle again, the speedboat's nose rose up in the air and sped forwards through the smoke when suddenly we emerged from the smoke screen to the oncoming patrol boat. Bernie let out a battle cry as he held our course, aiming our boat at the oncoming patrol boat when in the dying seconds of impact, Bernie pulled out of the way, allowing the patrol boat to speed past us and lose itself inside the thick curtain of smoke that now engulfed the Seine with the wind blowing it down river, making it harder for the patrol boats caught up inside the smoke to emerge at speed, giving us that vital edge over them as we continued our escape. We noticed the police cars racing alongside the Seine with their lights flashing and sirens blazing on either side of the river following us.

'When we're near the river wall, get ready to jump in and swim for the marker when I give the command,' Bernie told us.

'What about you?' I asked him.

'Don't worry about me, I'll be right behind you,' he replied.

'Do we have to get wet?' Jacques yelled at Bernie.

'Either that or spend the next 50 years in a French jail,' Bernie yelled back at him.

'Water it is, brother,'

'On my mark, shipmates,' Bernie shouted as he swung the speedboat around close to the Seine Wall, where another blue fluorescent glow-stick hung attached to a rope ladder, 'JUMP!' Bolt cried out.

Unhappily, we both jumped overboard into the cold dark water of the Seine and swam for the rope ladder as Bernie set the speedboat at full throttle, directing it back up river and leapt out himself and began swimming for the ladder. The police cars screeched to a halt and turned back around chasing the speedboat up the river, where it got engulfed by the smoke screen when a few seconds later there was a large explosion on the other side of the river from the speedboat crashing into the rivers wall. I and Jacques were out of the cold Seine water and at the top of the ladder peering around to see if there were any other police cars loitering near us and with none in sight, we quickly proceeded over the top, calling quietly down to Bernie to hurry up while we still had an advantage on our side.

Bernie came over the top of the wall with the three of us drenched, looking like drowned rats, we began making our way to the getaway car, squelching with every footstep we took. It sounded like we were all farting which gave us all the giggles.

And the more we hurried along, the funnier the squelching sounds became as did our giggles that eventually turned into fits of laughter from us all. We did our best to duck and dive as not get seen, as we continued with our escape only to bump into a pair of romantics hand in hand taking an evening stroll, who hardly bat an eye at us thanks to our lucky stars. Making it to the first getaway car, Bernie retrieved the key from under the front wheel arch and pressed the fob opening the doors.

'Thank fuck for that!' he exclaimed sneezing.

We drove through the quiet streets of Paris before we joined the Autoroute de l'Est, staying just under the speed limit with the car in front. While Bernie drove, Jacques and I changed into our getaway clothes whilst the Bolt's only comfort was from the car heaters on full blast; again he sneezed causing us to swerve slightly.

'Steady, Bolt,' I told him.

'It's okay for you two cosy bastards all nice and warm in dry clothes,' he snarled back.

'Let me drive while you change in to your dry clothes,' I suggested to him.

276

'No, you'll get lost, Mac,' he grumped back.

'You can direct me.'

'No! Like I said, you'll get lost,' he grumped again.

'How can I get lost, it's a straight fucking road for Christ sake!' I told him.

Bernie pointed at an overhead sign and asked me, 'What does that say up there?'

'How the hell would I know, it's in French,' I replied.

'What does this sign mean?' Bernie asked smiling, sticking his middle finger up at me.

Jacques pissed himself laughing as Bernie swung off the L'Autoroute and into the side streets and a few minutes later, Bernie quietly parked in a car park behind a block of flats. Amid his sneezes, Bernie changed into his dry clothes as I opened the second getaway car and took a can of petrol from the boot and walked over to the first car and opened all the car doors before dousing the interior with petrol. Jacques came over and threw our wet clothes inside as I ignited my lighter and tossed it inside the car, igniting it in a ball of flames. I quickly jumped inside the second getaway car, telling Bernie to go and as Bernie casually drove out of the car park and turned onto Rue Victor Hugo, we all heard the loud explosion of the first car. I turned around and looked through the rear windscreen and saw a fire ball rise into the night air. Bernie put his foot down on the accelerator and headed for Agde.

Jacques took the mobile phone out from the glove compartment and handed it to me saying, 'You had better call Fox, mate.'

I turned the phone on and dialled the only number stored in it and after three rings, a voice said, 'Lips...'

'Sealed,' I replied.

'Thank God!' Fox said relieved.

'Are you okay, love?' I asked her.

'Several millions okay, thank you very much,' she replied ecstatically.

'Are you in your hotel?'

'Yes, babe.'

'Were there any problems with you getting there?'

'No, babe, I put the rucksack on my back and walked off like a backpacker reading a map in my hand straight through the thick of it all,' she replied laughing.

'You're amazing,' I told her.

'I know, babe, and so are you. Mwah! Mwah!'

'You need to get some sleep,' I told her.

'Don't think I can, babe,' she replied excitedly.

'Do your best, love, and we'll see you tomorrow,' I told her.

'Okay, love you millions and millions,' she replied giggling.

'I love you, too.'

'Oh, babe.'

'Yes?'

'Give my love to Jacques and Bolt,' she said.

'Fox sends her love, guys,' I told them.

'We love you back,' Bernie shouted out and sneezed.

'Good night, babe.'

'Sleep tight,' I replied.

I opened the back of the phone and removed the sim card and snapped it in half before tossing it out of the window along with the phone. I lit up a cigarette and inhaled deeply relieved and after blowing the smoke out through the open window, I began laughing manically with the Bolt and Jacques joining in that soon turned into roaring fits of laughter as we left the Musee du Louvre behind us along with Paris.

Chapter 19

Prague –'Ello Mr Wolf!

Life returned back to normal again for a few peaceful days as it seldom did when Jacques got the phone call from Oralik on the Monday evening that we had been anxiously waiting for while we were all sat out on the terrace out the back of the restaurant overlooking the little harbour back in Agde while eating and drinking cold beers as the sun was setting. Jacques informed us that Oralik had set up a meeting in Prague in the old Jewish quarter of the city for the second coming weekend ahead where we would exchange the stolen masterpieces for the millions of pounds we had been promised by Oralik, who stated that the money would be transferred to our offshore bank account once all the paintings were verified as genuine. Jacques had asked Oralik who the buyer was and very reluctantly Oralik told Jacques that the buyer was the Russian billionaire, Demyan Volkov, otherwise known as "The Wolf" to all in his vicious circle of friends.

Nonetheless, Oralik's assurance was all that Jacques needed to be convinced that the Wolf was somehow decorous and of good creed. I on the other hand kept my thoughts to myself for the time being as not to upset Jacques as he and Oralik did class each other as brothers, and I didn't want to cast any doubt in Jacques' mind. But as history has taught most of us other siblings in life, there will come a time when siblings will inevitably fall out with each other.

This thought grew darker in my mind as the sun set over Agde's little harbour along with a chill that filled the air as dark clouds started to fill the early evening night sky. A rumble of thunder echoed way off in the distance; *a storm was coming*, I thought to myself… the sky grew darker!

I, Fox and Jacques arrived in Prague and settled ourselves into a quaint but lavishly decorated little hotel in the old part of the city arriving ahead of Bernie who was driving to Prague with the stolen masterpieces hidden in his car, allowing us three a little more time to get to know our bearings and take in our surroundings. We acted just like any other tourists ambling through the streets with a map in hand and taking snapshots of ourselves at various landmarks and points of interest. Though we were genuinely inspired by this little jewel of a city, along with its architecture and mixture of life and a feeling for Prague's new culture that had risen from the hardships of the early years and the torments to the city that had been buried into the history books housed in the vaults of the public library for safe-keeping, fragile and gathering dust along with its dark secrets kept away from the public.

Oralik and Anna arrived a few hours after us and were staying in the Grand Prague Hotel with all its luxuries and grandeur which thwarted our modest accommodation, yet we were suitably comfortable for our short stay in the city and with our hotel being a tad closer to all the sights and nightlife, the hotel was perfectly situated. Bernie arrived a full two days after us, looking very tired and miserable after his long hard drive from Agde and went to his hotel room putting the do-not-disturb sign on the outside door handle before taking a refreshing shower and got into his comfortable bed, falling asleep as soon as his head hit the pillows.

Oralik and Anna were as dedicated as ever, still making the passion but the complaints flooded in to the hotel management of their loud passion-making by the other guests from all the other floors of their hotel, even though they were on the top floor in one of the two penthouses that overlooked the main street below. Both Oralik's and Anna's love-making didn't go unnoticed by the neighbours either that were living close by in the opposite apartments across the street as well as the other hotels opposite them, as Oralik and Anna left the penthouse windows wide open (no doubt to use the chill in the air to cool themselves down?), but funnily enough in a twisted way, it was Oralik's and Anna's inspiration to the other couples across the way in the nearby hotels that Anna's passion-making love cries (was to a point of driving some people insane) became deafening with everybody else at it making love. And when Anna finally heard the noises of the other couples' loud love-making, she gave Oralik an evil stare. Oralik looked at his Anna a little confused and asked her, 'Why do you stare at me with eyes of a demon?'

'The noisy bastards with their passion, it is driving me mad. It makes my head ache and I can't sleep.'

Oralik sat bolt upright in bed and looked deep into Anna's eyes and said to her softly, 'I sort this problem out for you, my love of my life.'

Anna slowly sat up in bed and put her hands across her midriff and swayed from side to side all coy while eyeing Oralik and said, 'Really?'

He kissed her lightly on her head and said, 'No problem,' then he leapt out of bed and strode out onto the balcony bollock-naked and at the top of his lungs shouted out, 'Everybody stop doing the fucking passion, it giving my Anna a headache.'

About two seconds later from across the street, a man shouted back to Oralik, 'Get your cock in her mouth!

Oralik screamed back at him, 'I stick my cock in your mouth!!'

A male voice called up from a few floors from below Oralik, 'You can stick it in my mouth!!'

'And mine,' a female cried out from an apartment across the street.

'Fuck you all,' Oralik shouted at them all and came back inside off the balcony, only to see his Anna spread out naked on all fours on top of the marble coffee table with her back arched low to the table, displaying two fingers inside herself which she removed whilst keeping her erotic fixation upon Oralik.

'Fuck me!'

'You like the fuckers over the street always wanting to make the passion but with no result for my child.'

'Don't rush beauty,' she replied.

Oralik thought for a moment before he said, 'My love, you have a good point.'

Then thrust his cock in her mouth!!

Fox slipped her arm through mine and gave me a smile, and for the first time in my life, I struggled to smile back at her during the taxi ride to the meeting place at the Church of Our Lady before Týn. It was Sunday morning and we were to arrive at 09:00 am on the button as instructed by Oralik three hours before the church was due to open to the public at 12 pm. Fox squeezed my arm gently and gave me a forced smile then turned her head away from me and looked out the side window of the taxi in silence. I put my hand on top of Fox's hand and gently squeezed it without saying a word. Jacques was with his own thoughts of silence along with me and Fox.

The taxi came to a halt outside the Church of Our Lady before Týn and as I exited the taxi last, I pushed the taxi door to a close with a loud clunk which made Fox jump slightly, letting us know that she wasn't the only one getting a little on edge especially as we were all unarmed and not daring to risk being frisked, and a weapon being found on either of us, god-knows-what may happen. We knew the Wolf would not be alone and would have body guards that would be armed so for us to be armed would be a mistake and a dead cert to get us all killed. I looked at the Church of Our Lady before Týn with all its ugly menacing gargoyle figurines protruding from its stone walls, peering down at us like they were watching us, inspecting us, inviting us to come inside the belly of their lair.

'We are probably being watched,' I said lowly.

'For sure,' Jacques replied whilst slowly viewing the surroundings.

Fox said in a coarse tone, 'I got a bad gut feeling about this guy.'

'Keep a grip on your wits and stay aware. Let's try not to get too paranoid about all this,' I urged her.

'Ready, Mac?' Jacques asked.

'Let's get this over and done with and get the fuck on our way,' I replied, trying to sound confident and walked up to the doors of the church.

Firstly on reaching the doors, I tried pushing them open, they were locked. I knocked on the door and waited...nothing happened. I sighed and knocked a little harder and waited... again nothing happened. Fox stepped forward and booted the heavy door three times with her foot then stepped back away from the door. Suddenly the door opened a third of the way with a man's face appearing from around it and said, 'We have been expecting you,' then he withdrew back behind the door out of sight.

'After you, Jacques,' I said, nodding him through the door.

As he walked past me, he said, 'Thanks, Mac.'

I and Fox followed him inside and no sooner were we all inside, the door slammed shut behind us and a voice hissed, 'Put your hands up where I can see them.'

We had anticipated this kind of greeting but now that we were there, the surrealism of the man's orders hit home hard on our nerves. Slowly, all three of us raised our hands up in the air above our shoulders and held them there when the man said, 'That's good. Now just keep them up while I search you.'

'We are unarmed,' I told him.

'Good for you, but better for me to be safe rather than sorry. No more talk. Silence!' the man demanded.

With Fox being the last through the church door, she was frisked first then told to walk forward to the altar and wait while I was being frisked, then told to join her and finally Jacques was frisked, and he too was ordered to join us at the altar and wait. I started to say a nice greeting but was told by the man from somewhere behind us, or possibly off to the side of us somewhere within the shadows, 'No talking.'

From somewhere in front of us, a man appeared and stood behind the altar and called out, 'Kolzak!'

'Yes, boss.'

'Did you search our guests?'

'Yes, boss.'

'Did you find anything of any threat to us?'

'No, boss.'

'Then be nice to them. Understand?'

'Yes, boss,' Kolzak hissed back.

'Forgive Kolzak and his manners, he is how you would say, not the most sociable of creatures when it comes to being of society's understandings of normal living. He had a very unfortunate childhood to the extent of being orphaned at an early age of seven to be precise and was a difficult child in god's hands at the Orthodox churches' orphanages. Still, he learns new things every day, don't you, Kolzak?'

'Yes, bosssss,' came his hiss from somewhere over my left shoulder.

I said to the man behind the altar, 'Would I be right in guessing you are Mr Volkov?'

'I am afraid you would be guessing wrong,' he replied, pleased that I had made an error in assumption.

'Then why did he...wherever he is...call you boss?' I asked looking around for Kolzak.

Fox leant into me and whispered, 'Do you think it okay to question him?'

The man gave Fox a hard scowl and said to her, 'Do you think it not rude to whisper, Miss Fox-Wright?'

Fox looked at the man stunned that he knew her name. Her cheeks turned red from blushing and like a child that had been told off, she hung her head low and shyly apologised, quickly saying sorry. The man smiled to himself relishing the moment of Fox's degrade, before he turned his attention to Jacques, giving him a cold hard look. Jacques gave the man an even colder look back that made the corners of the man's mouth stretch slightly to the point of a possible smirk, followed by a small inclination of his head to one side as if paying Jacques a compliment.

The man and Jacques both continued to stare each other out when the man broke it off by reeling off, 'Mr Jacques Couture, ex French Foreign Legionnaire. Served three years with the 1st Rep. Small arms expert up to 30 calibre, reconnaissance diver specialising in the use of underwater explosives and demolition. Spent two long years in the highly skilled art of jungle warfare, credited with numerous medals for bravery that you threw away as soon as your commandant's back was turned, if I am correct?'

Jacques gave the man an incline of his head and said, 'Something like that.'

The man's mouth tightened again then he calmly asked Jacques, 'Why did you throw your medals away after all you had been through?'

Jacques's reply was filled with sarcasm, 'Because it kind of weighs you down if you know what I mean, but then again you wouldn't, would you?!'

The man let out a small laugh and said, 'I too have been credited for services to my country, whereas you Mr Couture…'

'Like I give a fuck where as you did!' Jacques told the man pleased with his taunt.

Fox cut their bickering short by saying, 'Can we just get on with what we came here to do!'

The man was a little taken aback looking at Fox amused and said, 'I think you have a point, Miss Fox-Wright.'

'If you're not Demyan Volkov, then who the hell are you?' I asked him.

'Ah…forgive my manners. My name is Veniamin Romanov, first to the right hand of Mr Volkov.'

'And where is Mr Volkov now?' I demanded looking around.

Veniamin winced before he said sternly, 'Enough of your questions! You shall meet Mr Volkov all in good time but firstly I ask that you have a little more patience and wait a short while longer for his arrival.'

'You mean he's not here yet?'

'Sorry for this small delay and please except his apologies on my behalf. Now I have to leave you for a short time under the watchful eye of Kolzak somewhere in the shadows.'

Veniamin walked away from the altar and vanished through a stone-arched doorway suddenly reappearing again and softly said, 'Please feel free to take a pew and discuss the magnificence of this splendid cathedral amongst yourselves.' Then he vanished through the stone-arched doorway again.

How ironic, I thought to myself, take a pew. Veniamin's irony started to take a hold of our minds as we all sat there in silence while taking a pew. I started to look around the cathedral and indeed the splendour of its interior was truly breath-taking as its éclat echoed from wall to wall with its many large stained-glass windows depicting various religious scenes with two of its windows either side of the nave, reminiscent of a kaleidoscope. Each stained-glass window allowed enough early morning light to shine through and partially illuminate the nave's directing passage to the altar's polished stone with intricate decorative vines carved all along the top and sides framed the altar as the centre piece of focalisation.

The top of the altar was less intricately decorated, only having a simple but lavish purple runner through its centre with the edges having gold yarn spun into it that draped over both ends of the altar neatly to the floor. Upon the runner at either end of the altar sat two large thick-stemmed silver candle sticks both mounted with single half-burnt white candles, their wax encrusted down the candle stems as if tears had been frozen in time. In the centre of the altar sat alone but flagged by the candle sticks was a large plain shallow disk-like bowel that was made of fine solid silver.

My solace eyes looked to the wall beyond the altar where a large cross loomed out at me, depicting the crucifixion of Christ impaled upon it with his crown of thorns upon his head with his blood running down over his face onto his chest. I was drawn to his eyes that radiated with empathy or were they broken... porous...empty...sorrowful...perhaps even filled with guilt? Only God would know the truth, if ever there was a God. I lowered my head and closed my eyes, and what became more apparent was how the cathedral silenced the deluge of everyday life beyond its walls, drowning out the noises of traffic and people going about their daily lives, oblivious to all contributes that we so take for granted. Yet the cathedral reposes such activities, casting them from its inner sanctum like a sin. Strange, I thought to myself, how I hadn't noticed this analogy whence first I stepped through the cathedral's doors or possibly I had, but got distracted from it by Kolzak.

I wasn't being allowed to overlook or fail to feel the justice of the church's inner sanctum now with its aura letting itself be known to me as I concluded how strange this feeling or notion was gripping my conscience. The hairs on the back of neck spiked themselves to be known and rose to meet my inner sanctum. I wanted to get out of here but at the same time stay in the clutch of this place away from all of society's inhumane atrocities. It felt safe here. I opened my eyes and began appreciating my silent thoughts when Fox shattered the moment or if not, she saved me from the cathedral's clutches when she abruptly blurted out, 'I need to use the bathroom.'

I shook my numbed head, discarding my conscience and asked her, 'Do you think our elusive friend Kolzak will allow you to go?'

Fox snapped back, 'For Christ's sake! Do you think I'm going to sit here and pee my knickers waiting for this guy Wolf to appear, because I damn well ain't!!'

I called out to Kolzak without turning around, 'Hey, wherever you are, the lady needs to use the bathroom.'

There was a moment of silence before Kolzak replied, 'The lady has to wait.'

Vehemently, Fox told him, 'I can't wait any longer! I've been holding it in and now I can't hold it in any longer, and I don't want to pee my knickers in a goddamn cathedral in front of Jesus Christ nailed to a cross! That is definitely not good for one's soul or one's reputation!!'

Kolzak hissed back at Fox, 'I not understand what you say. You have to wait for the bigger boss to see you.'

'What!!' Fox exclaimed. 'Your bigger boss wants to see me pee?'

'Maybe we are dealing with a bunch of voyeuristic mobsters here?' Jacques said through a tiny fit of giggles which started me and Fox off giggling at the thought of the Wolf being a voyeur, when a hellish giggle came from somewhere in the shadows and stopped abruptly.

'Was that Kolzak?' Fox asked, freezing like a statue.

'I think so, love,' I replied.

Fox laughed aloud and through her laughter she said, 'Holy Christ! That guy is really starting to creep me out.'

'I think he's getting off on the thought himself.'

Fox put her hands between her legs and threw her left leg over her right leg and doubled at the waist and said through gritted teeth, 'I'll fucking kill this Wolf guy if I pee my knickers sat here in front of Jesus, and you two and him, wherever he is!'

Jacques cracked up laughing and put a hand over his mouth to stifle his laughter. Fox still bent over at the waist, turned and looked at Jacques with dagger eyes which instantly killed Jacques's laughter, reducing him to silence. At that moment, Veniamin appeared at the altar looking quite puzzled and asked, 'What is so funny?'

Fox's head shot up backwards, throwing her hair into a mass of what can only be described as if she had been pulled through a hedge backwards with an expression on her face resembling someone who was possessed and needed to be exorcised. Staring viciously at Veniamin, she explained to him through a series of gargling low growls that sounded like a demon was talking through her, 'I need to pee before I piss my fucking knickers!!!'

Me and Jacques grabbed hold of each other and looked at each other scared shitless then we both quickly looked at Veniamin, who had whipped out his pistol with a silencer fitted to it in his hand, pointing it at Fox, horrified at her demonic state. Veniamin gulped twice as if trying to find his voice and asked her, 'Please, Miss Fox-Wright, what is the dilemma?'

Fox seemed to revert back to her normal self apart from the hair. She cleared her throat and calmly told Veniamin, 'I'm going to pee my knickers.'

Veniamin shook his head and shrugged his shoulders, putting his pistol away inside his jacket and grabbed at his chin with his thumb and forefinger, and began caressing it whilst looking at each of us in turn before he said, 'I don't get it.'

The three of us sat there and cracked up laughing at his inability to grasp Fox's anguish when Jacques diplomatically informed Veniamin, 'The lady needs to use the bathroom to relieve herself.'

Veniamin shrugged his shoulders again and said to us, 'You are strange people if you think going to the bathroom is hilariously funny!'

'Yes! Yes! Yes!' Fox cried out painfully.

Nervously, Veniamin said to us, 'Please, if you would follow me this way to the bathroom. And no tricks,' he gave Kolzak a gesture with his head to follow us.

We followed Veniamin through the stone-arched doorway to the left side of the altar and down a narrow stone stairwell with its steps that spiralled endlessly, eventually opening out into a long wide corridor with arched wooden doors set into the walls on both sides with a much larger wooden door to the far end of the corridor facing us dead ahead. Following Veniamin along the corridor, he suddenly stopped and pointed to a door on his right that had a small white opaque plaque fixed to the centre of the door that depicted a winged cherub peeing into a toilet.

Veniamin smiled at Fox and said, 'The bathroom, Miss Fox-Wright, if you please.'

Fox was through the door faster than a rat up a drain pipe, slamming the door hard behind her. Patiently, we waited for Fox and all pretended to glance around at nothing in particular in the silence of her absence when notably we heard Fox's trickling pee in the toilet from inside the bathroom that went on for quite some time before the trickling stopped, leaving us back in our silences only for the trickling to start again but not for so long a period as previously when it stopped again. I and Jacques raised our eye brows at each other while Veniamin fidgeted with his wrist watch, pretending to adjust the time when suddenly the trickling started again, briefly followed by a few tiny barrages of trickling pee.

I looked at the floor whilst Jacques stared at the arched ceiling, pretending he had noticed something of interest while Veniamin pretended he had had something under his fingernail and was trying to clean it out with another fingernail when we heard the toilet flushing to our relief. The toilet door opened with Fox reappearing better for colour but noticing the looks on our faces, she began to blush then she scowled at us and slammed the toilet door shut behind her and yelled out, 'What!!'

Veniamin blurted out, 'Is that normal?'

There was demonic irascibility in Fox's voice when she replied to him saying, 'Is what normal...taking a pee with the door closed?!'

Veniamin reeled back and said, 'So long.'

'Are you leaving us?' Jacques asked him.

'What for?' Veniamin replied baffled.

'You said so long,' Jacques reminded him.

'I am not going anywhere. I just meant so long in the bathroom.'

'She pees for Wales,' I informed Veniamin.

'I have never heard of such a thing before.' Veniamin paused for a second then asked, 'Are they big close up?'

'Are what big close up?!' Fox asked him fuming.

Veniamin looked puzzled but said, 'Why, whales of course.'

'I should imagine so, for their size,' I told him trying not to laugh.

Veniamin looked deep in thought. He sheepishly looked at Fox and asked her, 'Do you do the pee for dolphins too?'

Fox let out a little laugh grasping Veniamin's confusion and playfully told him, 'I only pee on Sundays when the dolphins are close to the shore and if no other persons are around to watch me.'

Veniamin fell silent, deep in thought again. Me and Jacques was smiling from ear to ear at Fox who gave us both a sly wink when Veniamin snapped himself out of his thoughts with a shake of his head and said, 'Interesting, Miss Fox-Wright.'

Fox folded her arms and smiled warmly at Veniamin and said, 'You learn something new every day in this life.'

Veniamin agreed saying, 'Yes,' and added, 'maybe so, but now I think it is time we carry on with the matters to hand.'

'I think it's more than time we got on with meeting Mr Volkov,' I told him.

Veniamin smiled at me nodding his head in agreement then turned his attention to Fox, looking her up and down, transfixing his eyes with Fox's and said, 'I'm sure the pleasure will all be Mr Volkov's.'

'We shall see about that,' Fox told him incensed.

Veniamin's last words of insult didn't go unnoticed by myself nor Jacques and as I stepped forward with fists clenched to punch Veniamin's head off his shoulders, Jacques grabbed hold of my arm, restraining me from my onslaught upon Veniamin. Jacques' restraint did not go unnoticed by Veniamin who made a low grunt and walked off towards the large wooden door. asking us to follow him where he stopped and knocked upon it. Instantly, the door opened; Veniamin beckoned us to follow him inside when from nowhere the sulky Kolzak appeared to our side, like an apparition of a ghost, and said, 'Move.'

Passing through the door into the room beyond, it was difficult to know exactly what the room held or who was in it, as it was too poorly illuminated by a small round single shaded light hanging from the arched stone ceiling which only emitted a small pool of light on the floor that stretched half way up the walls on either side of us. But it was plain to see that the room extended much further back beyond the pool of light, though it was hard to make out how far back the room actually stretched hidden away in the darkness...it felt eerie.

From behind us, there was a loud clunk of a heavy bolt being locked in place across the back of the wooden door that we had come through. Was that a draft in the air? Or was it my body feeling the cold air that this damn room possessed? It made the hairs on the back of my neck prickle to the point of creepiness...I shuddered. I noticed out the corner of my eye Fox take a side step closer to me, brushing her hands up and down her upper arms to fend herself from the cold. Looking around inside the pool of light that safeguarded us from the darkness beyond, I noticed many old religious relics piled against the stone walls on either side, along with piles of Bibles stacked neatly up the walls and clusters of chairs piled high into the darkness, when it suddenly occurred to me that we were stood in the vestry of the cathedral, the room used for storage.

I felt Fox's hand slip into my hand and gave her hand a reassuring squeeze; her hand was cold, very cold. She lightly gave my hand a squeeze back and whispered to me, 'I don't like this, Mac.'

I told her, 'Relax, darling, everything is going to be alright.'

Suddenly, there was a *clunk, clunk, clunk*. And with every *clunk*, another light came on, emitting three more pools of light that illuminated the rest of the vestry. At the third pool of light, there was a long broad table that had twelve chairs around it, with one man sat at the head of the table and a man sat on either side of him. The man on the left was roughly in his mid-sixties with a polished bald head and wore round wired spectacles, dressed in a dark suit, wearing a tie neatly to the collar of his white shirt. ·

On the table in front of the bespectacled man was a largish brown leather briefcase with his hands resting on the top of it, with the fingers of both hands interlocked. His stare was enough to notice us but never was there so much as a gesture or an acknowledgement from him. The man to right of the man sat at the head of the table was younger and looked to be in his mid-thirties with short cropped dark hair, with rugged hard looks, with sunken eyes and a flattened nose that had been broken several times over the years. Probably an ex-boxer, I thought to myself. He wore a black leather box type jacket with a black turtle neck jumper underneath it. His hands were the size of shovels and covered in tattoos.

Veniamin stood behind the thick-set man sat at the head of the table whose complexion was radiant, his skin was smooth, his eyes calm and alive with perhaps a look of pleasure. I slowly turned my head and looked at Fox then turned back to face the man again sat at the head of the table…he smiled momentarily at me then the smile vanished from his face, but his calmness remained steadfast.

I noticed a large wooden bowl filled with an assortment of fruits on the table end nearest us, along with three silver goblets and a bottle of red wine. A thought crossed my mind…The Last Supper? This is the Wolf, I thought to myself. I felt sickened.

The man sat at the head of the table beckoned Veniamin closer to himself with his finger and mumbled something in Russian in Veniamin's ear.

Veniamin smiled at us and said, 'Please come and sit down.'

We did as Veniamin asked and sat down in the chairs provided for us, with Jacques to my left and Fox to my right. The thick-set man spoke in a mild if not enchanting tone in surprisingly good English for a Russian.

'Please, if you will, enjoy the fruits and drink as you see fit and may I thank you for coming here, and also I would like to congratulate you all on pulling off such a great job at the Louvre. It was quite an achievement on your behalf. Never did I think that you could have pulled it off.'

'I assume you are the Wolf?'

The man reeled back in his chair scowling hard, staring at me, studying me for a few seconds before he calmly replied, 'You assume me correct, but please let's be less informal here and call me Demyan Mr Mac...'

I instantly cut him short saying 'I'd rather keep to formalities if that's okay with you, Mr Volkov!'

Jacques kicked me in the ankle while Fox pressed her foot on top of mine. The Wolf smiled generously at me and said, 'As you wish.'

I returned the smile but thought of the story Oralik had told me of the Wolf when we were all in Milan, that story began flooding through my mind again as Volkov began talking to his comrades in their mother tongue.

Demyan Volkov started out in life much the same as any other unfortunate peasant born under the hammer and sickle of the Cold War, living a depressed life of poverty in the surrounding suburbs of Moscow, in a small run-down house in a crime-ridden district filled with smog and stenches that would turn any city folk's stomach inside out on to the already filthy streets. Demyan's father was a drunken coward who spent the little money he earned on alcohol and gambling, and every time Demyan's father came home drunk, his mother would take another beating as did Demyan occasionally when his mother was not there to take it for him. By the time Demyan was 15 years old, he had nothing but hatred for his father who came home drunk for the last time one bitterly cold winters evening and as always, as soon as he came through the front door, he slumped himself down in his wooden chair in front of the fireplace and called out to his wife in his drunken slur, but on this night, she was not at home as she was selling her once dignified body and pure soul to the workers of the iron works to pay for the rent and make ends meet that her drunk of a husband could no longer maintain due to his alcohol and gambling habits. Neither her husband or Demyan knew of her fornications in the alleyways surrounding their home, so he turned his drunken afflictions on young Demyan this night, who was trying to stay hidden in the shadows of the room that was only illuminated by the flickering firelight which bathed his father's wretched face and those dreadful bloodshot eyes.

'Why do you hide from me in the shadows, boy?' he growled out at Demyan.

Demyan's voice trembled when he replied from the shadows, 'I'm not hiding, Papa.'

'Then why don't you greet me like a father when I come home?' he growled again.

'I'm keeping warm over here, Papa,' Demyan replied, his mouth beginning to dry.

His father's voice turned the room cold when he spoke next. 'Then why don't you come to Papa who will keep you warm?'

'Yes, Papa,' Demyan managed to say as he emerged from the shadows shaking from head to toe as he slowly made his way over to his father and stood in front of him afraid.

'Take off my boots, boy,' his father ordered.

Demyan did as his father asked, untying the rope laces and slipped each boot off to the foul smell of the piss that had run down his father's legs into his boots. 'There, Papa.'

'Good boy, now take down my pants,' his father growled.

Demyan's heart began smashing into his chest, he couldn't breathe, he had no air, he began to choke. 'But Papa…' he began.

The drunken savage hand of his father shot out at lightning speed and grabbed poor Demyan by the ear, pulling Demyan to within three inches of his father's foul-breathed twisted face and those devilish eyes. 'Don't ever but me, boy! Now take down my pants!!' he yelled, slapping Demyan hard across the face with his other hand, hitting Demyan to the floor.

With trembling hands, Demyan undid his father's belt to the sound of his father's drunken slurry of expulsions and delight. The fire in the hearth rose up and danced wildly as Demyan unbuttoned his father's piss-stained trousers and pulled them down around his father's ankles. Tears silently flowed down the boy's cheeks.

'There, Papa,' Demyan managed to say through a sobbing whisper.

'Now take my manhood out, boy!

Demyan's body shook violently as he got to his own feet and took a step back from his beast of a father before he cried out, 'No Papa! No Papa!!'

The fire in the hearth rose up triumphantly as it danced and flickered wickedly, casting shadows all over the walls as Demyan's father awkwardly rose up out of his wooden chair, his beastly shadow crept up the wall and across the ceiling towards Demyan, who took another step backwards towards the wicked fire.

'You little bastard boy!' his father said through gritted teeth and lunged forward at Demyan.

In that instant of terror, Demyan closed his eyes and fell to his knees and bowed his head traumatically exhausted and clasped his hands together as if in prayer and screamed out, 'No papa!! No papa!! No papa!!

Demyan felt his father's body crash on top of him and heard a thud. The beast that now lay on top of Demyan was heavy and motionless without a growl... Demyan fainted from mental exhaustion.

When Demyan regained consciousness, he opened his eyes and was reminded he was still underneath his father's beastly weight. A putrid smell of burning flesh filled the air. 3his stomach began to heave uncontrollably as he tried to breathe. Demyan slid from underneath the beast's body and began trembling again as he turned around and looked down at the fallen beast whose head was face down in the heart of the fire with all its hair burnt away, its head blackened and blistering burnt to a crisp...dead! Demyan's legs began to struggle to keep him upright so he sat down in the beast's chair and watched as the triumphant flames danced over and around the beast's head.

A calamitous calmness crept throughout Demyan's body as he relaxed back into the dead beast's wooden chair and smiled to himself with no feelings of emotion. For several minutes, Demyan watched the flames dance idly over the beast's head before he leapt up out of the wooden chair and smashed it to pieces, putting every last splinter of wood in the fire cooking the beast's head to a further black crust. Demyan then removed the piss-stained trousers from around his father's ankles, the downfall of the beast who would harm him and his mother no more, and took the few coins from the pockets and tossed the piss-stained trousers into the fire and watched them burn as the flames danced victorious once again. From this grossness, Demyan's soul was blackened, just like his father's skull, and a more sinister being was born in those horrific moments, and so came about the rebirth of "The Wolf".

On Demyan's 16th birthday, he found out by chance that his mother was prostituting herself and found this insidious revelation tearing his soul apart, shattering his love for his beloved mother which left him impalpable in his dark thoughts. Early that evening, Demyan's mother told him she had to go out and would be back in an hour or two to celebrate his 16th birthday with him. She smiled warmly at him before closing the door behind her. Demyan opened the door and saw his mother disappear from sight into the dim of an alleyway. Demyan was quick to follow his mother, stalking her from the shadows, having to endure the drunken moans and groans of men against his mother in the shadows ahead that persecuted him until he could bear those torturous sounds no longer. 'You have to stop it!' the Wolf cried out. Finally, he followed her into a dark deserted alleyway that cut between two streets and called out from behind her, 'Mumma.'

Startled, his loving mother struggled for words but replied, 'Oh! What brings you up here? I was just on my way home.'

Demyan paused before he said, 'I love you, Mumma.'

'And I love you too, son.'

Demyan walked towards his mother who had her arms outstretched to hug him and when he was within striking distance, the Wolf raised his iron bar over his head and brought it down upon her head, bludgeoning her to death, then raised it above his head in two hands over his mother's lifeless bloody corpse laying in a pool of blood on the alley floor and brought it down full force, piercing her chest and straight through her heart for the shame that she had inflicted upon his heart, his soul and his once love. Demyan knew that his mother's battered body lying there in the dark of the alley would soon be discovered but he also knew that it wouldn't raise any investigation outside of the suburbs, as murder was rife in the area anyway, so he made his way home sticking to the shadows, doing his best not to get noticed by any people passing by, eventually reaching the safety of his small house. He burnt his blood splattered clothes in the dancing fire and then washed her blood from his face and body. Demyan got dressed in a ragged set of clothes and fell asleep on the floor in front of the flickering fire, waiting for the ill news to come to him – the Wolf slept too!

The loud banging upon the door startled him awake from his sleep and quickly sprang to his feet remembering what he had done hours earlier. Demyan composed himself as the banging on the door continued in a rapid volley.

Demyan opened the door to an Orthodox priest dressed in his black costume with his head bowed before looking at poor Demyan with sorrowed serenity. The priest spoke, 'It's your mother.'

Collectively, Demyan said, 'Yes.'

The priest's eyes narrowed, his expression remained sorrowful. 'She was found murdered.'

Demyan dropped to his knees and playfully put his hands over his eyes and pretended to sob. The priest reached out a hand and placed it on Demyan's head and said, 'I'm sorry, my son. May God be with you,' and walked away.

Demyan left the suburbs and headed for Moscow with all its glory where after several weeks of sleeping rough and begging on the streets, he got involved with a petty gang of criminals stealing anything of any value. Demyan was quick and nimble, and very good at it his newfound life which didn't go unnoticed by a certain Mafia boss, who took Demyan under his wing, where Demyan's tested loyalty earned him a good life, sailing up through the ranks with great respect, earning Demyan the title of right-hand man to his boss. But after several years of loyal service, Demyan was not happy at seeing all the wealth his boss had accumulated, mostly by Demyan's hand, and Demyan himself felt he deserved better rewards for his services and was fed up of taking orders, so he decided to kill his boss by lacing a bottle of vodka with a powder that once in contact with liquid, turned into a destructive acid which Demyan sat and watched his boss drink along with four other Mafia bosses after an afternoon's meeting in his mentor's home.

No sooner had all five bosses downed the large vodka shot in one gulp, did they all start to clasp their throats with their hands as the acid instantly took effect, burning holes in their throats, disintegrating their cheeks to the jaw bones. The Wolf watched wide-eyed in amazement as blood spurted from their mouths as they spat teeth out on the floor with bits of tongue and other bloody fleshy parts, as all the bosses fell to the floor in horrific agony, thrashing their arms and kicking their legs wildly about until they all ceased to move. The damage was done and so were all the five bosses, and as for their intestines and other organs, only the coroner would truly appreciate the extent of the acid's destruction. The other gang members in attendance on this horrific day were all on their knees horrified, vomiting and clueless as what to do next, but Demyan took hold of the situation they were all left in and in those horrific minutes that he killed all five mafia bosses, Demyan Volkov became head of the five biggest crime organisations in Moscow.

At first, Demyan was all too generous to all the gang members but he shrewdly had them all killed off one by one and replaced by henchmen of his choosing, and with new members came new beginnings for all. Demyan Volkov aka "The Wolf" soon became a very powerful man inside of the old USSR system of communism and all the injustices that that era carried throughout the Cold War years. Though Demyan was poorly educated, it didn't take him long to pick up on the money side of things regarding business deals, from listening intently to his once beloved boss and how his now dead boss conducted his affairs, only for Demyan to capitalise on them, but kept these thoughts to himself to use at a later date. Demyan made a point of making friends with politicians, bankers and high-ranking business people alike, shaking many powerful hands whilst climbing the ladder of fortune to power, but nobody knew for sure how he ended up in the oil and gas business, but what is known is that most of his associates at this high end of his business sector, who Demyan had made his billions with, died suddenly or disappeared without a trace.

People became very, very afraid of Demyan Volkov and those that tried desperately not to have business dealings with him, were killed or never seen again. In general, people found it easier to get along with Volkov and live a couple more years, days in some cases, rather than suddenly vanish off the face of the earth or end up in a closed casket. Now "The Wolf" was a billionaire and more powerful and ruthless than ever at the ripe old age of 59 years, but time had favoured him well in his looks (or a plastic surgeon once had?) for he only looked a swell 40 years old. His face was round with chiselled cheek bones, to the point of somewhere between rugged and handsome, with immaculate shoulder-length silver hair swept neatly across the top to the left and back at the sides, weighing in at 120 kg, standing at a tad off six foot tall, his wrath had never idled as the days and years graced by.

I was drawn back to the Wolf's voice as he spoke to the bald-headed bespectacled man, who immediately flipped open the briefcase so both sides were lying flat on the table. The bald man removed his wire spectacles and quickly cleaned the lenses before putting them back on his face. He began taking from the briefcase various glass test tubes and inserted them upright into a simple wooden frame to hold them. Next, he took out from the briefcase a few small bottles of different coloured liquids along with what looked like to be a scalpel and finally a microscope. The bald-headed man looked over the items before him on the table and said to the Volkov, 'I am ready to start the testing.'

The Wolf nodded several times before he spoke, 'I can clearly see that you do not have the Mona Lisa with you or any of the other paintings which for the love of god has had me puzzled since you first walked in here,' he paused looking at each of us in turn before he asked, 'Do you not trust me?'

'Would you walk into a place with a few priceless paintings and just lay them on the table to someone you have never met before and hope they would just give you a few million?' I replied.

The Wolf let out a shallow laugh and said, 'From personal experience, I can say that I have. But from your point of view, I can understand your precautious approach.'

'Then you'll also appreciate my precautious approach for half the money to be wired to my account before the paintings are brought here as an act of good faith on your behalf.'

The Wolf turned to the man in the black leather jacket and said, 'Aleksi, set up the computer ready for the transaction.'

'Yes, boss,' Aleksi replied. He reached down to his right side and put a silver briefcase on the table and flipped up the lid and turned the laptop on inside.

'This will only take a few moments to complete and then can I have my paintings, yes?

'They'll be here in less than ten minutes.'

The Wolf smiled at each of us in turn before he said, 'Very good, but if you try to double-cross me in any sort of way, I will kill you all very slowly.'

'There will be no double-crossing, I can assure you of that, on our lives.'

Again, the Wolf smiled before he said, 'Your lives depend on it.'

Aleksi informed the Wolf that they were ready to complete the transaction to our account. The Wolf nodded at Aleksi and then said to us, 'Would two hundred and fifty million be a fair amount to start with?'

We all looked at each other and casually Jacques nodded in agreement to the huge offer as if it was no big deal. Fox's foot pressed down hard on top of my foot and when I looked at her, she had pound signs in her eyes. My heart was racing a championship all of its own, my mouth had gone as dry as a salt flat with the palms of my hands as sticky as a gecko's feet! But as casual as Jacques, I nodded back in agreement to Jacques and Fox and then turned to the Wolf and in a I-don't-give-a-fuck manner, told him, 'That will be fine.'

The Wolf asked 'Do you have an account number Aleksi can send the money to?'

'Of course.'

The Wolf looked me hard in the eyes and barked, 'Then now would be a good time to give the account number to Aleksi.'

I dug into my side pocket and pulled out the piece of paper with the account number written on it and placed it on the table, pushing it away from me. Aleksi came and took it without so much as a glance at me and put it on the table in front of the computer and began typing in the numbers written on it. A few minutes had elapsed, Aleksi kind of smiled and said, 'The transaction is completed.'

I asked Aleksi 'Do you mind if I take a look for myself?'

Aleksi looked at the Wolf and said, 'Boss?'

The Wolf rolled his eyes in his head and said, 'Go ahead.'

I walked up to where Aleksi was stood, only for Aleksi to turn the computer around towards me on the table and sure enough on the screen, it showed the transaction of £250,000,000 was deposited. I felt ecstatic inside but concealed my jubilations and began walking back to Jacques and Fox when a thought occurred to me. I turned around and walked back to Aleksi and said, 'You wouldn't mind if I checked my account myself?'

Aleksi's face seemed to grimace then fade instantly. He looked over to the Wolf and said 'Boss?'

The Wolf's face looked twisted and menacing, and for a moment, devilish, even down to the tone in his voice when he said, 'Enough of this nonsense. No more wasting any more time here. Phone your courier to bring the painting of the Mona Lisa, so Heinrich here can perform the authenticity tests on it!

Jacques said to the Wolf, 'How about we perform our authenticity test on the account you just sent our money to?'

'That's right,' Fox added, folding her arms.

The Wolf leapt to his feet and screamed out, 'Fucking foolish idiots! Enough time has been wasted already. Veniamin, bring the woman here to me!!'

Veniamin moved swiftly from behind us with his pistol drawn in his hand and came like lightning towards us, and just as he was a few feet away, Jacques sprung to his feet and began saying, 'Now hang on a minute here...'

But before Jacques could finish his sentence, a shot rang out that echoed around the vestry. Jacques fell backwards knocking over his chair and landed on the floor, heavily clutching at his shoulder. He'd been shot by Veniamin!

Fox let out a shriek. I grabbed hold of her arm and pulled her to me out of her chair. The Wolf laughed dementedly.

Jacques looked up at Veniamin and yelled, 'I'll fucking kill you for this.'

Veniamin laughed and said to Jacques, 'Not while you're unarmed you won't.'

'I don't need weapons, fool.'

Veniamin walked over to Jacques and kicked him hard in his stomach. Jacques let out a low groan of pain but remained steadfast where he lay clutching at his shoulder. Veniamin grabbed at Fox's arm while pointing his pistol in my face and said, 'Don't be foolish, let her go.'

Fox was rigid but said, 'It's okay, Mac. Let me go.'

I let my hand slip away from her arm and said to Veniamin, 'You slimy fuck. If you hurt her, I'll kill you.'

Veniamin raised the pistol level with my eyes and said, 'Not if I kill you first.'

The Wolf growled at Veniamin saying, 'Veniamin, don't be foolish, we need him to bring the courier here with the Mona Lisa. Bring Miss Fox-Wright to me.'

'Yes, boss,' Veniamin's replied as he threw Fox forward in front of himself, only for her to stumble and fall down on the floor.

Fox picked herself up off the floor and uttered, 'Bastard!

Veniamin put his pistol in Fox's back and said, 'Move.'

The Wolf was enjoying every moment of what was unfolding and his mannerisms were now even more distraught, agitated to the point of manic! The bald man, Heinrich, was nervous but silent as was Kolzak, who had an awful grin on his face but was relishing every moment of what was happening. Aleksi was cool, calm and collected, eyeing everyone in the room contemptuously without revoke or care. When Fox reached the Wolf, he violently grabbed her by the hair which made Fox grimace and slammed her head down hard on the table and held her there, which made her cry out in pain.

The Wolf pulled out a switchblade from his pocket and held it against Fox's throat and said coldly, 'Now, if you would please call your courier and ask him to bring the Mona Lisa here. And if you give any sign that not all is well here, I'll slit your girlfriend's throat! Do you understand me?

Even though my blood was boiling inside, I was helpless and all I could do was as the Wolf asked. 'I understand but go easy on the lady.'

'You're in no position to tell me what to do,' the Wolf replied and smashed his fist down into the centre of Fox's back.

Fox's agonising cry was too much for me to bear; I turned away so I couldn't see her in her pain. I had never felt so little, so helplessly ashamed in all my years as the Wolf had made me feel now. Jacques was sat upright on the floor still clutching at his shoulder where he had been shot, but his look of rage was eminent. Kolzak was transfixed, amused, dancing crazily on the spot with his gun in his hand singing out, *la la la la la da!* over and over again to every step.

'For fuck sake! Just leave her alone!!' I cried out.

'I'll give you ten minutes to have the Mona Lisa brought here or her throat gets slit.' The Wolf looked at his watch then at me adding, 'Time's ticking,'

'Okay, okay, I'm making the call. What about the other paintings, do you want them brought here too?'

'I was never interested in them, you fool. I was only ever interested in the Mona Lisa.'

I called Bernie and told him to bring only the Mona Lisa. Bernie started to question why only the Mona Lisa was to be brought but I calmly told him not to waste time and to be as quick as he could. There was a slight pause from Bernie before he asked if everything was okay. I told him everything couldn't be better and reminded him to hurry and ended the call. I looked at the Wolf and said, 'He's on his way.'

'Then take a seat while we await your friend's arrival.' The Wolf then turned to Aleksi and said, 'Go upstairs and greet our friend, and make sure he is unarmed.'

'Yes, boss,' Aleksi replied leaving the room.

The Wolf sat back in his chair and artistically began playing with the switchblade in his hand. Veniamin sat on the edge of the table with his pistol in his hand, eyeing me and Jacques intently. I got out of my chair and went to help Jacques up off the floor, only for the Wolf to tell me to leave him there on the floor. I tried to protest and got a punch to the side of the head from Kolzak. Jacques shook his head at me and told me to leave him and just sit down. I looked across the table at Fox who had blood running from a cut just above her eye when Volkov slammed her head into the table, yet she remained focused, managing to give me a sly wink.

I asked the Wolf, 'Do you intend on killing us once you have the Mona Lisa?'

Kolzak hit me across the back of the head with his pistol which sent me forwards. The pain was agonising and instinctively I reached for the back of my head with both my hands to smother the pain. The Wolf raised his hand to Kolzak and said, 'If she is a fake, then yes.'

I removed my bloodied hands from the back off my head and told him, 'It's not a fake.'

'Then that should make things easier for me.'

'In what manner?'

The Wolf replied sternly, 'In any manner I see fit.'

'Why not just take the painting and let us go?'

'I'm taking the painting anyway but as for letting you all go is another matter.'

'So you don't intend on killing us all?' I asked, trying to work out the Wolf's intentions.

The Wolf glanced at Fox then back to me and said, 'Not all of you.'

'Do you mind if I have a cigarette?' I asked like a condemned man waiting to be executed.

The Wolf sat upright and frowned, thrown by the question, and after a brief pause, he smiled with amusement and said, 'Go ahead, it may be your last one.'

Fox said, 'I could do with a cigarette myself.'

The Wolf's face reddened and looking at Fox, he told her, 'I'm sorry, dear, but I don't like women who smoke, it is another filthy trait some possess.'

'Then you definitely won't like me,' Fox told him.

The Wolf leant forward and stared into Fox's eyes and said, 'Is that so?'

Fox squinted back at the Wolf searching his eyes when she asked him, 'Is that eye liner you're wearing?'

The Wolf reeled backwards into his chair and looked away from Fox and said, 'Yes.'

'Wwwhy?' Fox stammered.

The Wolf looked at Fox with a screwed-up face and through gritted teeth he told her, 'Because it reminds me of my mother!' Then plunged his switchblade into the tabletop by her hand and barked, 'Shut up!'

It made Fox jump in her chair and cower away from him. The Wolf closed his eyes, tilted his head backwards, running both his hands through his silver hair while letting out a long sigh. He lowered his head back down and slowly opening both of his eyes, revealing the whites filled red with an unnerving evil glare! Suddenly there came a knock on the vestry door which made the Wolf jump slightly; he ordered Kolzak to open it and in Bernie casually strode, none the wiser to the situation, with a backpack slung over his shoulder.

Bernie was smiling away and started to say, 'Hey Mac, hey Fox. What you doing sat on the floor, Jacques...' Then the penny dropped when Aleksi put his gun in the back of Bernie's head to which Bernie said, 'Oh shit! Have I come at a bad time?'

'Isn't it obvious?' Jacques told him.

Bernie placed the backpack on the table and said, 'I'll come back later,' and turned to leave us all, only to be confronted by Kolzak and his pistol. Bernie put his hands up in the air and said to Kolzak, 'Reach for the stars, right?'

Kolzak told Bernie, 'Sit down.'

'On the chair or on the floor?' Bernie asked.

Kolzak spoke slowly through gritted teeth to Bernie saying, 'On...the...fucking...chair!'

'This chair or that chair?' Bernie replied looking puzzled.

Kolzak scratched his head and said, 'Any fucking chair, so long as you sit!'

'Oh okay. I'll sit next to Mac,' Bernie replied, sitting down next to me.

The Wolf told Aleksi to bring the backpack over to Heinrich. Heinrich opened the backpack, took out the cylinder and opened the lid carefully, and removed the Mona Lisa, laying it flat out on top of the table. The Wolf rose from his chair and stood beside Heinrich and admired the painting in brief before he said to Heinrich, 'Conduct the tests.'

'Yes, Mr Volkov,' Heinrich replied.

We all sat in silence and watched the bald-headed man Heinrich get to work on testing the Mona Lisa. Firstly, he carefully cut off a tiny amount of paint from the edges of the Mona Lisa and put it in the test tubes, adding some liquids into each of the tubes before placing them upright in the little wooden rack. The Wolf asked him, 'What are you doing?'

Heinrich replied without looking up at the Wolf and said, 'I am conducting the chemical analysis on the oil paint, used to see if it's consistent with the age of oils used in 1503–1506 when this painting was produced by Leonardo da Vinci. It shouldn't take too long, Mr Volkov.'

'The sooner the better,' the Wolf told him.

'You cannot hurry the chemical analysis, Mr Volkov. It is a process that has to occur naturally,' Heinrich told him.

The Wolf scowled at Heinrich and said, 'So be it,' and sat down on top of the table edge next to him.

Next, Heinrich took the microscope and carefully placed it on top of the Mona Lisa and raised his wired spectacles so they were sat on top of his head and looked through the scope, adjusting the magnifying wheels a few times back and forth. Again, the Wolf asked him with interest what he was doing. Heinrich told him that he was now conducting the microscopic stereo test, also to determine the age of the painting but specifically looking in the area around her left elbow that was damaged when someone threw a stone at it many years ago that had to be repaired and also at the craquelure formations, which are tiny rectangular blocks in shape and are typical with Italian paintings of the Renaissance period.

Bernie whispered to me, 'You learn something new every day,'

Kolzak clunked Bernie on the top of his head with his gun and told him, 'Quiet.'

I raised an eyebrow at Bernie who had both his hands capped on top of his head. Bernie's face was one of puzzlement with pain when he looked at me and shrugged his shoulders as if to say what did I do wrong? I motioned with my fingers across my lips, silently telling him to zip it! Bernie rubbed the top of his head vigorously with the palm of his hand. Smiling at his handiwork, Kolzak pretentiously waved his pistol at Bernie; Bernie sulked in silence! I looked to my left at Jacques who was still sat on the floor holding his shoulder; he had a smirk on his face, happy that Bernie had been clunked on the head by Kolzak. I couldn't help but think even in what was to be our final hour, Jacques and Bernie silently had this crazy rift between them that sometimes begs belief – I sighed happily.

Heinrich removed a test tube from the rack one at a time before replacing them back in the wooden rack, smiling to himself.

The Wolf on noticing Heinrich's smile, walked over to where he had left the switchblade stuck in the table top and removed it, hiding it in the palm of his hand and then walked over to Veniamin and whispered something in Veniamin's ear. Veniamin nodded slowly a few times in agreement as the Wolf whispered to him. Heinrich broke their private counsel, 'Mr Volkov.'

The Wolf peeled himself away from Veniamin's ear, 'Yes, Heinrich.'

'I have conducted the necessary tests required on the painting and can safely conclude that this is without any question the genuine Mona Lisa and is not a fake.'

The Wolf spread his arms out wide as if he was a bird and spun around full circle on his heels, laughing wildly before clasping his hands together before he asked, 'Are you sure?'

'Why of course, Mr Volkov. I am one hundred percent sure.'

The Wolf ran his hand through his hair saying, 'Good, very good, Heinrich. You will be rewarded generously for your expertise.'

Heinrich replied earnestly, 'Thank you, Mr Volkov.'

'No. It is I who has to thank you.'

'Not at all, Mr Volkov. I'm just doing my job that is all.'

The expression on the Wolf's face changed then he said to Heinrich, 'So you have, so you have. Oh, one more thing, Heinrich.'

'Yes, Mr Volkov?'

'Can you put my painting back inside that tube?'

'Yes of course, Mr Volkov.'

Kolzak was now stood to the side of Jacques with his gun in his hand, Veniamin was off to Fox's right, while Aleksi remained seated at the table. Jacques threw me that look of readiness. I looked down the table at Fox who looked straight back at me and moved her eyes to her right at Veniamin. I moved my eyes downwards to the floor; Fox frowned back at me so I silently mouthed to her FLOOR! Fox winked back at me. Bernie was signalling me the okay sign under the table with his thumb and forefinger. I gave him the thumbs up sign with my hand that we understood each other. By this point in time, Heinrich had carefully put the painting back inside the cylinder and as he was putting his equipment back into his briefcase back on the table, the Wolf silently strode up behind Heinrich and grabbed him around the mouth and jerked his head to the side and plunged the switchblade into Heinrich's jugular vein in his neck. The shock on Heinrich's face was terrifying as the Wolf pulled the switchblade out and stepped back. The blood began squirting high into the air and all over the table. Heinrich's whole body was shaking uncontrollably in the chair where he sat as he panicked, trying to stem the flow of blood gushing out of his neck with his hands. Heinrich's efforts were useless and a few seconds later, he fell sideways off the chair onto the floor dead.

The Wolf began laughing hysterically with Kolzak joining in with him when suddenly Jacques moved like a ghost, sweeping Kolzak off his feet with his hand so hard that Kolzak hit the floor head-first rendering him unconscious. Fox was already underneath the table, crawling on along the floor on her hands and knees as fast as she could towards me. Jacques had Kolzak's pistol in his hand and shot Aleksi in the head which sent him crashing to the floor. I was under the table with my hand outstretched towards Fox, beckoning her to me and as her outstretched hand met mine, I pulled her as hard as I could towards me, throwing my body over the top of hers to protect her. I could hear Bernie screaming, 'I've been shot!! I've been shot!! I've been shot!!'

Jacques was in a shoot-out with Veniamin, which ended when Jacques rolled under the table and shot Veniamin in the legs, sending him crashing to the floor in crying agony. I heard Jacques utter no mercy for the wicked before he fired his final shots into Veniamin's upper chest, killing him instantly. Then there was silence for a few seconds which was broken by Kolzak muttering, coming around from his unconsciousness which Jacques silenced with a bullet to Kolzak's head!

'Is everyone okay? Jacques asked.

'We're fine, but Bernie's been shot,' I replied.

Jacques looked to us and asked puzzled, 'Where's Bernie?'

Bernie replied, 'Over here.'

I looked behind me and saw Bernie was sat propped against the wall smiling so I asked, 'What you smiling about?'

'I'm a hero, I've been shot.'

Jacques said, 'I'll shoot you, you smug bastard. Get over here.'

'No need, they're all dead, and Volkov disappeared through that secret doorway in the wall over there,' Bernie told Jacques nodding his head in the direction of the far wall.

Fox scrambled over to Bernie to look at his wound in his right side and when she lifted his shirt up, she smiled at him and said, 'You'll live, hero, it's just a graze.'

Bernie sprung to his feet and said smugly, 'I've still been shot as far as I care.'

'Where's the Mona Lisa? I asked.

'Volkov took it with him,' Bernie replied.

Jacques quickly collected the dead men's weapons and on handing me and Bernie a gun each, he said, 'Then we had better get after him. You and Fox take the stairwell back up to the church, and me and Mac will follow wherever that doorway in the wall leads to. And be careful.'

'You too,' Bernie replied.

Cautiously, Jacques and I entered through the secret doorway and entered into a narrow damp stone tunnel with just enough headroom to stand up in, which was lit up with the odd wall light here and there spaced along its walls. We ran the full distance of the tunnel and when we reached the end, there was a flight of stone steps which we assailed three steps at a time to catch up with Volkov and when we reached the top, we could see daylight and a trap door flung open onto the Cathedral's chancel where the priests sit during religious ceremonies.

Jacques slowly poked his head out over the top and fired a shot off, only it was echoed by another shot which hit the wooden bench, sending splinters of wood flying in all directions.

'It's the Wolf,' Jacques exclaimed taking cover.

'We can't let him get away.'

'I know,' Jacques replied.

A shot rang out followed by another shot, we both looked at each other and peered over the top and saw Fox and Bernie taking cover behind the altar. Fox noticed us and called out, 'He's amongst the benches about half way up!'

'Stay where you are,' I called back to her.

'Okay,' Fox shouted back.

Jacques said, 'I'm going to make a run for that pillar over there. When I reach it, I'll give you covering fire.'

'Okay, pal. Just keep your head down,'

'We need to take him alive.'

'Really, what for?' I asked him puzzled.

'I want our goddamn money, mate,' Jacques replied and made a dash for the pillar.

As Jacques neared the pillar, the Wolf sprang up from between the rows of benches, and fired off a shot at him before he disappeared down behind the benches again, only I could see the Wolf was making his way along the bench and then he darted to a pillar on the opposite side of the church and took cover behind it momentarily before he made a mad dash to the next pillar along and in doing so, I made a hasty run to the pillar where Jacques had been, only he had run at the same time as the Wolf, moving along to the next pillar, firing off a shot at the Wolf as he ran. The bullet hit the pillar, narrowly missing the Wolf. The

Wolf quickly swung his arm from around the pillar and fired off an aimless shot back which missed Jacques' head by several inches, hitting the pillar behind him. Fox and Bernie had bolted from behind the altar to the front row of benches and were now taking cover down behind them, slowly edging their way along to the far end where they would be in line almost to the Wolf's line of fire.

Suddenly, the Wolf let off a quick volley of shots as he ran to the next pillar up. Jacques fired back and ran to the next pillar up too and I followed suit, running and taking cover behind the benches until I reached a pillar and took cover behind it. Breathing heavily, I wiped the sweat away from my brow. The Wolf was now one pillar away from the vestibule, the small entrance between the outer doorway and the inside of the cathedral; if the Wolf made it outside, all would be lost and so would our money.

But we were too late and in a flash of hailing bullets from the Wolf as he ran from behind his pillar, ducking and weaving as he ran, he was through the vestibule and out into the street. Jacques was hot on the Wolf's heels and I was hot on Jacques' heels, with both Fox and Bernie sprinting up along the nave, chasing after us all.

Jacques was through the doorway and first into the street with me a second behind him, but there was no sign of the Wolf, only a man shouting and waving his fist at a car speeding off. 'That's him in the car,' Jacques said.

'Well, that's fucked it for us then,' I told him just as a man on a motorbike came around the corner.

'Not yet we're not,' Jacques said and stepped out in front of the motorbike and pointed his gun at the rider.

The rider came to a stop in an instant and held up his hands. Jacques told the man to get off his machine and taking the poor guy's helmet for himself. Jacques straddled the motorbike and told me to get on the back and handed me the gun and said, 'Hold on tight, Mac,' and sped off after the Wolf.

Fox and Bernie had just made it out of the church in time to see us accost the motorbike. Just as a car rounded the corner, Fox stepped out in front of it and aimed her gun at the driver who screeched to a stop. Keeping her weapon trained on the driver, she opened the driver's door and told him to get out, which he did instantly, shaking like a leaf and lay down on the floor covering his head with his hands.

Fox turned to Bernie and said, 'Get in and drive.'

Bernie jumped in the car and when Fox was sat in the passenger seat, he said to her, 'Seatbelt please,' and sped off after us and the Wolf with screeching tires, leaving two very angry and shaking disturbed people in a cloud of smoke and the smell of burning rubber.

The Wolf broadsided around the first corner in the car, nearly killing a guy on a bicycle, making contact with the cyclist's rear wheel which sent the cyclist crashing to the ground as the Wolf disappeared out of our sight into the old town square.

We sped past the injured cyclist on the ground and into the square to scenes of total chaos and carnage that the Wolf had caused, smashing into many of the tents and awnings of the Sunday market, scattering tables, chairs and people all over the place. Jacques made his way through the scenes of destruction and across the other side of the square and down a street, closing in on the Wolf at great speed, who was still in our sights and as we rounded the corner, Jacques had to hit the brakes hard and mount the pavement on the other side of the road as the Wolf had smashed into a load of refuse bins, scattering them all over the road along with the bins' contents. Jacques continued along the pavement past all the bins and strewn rubbish in the road, re-joining the road once clear of the debris, leaving a few scared people behind on the pavement that had managed to jump out of the Wolf's way.

We turned the next corner at the end of the street to scenes of more chaos as the Wolf was driving the wrong way up a one-way street, forcing cars out of his way with many wing mirrors hanging off the parked cars he had recklessly driven by.

One driver was stubborn and wouldn't pull over, so the Wolf jumped out of his car with the Mona Lisa and pulled the stubborn driver's door open and yanked him out of the car, shooting him in the chest and started reversing the car back down the street, firing two shots at us with one of the bullets smashing the headlight on the motorcycle. Jacques closed in on him to only a few metres away when the Wolf exited the street into the joining road, crashing into the front of an oncoming car that spun his car around to the normal flow of traffic and sped off again.

'Shoot his tires out!' Jacques yelled out at me.

I started shooting at his tires but with bad aiming, I shot out the rear windscreen of the car and put a hole in the boot.

'Careful, we don't want to kill him,' Jacques shouted out.

'Sorry,' I replied.

'Fox and Bernie are behind us.'

'How do you know?'

'I can see them in the mirror.'

I glanced around and sure enough they were; Bernie waved at me so I gave him a little wave back and said to Jacques, 'It's them alright.'

'They must have followed the carnage?' Jacques shouted out.

'I bet they have,' I shouted back at him.

I could now hear police sirens and looked over my shoulder to see two police cars behind Bernie, who slammed on his brakes hard, bringing the car to a sudden stop. The first police car slammed on his brakes with the second police car smashing into the back of the first police car in front. Bernie honked his horn and sped off after us again, leaving the two police cars behind him fucked!

A police motorcyclist shot out of a side street and joined in on the chase too, speeding behind the Wolf, who blindly fired a few shots out of his car window at the pursuing police motorcycle with a bullet hitting the policeman in his chest, which sent the policeman and his motorbike veering off to the right and crashing into a parked car, The Wolf drove on wildly, cutting up the traffic, and turned a corner into another one-way street and drove around the cars ahead of him, mounting the pavements several times and re-joining the road again, leaving a few injured and dead people in his wake.

We weaved through the onslaught of his destruction on the motorbike and noticed a woman crying her heart out cradling her child in her arms. I felt sick and maddened, and shouted out to Jacques, 'Get that bastard.'

Bernie and Fox had no way of making it through the carnage and deaths in the street, so he reversed the car to find another route when Fox cried out, 'Stop!'

Bernie slammed on the brakes and asked, 'What for?'

'Get out of the car and follow me,' she ordered him.

They both got out of the car and Fox ran over to a man who had just parked his motorcycle and was helping the injured people lying on the ground in the street and forced him to give her his helmet at gunpoint and threw the helmet to Bernie saying, 'Get on that bike.'

Bernie started the motorbike and stopped by Fox's side and said, 'Get on.'

Fox got on the back of the motorbike and looking at the owner crouching over the injured person sprawled out on the ground, she shouted, 'Sorry!'

'Hang on tight,' Bernie told her and sped off down the street after us.

The Wolf in his madness exited the one-way street and crashed head on into the side of a tram. The Wolf got out of the car dazed with the Mona Lisa and started to run on foot when he hailed a small lorry down with his gun. The driver of the lorry jumped out on the passenger side and ran for his life up the street. The Wolf turned his gun on us as we approached him on the motorbike and fired, only he was out of bullets and threw his gun at us then quickly scrambled into the cab and swung the lorry around and headed out over Charles Bridge, smashing vehicles out of his way.

Bernie and Fox pulled up alongside me and Jacques, and said, 'That guy is a fucking maniac!'

'Let's get out of here pronto, there's police sirens all over the place,' I said.

'Well, we know where he's heading, so let's go catch him up,' Fox stated.

'Follow us,' Bernie said and sped off with us in tow.

It didn't take us long to catch the Wolf up in the lorry on an open road outside the city. Though he was trying desperately to lose us, he stood no chance as we toyed with him, pulling alongside him. He began swerving from left to right only for us to drop back behind him again. He continued in this manner when the airport came into view in the distance and when he was close to the airport's boundary fence, the Wolf veered off the road onto the grass and rammed down the fencing and made his way across the airport to the hangars in the distance. We followed at a slower speed as the grass was moist and the motorbike tires couldn't grip properly, sending the back end of the bike sliding all over the place. The Wolf reached the hangar where his private jet was and jumped out of the lorry and ran with the Mona Lisa up the steps of his jet and pulled the steps up behind him, locking the door in its closed position, shouting out, 'TAKE OFF! TAKE OFF! TAKE OFF!' The Wolf froze to the spot instantly when a voice from behind him said, ''Ello, Mr Wolf!!'

The Wolf slowly turned around and saw Bootsie Burns grinning like a Cheshire cat flanked by his henchmen.

'Who are you?' the Wolf asked Bootsie.

'Don't trouble yourself with that right now. Just have a nice sit down and wait for the others to arrive,' Bootsie told him.

The Wolf asked puzzled, 'What others?'

'Our friends! Now sit down or dear George here will make you sit down with a bullet in your foot. Let's not get off on the wrong foot here, so just fucking sit down,' Bootsie told him.

The Wolf took a seat and sat in helpless silence looking at the grinning Bootsie.

'George,' Bootsie said.

'Yes, Guv?'

'Be a good fellow and make Mr Wolf here a nice mix, would ya?'

'Of course, Guv,' George replied opening the jet's door.

'Dave.'

'Yes, Guv?'

'Give George a hand with the mix, would ya?'

'Oh okay, Guv, sure.'

'Ta!'

Bootsie turned his attention to Volkov and said, 'Kindly slip your shoes off, Mr Wolf.'

'What?'

'Slip your fucking shoes off!'

'What for?' the Wolf asked puzzled.

''Cos I wanna see the colour of your fucking socks.'

'Eh!' the Wolf replied puzzled again.

Bootsie leant forward and shouted at the Wolf, 'SLIP THEM FUCKING SHOES OFF OR I'LL CUT YA FUCKING EARS OFF, YA DEAF CUNT!!'

The Wolf reluctantly leant forwards and started untying his shoe laces. Bootsie smiled at the Wolf and relaxed back into his seat and lit up a cigar.

The Wolf said to Bootsie, 'There's no smoking on my plane.'

'Are you testing my patience, Mr Wolf?'

'Eh!'

Bootsie puffed on his cigar and told Volkov, 'It was your fucking plane! Now shut the fuck up and keep untying those laces OR... I'll cut your fucking balls off!'

The Wolf hung his head low and carried on untying his laces. Then Oralik poked his head out from the cockpit and said, 'You've been a bad, bad wolf, Volkov!

The Wolf looked up and said stunned, 'Kalashnikov!

'You try to double-cross me and my brothers.'

'And sister,' Fox told Oralik, making her entrance into the private jet.

'Ah, Sister Fox. So good to see you alive,' Oralik replied smiling.

Fox acknowledged Bootsie by simply saying, 'Bootsie.'

311

'Fox,' Bootsie replied.

'Hello, everyone,' Bernie said, making his entrance followed by Jacques and me.

'Ah, brothers, you make it out alive like Fox here,' Oralik said smiling.

'Just about,' Jacques replied and lunged forward, smashing the Wolf in the face with his fist, knocking the Wolf out unconscious.

Bootsie spoke out, 'Hang on a minute, Jacques, I thought that was my job?'

'Sorry, Bootsie,' Jacques replied.

'Is okay, no offence taken,' Bootsie told Jacques laughing.

Just then Dave popped his head in and said, 'Guv, the mix is ready.'

'Good. Now if the rest of you don't mind having a seat, we got some work to do on this scum of the earth,' Bootsie said as Larry handed him a pair of very large green Wellington boots.

We all took a seat inside the jet and watched with interest as Larry bound the unconscious Wolf's hands and body to the seat, and then place the oversized Wellington boots on his feet. George pulled the top of the boots wide open as Dave poured in the mix of rapid setting concrete to the top of the boots and then tethered the Wolf's lower legs together with rope and sat down just as the Wolf stirred from his unconsciousness and to his despair, he looked down at the Wellington boots filled with concrete. The Wolf tried to struggle but Bootsie told him to be a good boy and sit still while the concrete sets, but the Wolf was having none of it and kept moving his legs around, trying to free his feet. Bootsie looked at George and gave him a slight nod with his head in the direction of the Wolf. George walked over to the Wolf and punched him in the face, splitting the Wolf's nose wide open and rendering the Wolf unconscious again.

When the Wolf came around conscious for the second time, he remained still but his nose had ballooned up and blood was running down his face; he looked a mess and rightly so too. Oralik fired up a laptop computer and said to the Wolf, 'I believe you owe a lot of money to my friends. Now if you don't mind transferring their money, with a lot of inconvenience money on top for their troubles, then you can be on your way.'

The Wolf looked at Oralik and said, 'Not a chance on this earth, for you will only kill me after I have made the transfer.'

Oralik pulled a funny face and said, 'I won't kill you, Volkov, I can assure you of that, but if you don't transfer the money, my new London friends here will.'

'Fuck you all,' the Wolf replied and spat on the floor.

Bootsie stood up and said, 'Okay, ladies and gentlemen, if you wouldn't mind waiting outside while we impress this Wolf with some East End persuasion.'

We all left the jet and waited outside in the hangar as Bootsie and his boys taught the Wolf some manners. The Wolf's screams and cries of pain were unbearable at times and after fifteen minutes, Dave poked his head out from the jet and said, 'Come on, the Guvna wants to see you.'

I was first to step back inside the jet and when I looked at the Wolf, I was horrified at what I saw, as the Wolf had several fingers missing and lots of teeth all strewn across the floor in front of him, so I told Fox to remain outside and not to come in as I felt she didn't need to see such horrible things. Bernie said he would wait with her to keep her company. Bootsie was sat back in his seat and said, 'He's ready to do business, Mac.'

The Wolf was trying to say something so I leant forward to hear him and he uttered the word account, which I told him and watched him struggling to type on the laptop with his thumbs, and after a few minutes, the Wolf started nodding and whispered done. I took the bloodied computer from the Wolf's lap and logged into my account and saw that five hundred million had been transferred. I was stunned into silence. Jacques asked if the money was there so I gave him the laptop to see the figure himself and even Jacques looked stunned momentarily till a wide grin broke out across his face then he looked up at me and I gave him a broad smile back.

Bootsie seeing us both smiling said, 'Well, gentlemen, I take it all is very well and good with the transaction?'

'Yes,' I replied.

'Thank fuck for that! Now if you don't mind, I have some business of my own to conduct with this fucker, SO if you wouldn't mind leaving us alone to conduct our affairs in private, I would be more than grateful,' Bootsie stated and held out his hand and told George to start the jet's engines.

Jacques shook Bootsie's hand and said, 'Thanks a million.'

'It's been a pleasure,' Bootsie told him.

I shook Bootsie's hand firmly and said, 'Thanks for everything.'

Bootsie smiled and said, 'Like I said, Mac, it's been a pleasure. Now don't keep your good lady waiting, she's got shopping to do. Look us up the next time you're in London, or Marbella if you're ever in Spain, and we'll have a good old knees-up.'

'I look forward to it,'

'Me too. Now go on, get out of here for fuck's sake,' Bootsie said giving me a playful slap on the back and gently pushed me outside, and once I was down the steps, Larry pulled them up to close, giving us all a smile and locked the door.

Fox asked me, 'What happened?'

'We're stinking fucking rich, love, that's what happened,' I replied.

Fox threw her arms around me and gave me a kiss then she kissed Bernie then Jacques and finally Oralik to his shock.

Fox jumped up in the air and shouted, 'WE'RE RICH!!'

The jet took off and at around one thousand feet, Larry opened the door and doused the Wolf in petrol. Bootsie whispered in the Wolf's ear, 'Bon voyage,' then set him alight and kicked him out of the plane in a screaming ball of flames hurtling towards the ground. Larry pulled the jet's door to a close. Dave picked up the cylinder off the floor and said, ''Ere, Guv, what's in this then?'

Bootsie raised his eyebrows and said curiously, 'I dunno, Dave. Bring it over here.'

Dave gave Bootsie the canister and when Bootsie opened the lid and pulled out the painting, he said, 'Fuck me! It's only the fucking Mona Lisa!'

Dave frowned at Bootsie and asked, 'Who's she?'

Chapter 20

A Shotgun Wedding

A few nights later back in Agde, we had all made our way down to the restaurant where Chantelle was working and were all sat out the back on the terrace eating and drinking when all of a sudden, the locals started spilling out onto the terrace at around 7:30 pm and began filling all the empty tables and chairs surrounding us. Soft Parisian music began to flow out of the speakers fixed to the walls which ignited the mood and made the atmosphere more relaxing and enjoyable under the full moon, when suddenly Chantelle appeared wearing a lovely floral patterned dress with her hair tied back. Chantelle sat down next to Bernie and placed her hand over the top of his and gently squeezed it, giving him a reassuring fruitful smile, but Bernie being Bernie, peered around nervously and was surprised to see that no locals were fast approaching him with a shotgun in hand and so relaxed a little and smiled back at Chantelle. Chantelle, Fox, Izzy and Marie Claire were in a fit of giggles along with me and Jacques on the quiet while Mick on the other hand just shrugged his shoulders and took a sip of his drink, taking no notice of the women.

Two waiters came over and cleared our table and then reset the table and placed three seafood platters in front of us with three large bowls of freshly tossed salad and three bottles of red wine.

I looked at Bernie who was breaking out in a cold sweat with a look of confusion on his face when he whispered across the table to Chantelle and asked her, 'What's going on?'

'Relax, my love, or you may get shot,' she replied, doing her best to conceal her giggling.

The next thing, a handful of waiters emerged with their arms full of table clothes that they covered all the locals' tables with and laid out cutlery for them all, before disappearing shortly only to return and place salad bowls and seafood platters on every table along with bottles of red wine. Bernie was now paranoid as hell, looking around in every direction at everyone but was making a very bad effort trying to keep his cool. Chantelle and our women started taking fish and prawns from the platters, and encouraged us to follow suit which we all did. Bernie was now shaking like a leaf and sweating profusely as his shaking hands tried to get fish on his plate, so I whispered across the table to him, 'This could be our last supper together, mate.'

'Best we take our time fucking eating it then,' he replied cautiously, looking over his shoulder, and scooped up a mass of salad and dropped it on his plate.

At that moment, the waiters placed three bottles of champagne on the table with fluted glasses, 'What's the occasion?' Mick whispered to me.

I whispered back to him, 'Enjoy the food and champagne, and just go with it.'

'Okay, but what's happening?'

'Shhhh, you'll find out soon enough,' I whispered.

I turned my attention to Fox sat opposite me and the girls turned their attention to their men whilst Chantelle was doing her best to keep Bernie calm and happy. I and the girls were thoroughly enjoying the scenario that was unfolding around us. An hour later at 8:30 pm, Chantelle's parents arrived whom she greeted warmly with a hug and a kiss on both of their cheeks, but her father looked at Bernie and shook his head very slowly from side to side with an un-cocked shotgun resting over his arm.

Bernie got my attention by throwing a prawn at me and said in a low voice, 'Fuck this, I'm dead! We jump over the side wall and make a run for it! Are the keys in the jeep?'

'I'm staying here, mate, but it's been great knowing you and it's a tragedy that it has to end this way.'

'Are you fucking serious, Mac?! You're not coming with me?'

'I haven't done anything wrong, ask Mick to do a runner with you.'

'Psst, Mick! Are you coming with me?'

'I'm new here, so you'll have to go it alone,' Mick whispered back.

'Pssst, Bernie.'

'What?'

'They have the place surrounded,' Jacques whispered to him.

'Shit!' Bernie said aloud.

'Face it like a man and don't resist,' I told him.

'Mac! Whose side are you on?' he asked red in the face.

Chantelle came back over and said to Bernie, 'It's no good, my love, you have to stand up.'

'What for?'

'Just stand up, my love.'

Rising to his feet, Bernie said to Chantelle, 'No matter what happens, I have always loved you.'

'And I have always loved you too, my sweet, sweet darling,' she told him with a tear rolling down her cheek and held out her hand for him to join her at her side.

The music cut out and the air fell silent as everyone's eyes were now on both Bernie and Chantelle, and in the silence, you could have heard a pin drop. Fox, Izzy and Marie had tears rolling down their cheeks and were dabbing their eyes with napkins while me and Jacques had big silly grins on our faces, enjoying every moment. As for Mick, he kept on shelling prawns and scoffing them until Marie Claire whacked him on the hand with a wooden fork from the salad bowl and pointed towards Bernie and Chantelle, and putting a finger to her lips, she motioned for him to be quiet and take notice. Chantelle's father rose to his feet with the shotgun resting over his arm and addressed everyone present in his native Parisian tongue, occasionally he looked across to our table but remained fixated on Bernie and Chantelle.

Chantelle's father spoke in a hoarse baritone and there were numerous ooohs and ahhs from all the locals as he pointed at Bernie that made Bernie sweat even more, saturating the back of his shirt, but Chantelle's father kept speaking and when her father turned and pointed at Bernie again, the crowd burst out into fits of laughter as if he was mocking Bernie. Her father continued speaking as all the locals' roars of laughter got louder. Then her father seemed to say something in an irate manner at Bernie who quickly took hold of Chantelle's hand as Chantelle's father held out his hand to her mother, who smiled at her husband and stood up. Chantelle's mother raised her hands for silence and spoke softly to everyone but in that brief moment of silence, her mother said something in French that made everyone fall back into fits of laughter again. Jacques by the way was laughing hysterically with them all.

Bernie was so agitated and scared that he pulled Chantelle closer to him so they were stood shoulder to shoulder just as Chantelle's mother finished speaking to everyone and sat down again. Chantelle gave Bernie's hand a tight squeeze and said to him lovingly, 'This is it, my love.'

Everyone sat in silence apart from Chantelle's father who stood up and broke the silence as he snapped the double barrels of his shotgun shut with a loud snap! Bernie stepped in front of Chantelle and raised his hands up in the air and cried out, 'WAIT! Listen before you condemn me.' He paused for a reaction of some sort but none came, so he carried on saying aloud so everyone could hear him, 'I love Chantelle wholeheartedly and I would not allow any harm to come to her. I know I haven't been honest from the beginning by declaring my love for her to her parents, but I'm declaring it now and I see no reason why anyone should try to ruin this for her and leave her with a broken heart.

'So I urge you to reconsider shooting me, so there! And if that isn't good enough a reason, then what is? But given the opportunity, I would have made her a damn fine husband and she would have made me a damn proud wife,' he declared to all present.

At first there was a stunned silence when all of a sudden, they all erupted into laughter with lots of applause with many a tear being shed, even Chantelle was wet with laughter which spooked Bernie all the more. Eventually, the laughter faded and everyone found their composure again. Chantelle's mother smiled at her, and her father gave her a nod of his head then Chantelle turned to Bernie and said, 'Oooh my sweet love, you are so funny and I love you.'

Bernie was confused to say the least and said to Chantelle, 'What the hell is going on here?'

'It's simple, my love,' she said squeezing his hand and continued saying, 'You have just declared your undying love for me in front of my parents and the whole of the town as well as your friends.'

'I what!' He paused for thought and said, 'I mean I did…now what happens?'

'We get married, but first you have to ask my father,' she replied giggling.

'Does he like me?' Bernie asked her frowning.

'Go and find out, my love. Ask him to make us proper.'

Bernie looked all around at everyone and when he caught my eye, I gave him a wink and encouraged him to go over to her father with a quick sideways nod of my head. Bernie took a deep breath and exhaled slowly and produced a smile and walked over to Chantelle's father and asked him for his daughter's hand in marriage to make it official.

Her parents did a lot of whispering in each other's ears and then beckoned Chantelle over to them both. Bernie rubbed his chin hard as Chantelle and her parents talked quietly to each other as not to be overheard and after a few minutes as the rest of us looked on in silence, Chantelle turned and addressed Bernie saying, 'My father asks that you rid yourself of that hideous jeep.'

'What!' Bernie cried out but then composed himself and said, 'Yes.'

'One more thing, my love.'

'What is it?' Bernie asked her with a tone of caution in his voice.

Chantelle produced a big smile and said, 'My mother would like me to move in with you right away.'

Bernie's face lit up like a Christmas tree and said, 'Of course, yes.'

Chantelle turned to her parents and said, 'Oui.'

Both her parents came forwards and kissed Bernie on both of his cheeks and then her father turned around to face everyone and threw his arms up in the air and shouted something out in French that made the whole crowd erupt in shouts of joy along with lots of applause. Bernie and Chantelle embraced with a kiss and again the cheers went up, but notably Bernie was ecstatic with joy with a smile that dynamite couldn't wipe off his face. Marie Claire lent over the table and grabbed Mick and planted her lips on his. Izzy grabbed Jacques and kissed him too, as Fox grabbed me and kissed me on the lips.

Everyone present including us went and congratulated Bernie and Chantelle as well as congratulating the in-laws. The music started out of the speakers again and the food and drinks flowed into the early hours with everyone dancing and celebrating. Tired and a little drunk, we made our excuses to everyone, leaving Bernie and Chantelle with her parents and made our way back up to the house tightly packed inside the hideous jeep.

THE END

Aftermath

BOOTSIE BURNS: On discovering the Mona Lisa, Bootsie made a few phone calls and managed to get the Mona Lisa rightfully placed back on show at the Musee du Louvre. Although he got paid a hefty lump sum for his part in returning the painting, he is now semi-retired but keeps a watchful eye over the East End of London when he's not in Marbella, Spain!

MICK & MARIE CLAIRE: Both are living a relaxed lifestyle growing their own vegetables in their fields and selling all the produce at local markets and have just acquired a large disused vine yard next to them with plans already in place to produce their own wines.

ORALIK & ANNA: Both are still crazy in love with each other and after months of hard work, finally the passion has paid off for both of them. And I am delighted to announce that the happy couple are now expecting twin girls. God help us!!

BERNIE & CHANTELLE: Our joint project on the house in Agde is now finally complete with both Bernie and Chantelle playing host to backpackers from all over the world. Bernie has even finished the swimming pool, though he only has eyes for his beloved Chantelle in her bikini. Both are hard at it making wedding plans with Chantelle's mother!!

JACQUES & ISOBELLE: Surprisingly, both are still together and have jointly ventured into the property development business, converting disused warehouses into posh apartments in and around the docklands in London. Izzy occasionally supplies the odd escort girls to the councillors in the land and property sectors to help secure the odd land deal here and there as well as keeping her regular punters happy.

ME & FOX: We are currently sailing around the Caribbean Island hoping and chasing the horizon as well as chilling out on the deck of our yacht or ashore on one of the many islands, sipping cocktails whilst watching the sun set in the evenings, and occasionally watching the sun rise in the morning, which are both awe-inspiring. But we will be back to see how the rest of the gang are doing at some point in the not-too-distant future and see what's on the horizon with them.

PS.
Stay safe.

9 781788 485678